Beginning REALbasic

From Novice to Professional

Jerry Lee Ford, Jr.

Apress®

Beginning REALbasic: From Novice to Professional

Copyright © 2006 by Jerry Lee Ford, Jr.

ISBN-13 (pbk): 978-1-59059-634-0

ISBN-10 (pbk): 1-59059-634-X

ISBN-13 (electronic): 978-1-4302-0169-4

Printed and bound in the United States of America 9 8 7 6 5 4 3 2

Lead Editor: Chris Mills
Technical Reviewer: Allan Kent
Editorial Board: Steve Anglin, Ewan Buckingham, Gary Cornell, Jason Gilmore, Jonathan Gennick,
    Jonathan Hassell, James Huddleston, Chris Mills, Matthew Moodie, Dominic Shakeshaft, Jim Sumser,
    Keir Thomas, Matt Wade
Project Manager: Richard Dal Porto
Copy Edit Manager: Nicole LeClerc
Copy Editor: Marcia Baker
Assistant Production Director: Kari Brooks-Copony
Production Editor: Lori Bring
Compositor: Pat Christenson
Proofreader: Linda Seifert
Indexer: Broccoli Information Management
Artist: April Milne
Cover Designer: Kurt Krames
Manufacturing Director: Tom Debolski

Distributed to the book trade worldwide by Springer-Verlag New York, Inc., 233 Spring Street, 6th Floor, New York, NY 10013. Phone 1-800-SPRINGER, fax 201-348-4505, e-mail orders-ny@springer-sbm.com, or visit http://www.springeronline.com.

For information on translations, please contact Apress directly at 2855 Telegraph Avenue, Suite 600, Berkeley, CA 94705. Phone 510-549-5930, fax 510-549-5939, e-mail info@apress.com, or visit http://www.apress.com.

The source code for this book is available on the accompanying CD. Any corrections to code and errata are posted for download/viewing at http://www.apress.com. Just search for the book by title, author, or ISBN, in the search bar on our homepage.

To Alexander, William, Molly, and Mary.

Contents at a Glance

PART 1 ■■■ Introducing REALbasic

PART 2 ■■■ Learning How to Program with REALbasic

PART 3 ■■■ Advanced Topics

PART 4 ▪▪▪ Appendixes

Contents

PART 1 ▪▪▪ Introducing REALbasic

PART 2 ▪▪▪ Learning How to Program with REALbasic

PART 3 ■■■ Advanced Topics

PART 4 ■■■ Appendixes

About the Author

JERRY LEE FORD, JR. is an IT professional with over 16 years experience in the industry. His background includes roles as an automation analyst, technical manager, technical support analyst, automation engineer, security analyst, and college instructor. Jerry has a master's degree in Business Administration from Virginia Commonwealth University in Richmond, Virginia. He is an MCSE and a CISSP. Jerry is the author of 17 other books, including *Microsoft Visual Basic 2005 Express Edition Programming for the Absolute Beginner, Microsoft VBScript Professional Projects, Microsoft Windows Shell Scripting and WSH Administrator's Guide, Learn VBScript: In a Weekend, Microsoft Windows Shell Script Programming for the Absolute Beginner, Learn JavaScript: In a Weekend,* and *Microsoft Windows XP Professional Administrator's Guide.* Jerry lives in Richmond, Virginia, with his wife Mary, and their children Alexander, William, and Molly.

About the Technical Reviewer

ALLAN KENT is a born-and-bred South African, who still lives and works in Cape Town. He has been programming in various and diverse platforms for over 20 years. Most recently, while on the hunt for a viable cross-platform programming solution, Allan chanced upon REALbasic and he hasn't looked back since.

Acknowledgments

This book represents the hard work and efforts of numerous individuals. I would like to thank Chris Mills, who served as the book's lead editor, for working so hard and for providing me with the opportunity to write this book. Special thanks go out to Allan Kent, the book's technical reviewer, for offering countless ideas and suggestions that helped make this a much better and stronger book. I would also like to thank Marcia Baker, the book's copy editor, for her dedication and professionalism, and for her patience in dealing with and fixing my many typos and grammatical errors. I also want to acknowledge and thank Richard Dal Porto, the project manager, for keeping me on schedule and making sure I didn't forget to tie up any loose ends, and Lori Bring, the book's production editor, for guiding this book through its final stages. Finally, I'd like to thank everyone else at Apress for all their hard work.

Introduction

Welcome to *Beginning REALbasic*! REALbasic is a programming language that provides you with everything you need to create software applications that can run on Macintosh, Windows, and Linux. REALbasic is an extremely powerful programming language that is capable of creating world-class software. Yet, at the same time, REAlbasic is easy to learn and makes a perfect programming language for first-time programmers.

Using REALbasic, you can create applications, utility programs, and computer games. If you are a Windows programmer, REALbasic provides you with all the tools you need to write just about any Windows application imaginable: the same goes for Macintosh and Linux programming. By supporting cross-platform application development, REALbasic significantly enhances your ability to distribute your applications. This means you can share your work with more friends and colleagues, and if you are in the business of developing commercial software, REALbasic can help you attract new consumer markets.

Why REALbasic?

Plenty of programming languages are available today that are similar to REALbasic in many aspects. On any given operating system (OS), they may come close to matching REALbasic's core set of features. However, none of the other major modern programming languages based on the Basic programming language support application development on all three major desktop OSs. This makes REALbasic unique and gives REALbasic programmers a competitive advantage over other programmers.

As far as modern programming languages go, REALbasic is easy to learn, yet it is every bit as powerful and full featured as any other modern programming language. So, whether you are a student, a hobbyist, or a professional programmer, REALbasic has something to offer you. REALbasic programmers are supported by a thriving user community and an array of third-party developer support. This means you won't have any trouble finding help or locating companies that do REALbasic software development.

Unlike other programming languages, REALbasic does not require a complex framework to execute. And, unlike Visual Basic .NET, REALbasic applications can run on older versions of Windows, such as Windows 95 or 98, where the .NET Framework is not installed. REALbasic is not restricted to a particular OS. In short, REALbasic is a modern, powerful, cross-platform, object-oriented programming language that is friendly to beginners, yet powerful enough to satisfy the most demanding programmers' needs.

Who Should Read This Book?

The primary purpose of this book is to teach you how to develop applications using REALbasic that can run on Macintosh, Windows, and Linux. Previous programming experience is not required, although it certainly is helpful. This book is also designed to assist Visual Basic programmers in making the jump over to cross-platform development using REALbasic. It accomplishes this goal by pointing out key differences between the two programming languages where appropriate throughout the book.

At a minimum, you need a good understanding of at least one of the OSs that REALbasic runs on (Macintosh, Windows, or Linux). So, whether you are new to programming or an experienced programmer eager to make the transition to cross-platform application development, this book can help you reach your goal.

What You Need to Begin

REALbasic supports cross-platform application development, meaning you can use it to create applications that can be run on Macintosh, Windows, and Linux. To demonstrate and reinforce REALbasic's cross-platform development capabilities, this book was written using versions of REALbasic that run on all three of these OSs. Therefore, you will see figures and examples of applications running on any combination of these OSs. Except where specifically noted, all the applications you learn how to create in this book run equally well on each OS. Because of differences in how each OS is designed, however, you may notice small differences in the appearance of certain application features. I make every effort to point out where differences occur and to ensure that the examples presented work equally well on Macintosh, Windows, and Linux.

If you do not already have a copy of REALbasic installed on your computer, we have provided Macintosh, Windows, and Linux trial versions on the book's accompanying CD, along with the source code for all the examples featured in the book. Once you have REALbasic installed, you are prompted to enter a license key when you start it up. If you purchased REALbasic online, you receive your license key via e-mail. If you did not purchase REALbasic online, you are prompted to automatically request a demo key via your Internet connection. This enables you to try REALbasic free for ten days. Once this is done, you are ready to go.

Along with this book, we provide everything you need to begin developing world-class software applications for Macintosh, Windows, and Linux!

How This Book Is Organized

Beginning REALbasic is organized into four parts.

Beginning REALbasic is designed to be read sequentially from cover-to-cover. However, more experienced programmers and programmers with previous BASIC programming experience may want to use this book by reading the first few chapters, and then skipping around and selecting the chapters that interest them the most.

Part 1: Introducing REALbasic

This section is made up of two chapters that are designed to provide you with a solid introduction to REALbasic and its integrated development environment.

Part 2: Learning How to Program with Realbasic

This section consists of six chapters, each of which addresses a specific programming topic. These topics include interface development, menu development, storing and retrieving data, conditional logic, loops, and object-oriented programming.

Part 3: Advanced Topics

The Advanced Topics section, which is made up of four chapters, covers processing files, creating and accessing databases, and working with graphics and audio.

Part 4: Appendixes

This section is made up of three appendixes that address porting a Visual Basic application over to REALbasic, the contents of the book's CD-ROM, and different resources available to you as you continue learning about REALbasic.

Conventions Used in This Book

One of the goals I had in writing this book was to make it as clear and easy to understand as possible. Throughout the book, you will find a number of special elements designed to make reading and working with the presented material easier. The following provides a quick review of these special elements.

■**Tip** Tips are suggestions that point out different ways of accomplishing tasks or helping you to work more efficiently and effectively.

■**Note** Notes are designed to provide you with additional information about a topic being discussed or to bring additional emphasis to a particular point.

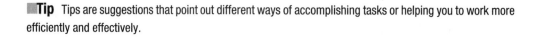

SIDEBAR

Sidebars are designed to provide you with information that, while not necessarily essential to the topic being discussed, is still important and worth learning. Sidebars are also used to identify real-world situations where REALbasic can be applied.

PART 1

Introducing REALbasic

CHAPTER 1

■■■

An Introduction to REALbasic

REALbasic is a cross-platform programming language designed to facilitate the creation of software applications that run on Macintosh, Windows, and Linux. REALbasic is a great tool for developing commercial software. It is also an excellent choice to learn as a first programming language. A great deal of time and effort has gone into making REALbasic both powerful and easy to use. In this chapter, you get an overview of what REALbasic is and the kinds of things you can do with it. You also get to see how REALbasic stacks up against competing application development tools that run on Macintosh and Windows. Finally, you jump right in and get your feet wet through the development of your first REALbasic application. Through the creation of your first REALbasic application, you

- Get a introduction to components that make up a REALbasic application

- Learn the steps involved in building a REALbasic application

- Get the chance to compare REALbasic to other application development tools and programming languages

- Learn how to compile a REALbasic application to run on different operating systems(OSs)

Overview of REALbasic

REALbasic is a software development tool that provides programmers at all levels with everything they need to create just about any kind of software application you can think of. This includes everything from major enterprise applications to small personal utility programs or even computer games. With REALbasic, the name of the game is cross-platform software development. What this means is that REALbasic enables programmers to create and deploy software applications that can run on different OSs, including Macintosh, Windows, and Linux.

REALbasic is an object-oriented implementation of the BASIC programming language. REALbasic is also a visual programming language, meaning you visually create your REALbasic application's graphical user interface (GUI) by dragging-and-dropping prebuilt controls onto windows generated by REALbasic. The graphical user interface is the part of the application that the user sees and can interact with using the mouse and keyboard.

Note The term "BASIC" stands for Beginners All-Purpose Symbolic Instruction Code. BASIC was created in 1963 at Dartmouth College.

Using REALbasic, programmers create stand-alone applications. *Stand-alone,* in this instance, means that once written and compiled, an application can run natively on the OS for which it was created. Nothing else is required. *Compiling* is the process of translating programming statements into a format that can be executed on a particular OS.

REALbasic is made up of a graphical integrated development environment (IDE), an object-oriented programming language, a debugger, and a cross-platform compiler, as Figure 1-1 shows. REALbasic provides a powerful collection of tools that any professional software developer can appreciate. At the same time, first-time programmers and computer hobbyists will find that REALbasic is easy to learn and fun to work with.

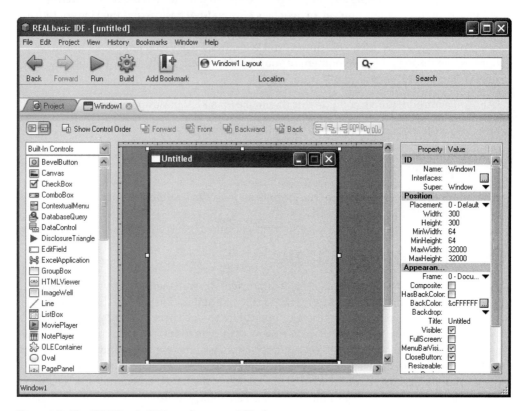

Figure 1-1. *The REALbasic IDE, as shown on Windows*

COMPETING PROGRAMMING LANGUAGES

Plenty of other software companies have developed various programming languages based on BASIC. These companies include Microsoft's Visual Basic, Pyxia's iBasic, Shoptalk Systems' JustBasic and Liberty Basic, the GameCreators' DarkBasic, and many more. However, all these BASIC implementations are designed to run only on the Windows OS. Each of these BASIC implementations has its own particular set of strengths and weaknesses, but none can complete with REALbasic when it comes to cross-platform software development.

From its introduction, REALbasic has been recognized as a programming language that is easy to learn, yet powerful enough to build complex applications. REALbasic quickly became popular for a number of reasons, including

- REALbasic facilitates drag-and-drop GUI design.

- REALbasic is an object-oriented programming language.

- REALbasic supports rapid application development (RAD).

- REALbasic provides for cross-platform application development.

Drag-and-Drop GUI Design

One of the features that makes REALbasic popular is the capability to create professional GUIs without requiring that you write a single line of code. Each time you start REALbasic, its IDE appears and you are presented with a new project. A *project* represents the collection of resources that make up a REALbasic application. Included in every project is a new blank window. You can use this window to create your application's GUI by dragging-and-dropping predefined controls supplied by REALbasic on to it.

Note An Integrated Development Environment (IDE) is the workspace you are given to work with when creating your application, along with all its associated menus, toolbars, windows, and built-in editors.

REALBASIC'S TIMELINE

REALbasic is developed by REAL Software, Inc. (www.realsoftware.com), which was founded in 1996. REALbasic started out as a software development tool for the Macintosh OS. REALbasic was first released on the Apple Macintosh in 1998, where it quickly received much acclaim and praise. In 2003, the Windows version of REALbasic was released. Later, in February 2004, REAL Software added the capability to compile software that could run on the Linux OSs to both the Macintosh and the Windows versions of REALbasic. However, REALbasic itself still only ran on Macintosh and Windows. This situation changed in September 2005, when REALbasic 2005 for Linux was released.

REALbasic provides a large collection of controls, representing features like PushButtons, EditFields, ProgressBars, and so on. Once added to a window, REALbasic assists you in moving and resizing them by automatically providing you with visual indicators that show when they are aligned with one another.

Object-Oriented Programming

REALbasic is an object-oriented programming language (OOP). An *OOP* language like REALbasic sees everything that makes up an application as an object. For example, a window is an object. A PushButton on a window is an object, as is a CheckBox or a ProgressBar.

In OOP, objects are semi-independent entities, meaning they store information about themselves and are responsible for controlling their actions. For example, a *PushButton control* stores attributes defining its appearance, such as its size, color, and position within a window. A PushButton control also stores program code that controls its actions, such as what to do when it's clicked or double-clicked.

RAD

REALbasic supports rapid application development (RAD). *RAD* is a process that supports a speedy software development process. One important RAD feature is prototyping. *Prototyping* is a programming technique in which the programmer creates a mockup of all the windows that will make up an application. This initial version of the application has no program code. It is designed to show the user or customer what the end result will ultimately look like. This enables the programmer to collect early feedback and to incorporate this feedback into the design of the application. RAD provides programmers with the capability to ensure the application that is ultimately created will meet customer expectations.

Cross-Platform Application Development

The REALbasic IDE looks and operates the same way on Macintosh, Windows, and Linux. Its toolbars, menus, windows, and options all look and work exactly the same way. The applications you create will all look and act the same when run on any of these OSs, except for cosmetic differences that have to do with the differences in the way Macintosh, Windows, and Linux OSs display certain application features. For example, the appearance of the Minimize, Maximize, and Close buttons are slightly different on each OS. However, by allowing for these OS specific differences, REALbasic enables you to develop applications that look and act just the way your users expect them to on their specific OS.

What Can REALbasic Do?

As previously stated, REALbasic provides you with all the tools you need to create world-class commercial software, or to create your own custom applications or computer games. If you can imagine it, you can build it using REALbasic. For example, using REALbasic, you can create

- Desktop applications

- Utility programs

- Background programs and services

- Computer games

- Database applications

- Internet client applications

- Internet web server applications

One of the things that makes REALbasic a powerful software development tool is it hides most of the complexity involved in the creation of applications. REALbasic does this by automatically taking care of core application functionality. For example, when you create a REALbasic application, you needn't worry about how to create a window or a PushButton control. REALbasic automatically provides you with these resources and takes care of making sure that they work, as you'd expect.

By abstracting so much OS functionality, REALbasic greatly simplifies the application development process. As a result, you'll find you can create applications that can perform tasks such as creating reports and text files on Macintosh, Windows, and Linux OSs without having to concern yourself with the differences in the ways each of the OSs works with these types of resources. Similarly, REALbasic also masks the complexities of working with graphics and network resources, enabling you, instead, to focus on developing the higher level functionality provided by your application.

What's New in REALbasic?

REALbasic 2006 is the most current version of REALbasic. It is backwards-compatible with previous versions, meaning you should be able to compile and run any application created using a previous version of REALbasic with little, if any, modifications or problems.

Starting with REALbasic 2005, a number of new bells and whistles were added that are not found in previous versions. Highlights of some of the more interesting new features, include

- **A new browser-styled IDE**. REALbasic's IDE now has the look and feel of an Internet browser that supports tabbing, complete with controls for navigating forward and backward (such as are found in the FireFox browser). The new IDE also helps to provide more room to work by making it easier to share space with various IDE windows and screens.

- **Support for multiple projects**. REALbasic now provides the capability to open up and work with multiple projects at the same time. This makes copying and pasting code between your applications easier.

- **The capability to remotely debug applications**. This feature is available only on the Professional Editions of REALbasic. REALbasic now has a built-in remote debugging capability that enables programmers to remotely test and debug applications running on one computer from a completely different network computer. In addition, the two computers being used do not even have to be running the same OS.

- **Built-in support for the SQLite database**. Previous versions of REALbasic included support for REALbasic's REAL Database. In REALbasic 2005, REAL Database has been replaced with the SQLite database, providing REALbasic with an even more powerful industry-recognized database.

- **A rapid release online distribution model.** With the release of REALbasic 2005, REAL Software began providing fixes, updates, and upgrades for REALbasic every 90 days. This will provide REALbasic programmers with access to new features that other competing software developers may not incorporate into their programming languages for up to 18 months.

Supported Development Platforms

This book makes a distinction between the computers and OSs used to run REALbasic and create applications, and those computers and OSs where applications are ultimately run. The computer and OSs where REALbasic is installed (for example, your computer) is referred to as the *development platform,* whereas the computers and OSs where the applications you create will ultimately run (for example, your customer's computers) are referred to as the *execution platforms.*

Once installed, REALbasic looks and runs the same way on each of its supported development platforms. However, its minimum and recommended hardware requirements vary for each supported OS.

Macintosh

REALbasic Standard and REALbasic Professional both have the same minimum hardware requirements. Like most software applications, REALbasic runs better when additional hardware resources are available. Table 1-1 outlines REALbasic's minimum and recommended hardware requirements when running on the Macintosh OS.

Table 1-1. *REALbasic's Minimum and Recommended Hardware Requirements for Execution on Macintosh*

Resource	Minimum Requirements	Recommended Requirements
Processor	Any PowerPC capable of running Mac OS X	800GHz G4 or higher
Memory	512MB	768MB
Operating Systems	Mac OS X 10.2.8 or higher	Mac OS X 10.3.9 or higher

SUPPORT FOR MACINTOSH RUNNING ON INTEL

In June 2005, Apple announced that it was going to begin delivering a version of the Macintosh operating system that would run on the Intel processor, with the intention of transitioning all of its computer lines over from the PowerPC processor to the Intel processor by the end of 2007. The next day, REAL Software announced that it would add support for the MAC OS X on Intel processors, promising that most existing REALbasic applications made for the Macintosh would be able to be recompiled for the new Intel processor version of MAC OS X without any code changes. In addition, REAL Software announced that it would continue to support application development for the PowerPC processor.

Windows

REALbasic can run on any version of Windows, starting with Windows 98 and NT. However, for optimal performance, you should run it on Windows XP or Vista. Table 1-2 outlines the minimum and recommended hardware requirements for both the Standard and Professional Editions of REALbasic 2006 for Windows.

Table 1-2. *REALbasic's Minimum and Recommended Hardware Requirements for Execution on Windows*

Resource	Minimum Requirements	Recommended Requirements
Processor	1GHz	1.5GHz
Memory	256MB	512MB
Operating Systems	Windows 98, NT, or higher	Windows 2000, 2003, XP, or Vista

■**Note** Surprisingly, REALbasic is more flexible than Visual Basic .NET when it comes to what versions of Windows OSs its IDE can support. Visual Basic .NET 2005 only supports execution on Windows 2003 Server, Windows XP running Service Pack 2, and Windows 2000 running Service Pack 4.

Linux

Linux has been quick to gain acceptance in the enterprise. It started out being used mostly on the server, but has since make great strides on the desktop. As Linux supports grows, more and more individuals and companies are looking for desktop applications that match what is found on Windows and the Macintosh. Porting Visual Basic applications over to REALbasic provides an easy answer to serve this niche, as does the development of new REALbasic applications.

The Standard and Professional versions of REALbasic for Linux can run on any Intel-based Linux distribution that supports GTK+ 2.0, Glibc-2.3, and Common UNIX Printing System (CUPS) or any higher levels for any of these requirements. Examples of qualifying Linux OSs include

- Novell Linux Desktop

- SuSE

- Mandriva/Mandrake

- Red Hat Desktop

Table 1-3 outlines additional minimum and recommended hardware requirements for REALbasic 2006 Linux.

Table 1-3. *REALbasic's Requirements for Execution on Linux*

Resource	Minimum Requirements	Recommended Requirements
Processor	1GHz	1.5GHz
Memory	256MB	512MB

Supported Execution Platforms

When it comes to which OSs are supported, REALbasic's list of supported execution platforms is a little larger than its list of supported development platforms. Specifically, the list of supported Macintosh systems is larger, as shown in Table 1-4.

Table 1-4. *Supported Operating Systems*

Type	Supported Operating Systems
Macintosh	PowerPC Macintosh, including G3, G4, and G5 running System 9.1 or Mac OS X 10.1 or higher
Windows	Windows 98, Me, NT, 2000, 2003 Server, XP, and Vista
Linux	Any Intel-based version of Linux with GTK+ 2.0 or higher, Glibc-2.3 or higher, and the CUPS

Standard vs. Professional

REALbasic comes in two flavors: Standard and Professional. Both REALbasic Standard and REALbasic Professional Editions provide you with all the tools you need to develop Windows, Macintosh, and Linux applications. However, as you would expect, the Professional Editions of REALbasic provide additional features not found in the Standard Editions.

The Standard Editions are typically better suited for the first-time programmer who doesn't want to invest too much money to start learning the language. The Standard Editions are also suitable for hobbyists who are looking for a programming language that can help them create custom applications or to have a little fun. On the other hand, the Professional Editions of REALbasic are designed for professional programmers and software development companies in the business of developing and distributing professional commercial software.

■**Note** Just because the Professional Editions of REALbasic include additional features, doesn't mean you can't do some serious software development with the Standard Editions. In fact, in many cases, you'll find you don't need the extra capabilities provided by the Professional Editions to build commercial quality applications.

REALbasic 2006 Standard Edition

REALbasic 2006 Standard Edition comes in the following three versions:

- REALbasic 2006 Standard Edition for Macintosh

- REALbasic 2006 Standard Edition Windows

- REALbasic 2006 Standard Edition for Linux

Each of these three versions of REALbasic provides programmers with the same set of features, regardless of OS platform. With the Standard Editions, you get a full set of development tools for creating applications for a particular OS.

The following list outlines some of the major development features provided by the REALbasic Standard Editions.

- **A Window Editor**. Enables you to create windows by dragging-and-dropping any of over 40 predefined controls, and provides visual assistance in resizing and realigning those controls.

- **A Code Editor**. Provides automatic statement color-coding, as well as a built-in autocomplete feature that provides assistance with writing code using valid syntax.

- **Object-oriented Programming**. REALbasic's implementation of BASIC is fully object-orientated with support for classes, objects, methods, and properties, as well as support for such features as polymorphism, inheritance, encapsulation, and abstraction.

- **Graphic Support**. Provides the capability to incorporate bitmaps and vector graphics, and to implement 2-D and 3-D graphics, as well as to integrate QuickTime movies into your applications.

- **Integrated Help System**. REALbasic uses its status bar to provide context-sensitive help based on the work currently being performed. In addition, the entire REALbasic reference manual has been integrated into the REALbasic IDE.

- **Internet Development Features**. Support is included for HTTP, UDP, SMTP, and POP3 to provide the capability to create Internet client-side applications.

- **Built-in Database Support.** REALbasic comes equipped with a single-user version of *SQLite*, a fully functional database engine.

- **Royalty-free Deployment**. Any applications you create can be freely distributed. You can give away or sell your REALbasic applications without having to pay REAL Software a royalty free.

- **Platform-specific Application Creation**. Each of the three Standard Editions is capable of generating stand-alone applications for their associated OSs, as well as demo versions that can run on other OSs.

- **Extensibility**. REALbasic provides the capability to extend its capabilities by adding your own or third-party plug-ins to REALbasic.

■**Note** Each version of REALbasic Standard Edition is also capable of creating demo applications for other OSs. A demo application has all the features of the application, but automatically stops executing after five minutes. For example, using REALbasic 2006 Standard Edition Windows, you can create full-featured Windows applications, as well as create demo versions of those applications that can run on Macintosh and Linux.

REALbasic 2006 Professional Edition

REALbasic 2006 Professional Edition comes in the following three versions:

- REALbasic 2006 Professional Edition for Macintosh

- REALbasic 2006 Professional Edition for Windows

- REALbasic 2006 Professional Edition for Linux

Each of these three versions of REALbasic provides programmers with the same set of features, regardless of OS platform. The REALbasic Professional Editions provide all the features found in the Standard Editions. Also, the following additional features are available in each of the Professional versions.

- **Internet Development Features**. REALbasic provides the capability to develop secure Internet applications using Secure Sockets Layer (SSL).

- **Web Server Development Enhancements**. REALbasic provides support for ServerSockets, providing the capability to create web server applications capable of managing thousands of connections.

- **Enhanced Database Support**. Database support for numerous third-party databases has been added, including support for Oracle, Sybase, Microsoft SQL server, Openbase, Frontbase, FileMaker Server, MySQL, and any ODBC-compliant data source.

- **Multiplatform Application Creation**. All the Professional Editions are capable of compiling applications that can run on any of the OSs supported by REALbasic.

- **Cross-platform Remote Debugging**. Provides the capability to debug an application running on one computer from a different computer, using any combination of OSs supported by REALbasic.

- **Support for Console Applications**. Provides the capability to create background applications that can be executed without requiring user interaction or scheduled to run when no one is logged into the computer.

Downloading REALbasic

REALbasic is distributed online. REALbasic has three different distributions: one for Macintosh, one for Windows, and one for Linux. You can download all three versions of REALbasic from REAL Software's website at www.realsoftware.com, as Figure 1-2 shows.

Figure 1-2. *You can download a copy of REALbasic from the REAL Software website.*

Each of these distributions is activated by a software key, which you must get from www.realsoftware.com. Each distribution contains everything needed to install either the Standard Edition or the Professional Edition of REALbasic.

At press time, REALbasic 2006 Standard Edition for Linux was free. In addition, you could purchase a license key for the Macintosh or Windows version of REALbasic Standard Edition for $99.95. The purchase price for any of the three Professional Editions of REALbasic is $499.95.

Once installed, you can activate either the Standard or the Professional Edition of REALbasic by entering the software key you obtained from www.realsoftware.com. In other words, if you enter a key for the Standard Edition, REALbasic Standard Edition will run. However, if you enter a key for the Professional Edition, the REALbasic Professional Edition will run.

■**Note** If you don't get your software key before you install REALbasic on your computer, REALbasic prompts you to do so the first time you start it up.

REALbasic vs. Visual Basic

When it comes to the development of Windows applications, REALbasic's main competitor is Microsoft's Visual Basic programming language. If you are a Windows programmer with a background in Visual Basic, you are going to find that REALbasic is remarkably similar to Visual Basic. As a result, you can get up and running quickly and can leverage nearly all your Visual Basic programming experience. This is especially true for Visual Basic programmers with a Visual Basic 6 background. The reason is because REALbasic closely mirrors much of what is in Visual Basic 6. Programmers with a background based on Visual Basic .NET also find the transition to REALbasic relatively smooth and can bring over most of their Visual Basic programming experience, less any .NET-specific features.

Because REALbasic is so similar to Visual Basic, you'll find it is relatively easy to port your Visual Basic applications over to REALbasic. In fact, you'll probably find you can port your applications over in an hour or a day, instead of weeks or months, as would be the case if you moved from Visual Basic over to another programming language, such as C++ or Java. REALbasic and Visual Basic are similar to one another, but plenty of important differences exist. These similarities and differences are highlighted in the following sections.

The Development Environment

Both REALbasic's and Visual Basic's IDE are similar and their development process is nearly identical. You start by adding controls to a window (called a *Form* in Visual Basic). Then, you set window and control properties, and add code. Next, you test your application and, when you are ready, you compile your stand-alone application.

Language Similarities

Both REALbasic and Visual Basic are object-orientated programming languages. Both share a common set of keywords (If, Then, Else, and so forth). Both have numerous functions in common. Both also share a common syntax and both use dot notation to reference properties. The list of similarities goes on an on.

In many ways, REALbasic can be looked at as the next step in the evolution of Visual Basic 6, whereas Visual Basic .NET can be viewed more as being a new divergent form of the language. The end result is this: porting a Visual Basic 6 application over to REALbasic is usually easier and quicker than modifying it to run under Visual Basic .NET.

Platform Support

Visual Basic only supports Windows operating systems, specifically only those Windows OSs running the .NET Framework. REALbasic, on the other hand, is designed to support cross-platform development on Macintosh, Windows, and Linux. Of course, more platforms mean more customers and more sales.

Distribution Issues

Visual Basic 6 applications may required specific DLLs be installed on a computer for it to execute and it is, thus, subject to DLL Hell. *DLL Hell* occurs when a new application overwrites an existing DLL file with a newer one, breaking any applications that need access to the previous version of the DLL file. Visual Basic .NET applications require the .NET Framework to be installed for the applications to execute, thus requiring additional system overhead. REALbasic applications run natively on any supported OSs, without requiring the overhead of a framework or risking DLL Hell.

Windows Ready Applications

Visual Basic applications are, of course, automatically designed to work and act like any other Windows application. REALbasic applications that run on Windows are also automatically Windows theme ready, meaning they will run and look like any other Windows application running on Windows 98, Me, NT, 2000, XP, and Vista. REALbasic applications also support Windows technologies, such as ActiveX and COM, as well as the Windows registry.

Support for PDAs and Mobile Devices

One area where Visual Basic has capabilities not matched by REALbasic is Visual Basic's capability to support application development for PDAs and mobile devices, such as cell phones.

REALbasic vs. Apple's XCode

Just as REALbasic competes with Microsoft's Visual Basic as a tool for application development for Windows software, REALbasic also has plenty of competition in the Apple world. One competitor of particular significance is Apple's XCode. Like REALbasic, *XCode* is a tool suite and an IDE for software creation on the Mac OS X.

There is no doubt that XCode provides an effective and powerful software development platform. Programmers with a strong Macintosh background no doubt will want to give it serious consideration. However, unlike REALbasic, XCode's capabilities are strictly limited to Mac OS X development. Unlike REALbasic, XCode is not designed to support the development of applications on previous versions of the MAC OS.

XCode's focus is on providing a powerful software development environment that facilitates application development using any of an assortment of programming languages. XCode is also designed to provide programmers with access to the latest Apple technologies. The programming languages supported by XCode include

- C

- C++

- Objective-C

- Java

- AppleScript

XCode provides a powerful and robust IDE for the development of software designed specifically for the Max OS X. However, it falls short of REALbasic in many ways. For example, while REALbasic is based on a easy to learn, yet powerful, implementation of BASIC, XCode only supports AppleScript, Java, and variations of C and C++.

XCode also falls short in the area of cross-platform development. Programmers who develop an application using XCode and one of its supported version of C or C++ must be prepared to rewrite their applications to port them over to Windows or Linux. While versions of C and C++ exist on both Windows and Linux, the programmer needs to be prepared to deal with differences in the way the languages are implemented on other platforms. In addition, the programmer also must be prepared to learn to work with different IDEs on each platform to which the application will be ported.

Online REALbasic Support Services

You can download a copy of REALbasic and acquire a license key from the download pages at the REAL Software website, as you can see in Figure 1-3. Here you can also find plenty of information about REALbasic, including information and links to all kinds of REALbasic resources, such as user groups and sample applications.

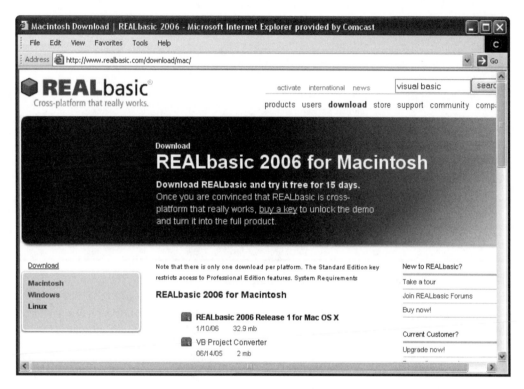

Figure 1-3. *Downloading the Macintosh Edition of REALBasic 2006*

In addition to learning more about REALbasic and visiting the REAL Software online store, you'll probably find the information presented on the Support page located at www.realsoftware.com/support/ (as Figure 1-4 shows) the most helpful.

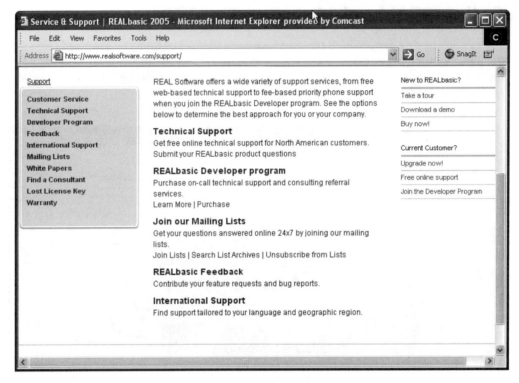

Figure 1-4. *A variety of support services are available for REALbasic.*

The Support page at the REAL Software website provides access to critical technical and information resources. The Support page provides access to the following resources.

- **Technical Support**. Free online e-mail-based technical support for North American customers. To use this service, you must supply your e-mail address and your license key. Allow up to 48 hours for a response.

- **REALbasic Developer Program**. Designed for professional software developers and software development companies, this feature enables you to purchase one of several different support options. These options provide for expedited technical support services, and bug fixes, as well as get your name or company listed in REAL Software's consultant referral program.

- **Mailing Lists**. Lets you sign up for any number of REAL Software sponsored mailing lists and search through archive listings. Lists are available for new users, news, game programming, and plug-ins.

- **Feedback**. Provides the capability to notify REAL Software of problems or bugs found in REALbasic, as well as to request new features and product enhancements.

- **International Support**. Provides access to links that non-North American users can use to find regional sources of information and support for REALbasic.

In addition to all the resources just listed, you can also find links to white papers, be able to request assistance in locating a REALbasic consultant, and get help if you have forgotten or lost your REALbasic license key.

Getting Started with Your First REALbasic Application

Now that you have spent some time learning about what REALbasic is, what it can do, and how it stacks up against other software development alternatives, it's time to see how REALbasic works. You can do this by creating your first REALbasic application. Learning a new programming language can be challenging and, at the same time, it can be a great deal of fun. For some, the idea of creating your first application before you have had a chance to learn all about the language seems intimidating. This is perfectly normal. However, there is no better way to learn than by doing. By creating your first application, you can get a solid understanding of what REALbasic is and what it can to, and you will be better prepared to understand the material in the following chapters.

First-time programmers should follow along carefully in this exercise, making sure to follow every step precisely. For now, focus on the overall process and the order in which things are done. Limit your attention to only the specific steps covered. Don't get caught up in trying to sort your way through all the different windows, menu options, toolbars, and controls that REALbasic makes available.

Programmers with a Visual Basic background should focus on the overall steps involved and look for similarities between REALbasic and Visual Basic. Programmers with a background involving a different programming language should vary their approach, based on what they bring with them from their particular programming background and its similarities (or lack thereof) to REALbasic. Regardless of your background, the most important fact is to focus on the big picture. Don't worry about the details for now.

Hello World!

As you will see as you go through the steps required to build the Hello World! application, REALbasic applications are typically created in five steps, as shown in the following outline.

1. Create a new REALbasic project.

2. Build the graphical user interface.

3. Modify window and control properties.

4. Add program code.

5. Test and compile the application.

If you have not done so already, go ahead and install REALbasic. Once the install is complete, start REALbasic. Once REALbasic starts, you will see its IDE. As Figures 1-5, 1-6, and 1-7 show, except for a few OS-specific cosmetic differences, the REALbasic IDE looks the same on Macintosh, Windows, and Linux.

As you can see, the REALbasic IDE is made up of a collection of menus, toolbars, tabbed screens, and windows. Through the creation of the Hello World! application, you get a gentle introduction to some of the major features of the REALbasic IDE.

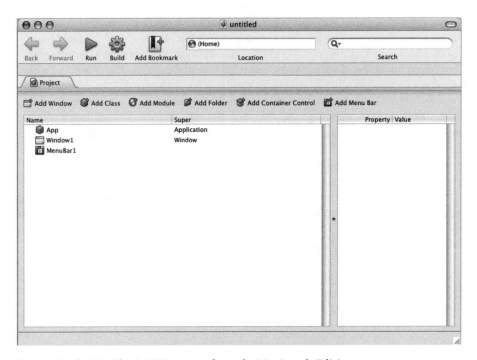

Figure 1-5. *The REALbasic IDE, as seen from the Macintosh Edition.*

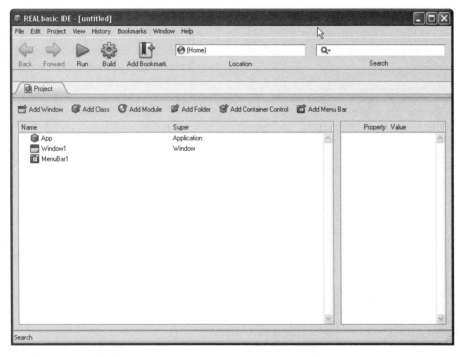

Figure 1-6. *The REALbasic IDE, as seen from the Windows Edition.*

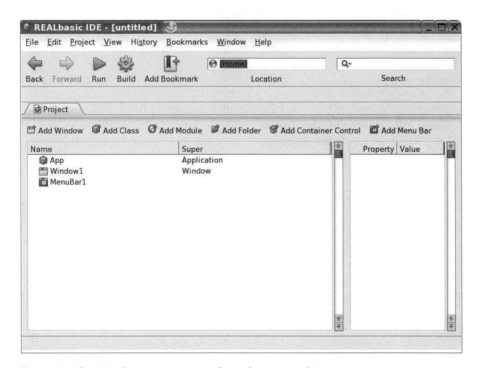

Figure 1-7. *The REALbasic IDE, as seen from the Linux Edition.*

Creating the Graphical User Interface (GUI)

Each time REALbasic starts, it automatically creates a new project for you. A project is a collection of items that, together, make up the building blocks of a REALbasic application. By default, all REALbasic applications start out with three items, as you can see in Figure 1-8.

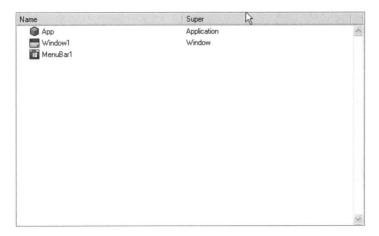

Figure 1-8. *A REALbasic project is made up of multiple items.*

These three items are

- **App**. This item contains information about the application.

- **Windows1**. This item contains information about the application default main window (Window1).

- **MenuBar1**. This item contains information about the main window's default menu bar.

The first step in creating the Hello World! application is to create its GUI. You begin this process by double-clicking the Window1 item on the Projects screen tab. This opens the Windows Editor, as Figure 1-9 shows, enabling you to design your application's GUI.

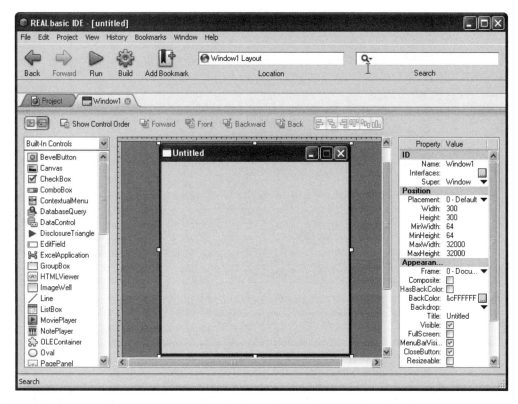

Figure 1-9. *The Window Editor provides you with all the tools you need to build your application's graphical user interface.*

Just to the left of the Window Editor, you can see a window containing a collection of predefined controls. These controls provide you with everything you need to create the Hello World! application.

To build the application's GUI, you need to add the appropriate controls to Window1. The easiest way to do this is by dragging-and-dropping a copy of the control on to the window. As you do this, the cursor changes to a crosshair. You can then drag the crosshair across the window and draw the size of the control. The first control you need to add is the PushButton control. This control is used to manage the display of a text message the application displays as it runs. Using the slider bar in the Control List window, locate the PushButton control, and then drag-and-drop on top of Window1, as Figure 1-10 shows.

■**Note** A *PushButton* is a control that looks and acts like a button. Typically, PushButton controls are used to initiate the execution of a particular command or task when the user clicks them.

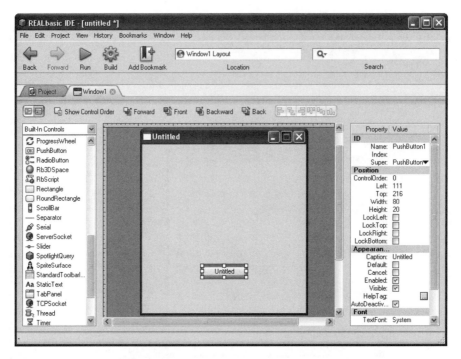

Figure 1-10. *Using drag-and-drop, you can quickly build your application's GUI.*

Once you have added a copy or *instance* of the PushButton control, you move it where you want it, using drag-and-drop. Notice that when the button is selected, resizing handles appear. Using these handles, you can change the size of the control to suit your needs. Place the PushButton control in roughly the same location as Figure 1-10 shows.

Next, you need to add an EditField control to the window, and resize and center it just above the PushButton. The EditField control is used to display the text message the user sees when the application runs. Note, as you move and resize the EditField control, the Window Editor assists you by displaying alignment indicators, as you can see in Figure 1-11.

The last control you need to add to your application is the StaticText control. Drag-and-drop an instance of this control onto the window, and align and center it just above the EditField control, as Figure 1-12 shows.

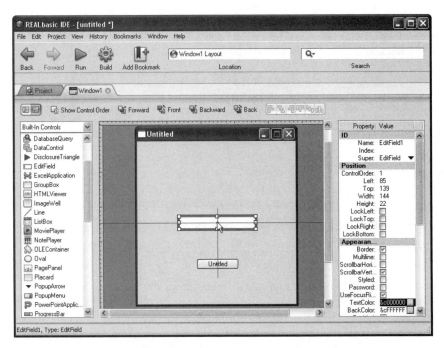

Figure 1-11. *Adding a EditField control to your REALbasic application*

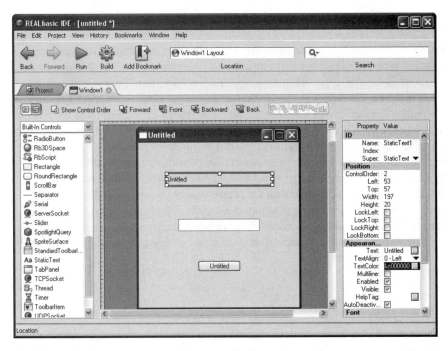

Figure 1-12. *The StaticText control lets you display text anywhere on your application's background window.*

■Tip Visual Basic programmers should recognize the PushButton, EditField, and StaticText field as being equivalent to Visual Basic's Button, TextBox, and Label controls.

At this point, the basic design of the Hello World! application's GUI is complete. If you want, you can go ahead and run your application by clicking the Run icon in the REALbasic's Main Toolbar, as Figure 1-13 shows.

The Run icon

Figure 1-13. *REALbasic lets you test your application from directly within its IDE.*

At this point, you can see REALbasic compile a development version of your application, which it then runs. As you can see, you application has a menu and displays the three controls you added to its main window. However, the application does not have a polished look at this point and it doesn't do anything. You can take care of addressing these issues in the sections that follow. For now, just exit your application as you would any application that runs on your particular OS. You will be returned to the Window Editor in the REALbasic IDE.

Configuring a Few Properties

The next step in the development of the Hello World! application is to spruce it up a bit by changing the appearance of its window and the controls you placed on it. For starters, click anywhere on the window. When you do, notice that resizing handles appear around the window. Also, you should see the Properties pane, located just to the right of the window Editor, is not populated with information. The information displayed in the Properties pane reflects the current state of Window1. To change an attribute or property of the window, all you have to do is assign a new value to one of the properties displayed in the Properties pane.

For your application, scroll down in the Property pane until you see the Title property, which is located in the Appearance group. Note, the property pane is divided into two columns: the first column displays a listing of all the properties for the selected object and the second column displays each property's associated value. By default, the Title property is assigned a value of Untitled. Click the Untitled value to select it and replace it with the word "Greetings," and then press Enter. You should see your application's title bar has automatically changed to reflect this new value.

Next, click the EditField control to select it. The information shown in the Properties pane now reflects the properties associated with the EditField control. You are going to change three properties associated with this control. For starters, in this application, the EditField control is going to be used to display a text string, as opposed to letting the user type a text string into it. To enforce this behavior, scroll down and locate the EditField control's ReadOnly property and select it.

Next, scroll up and located the Bold property in the Font section and select it. This causes any text displayed to appear in bold, to make it stand out. To set the final property for the EditField control, scroll up and locate the TextColor property in the Appearance section of the Properties pane, and then click the ellipsis icon. When you do, REALbasic displays a color palette, as Figure 1-14 shows. Select a color, such as dark blue, and then click the OK button. The color you selected should now be displayed as the background color in the Value row associated with the TextColor property. The actual background color of the EditField control does not change in the IDE, but it does display as expected in the compiled version of the application.

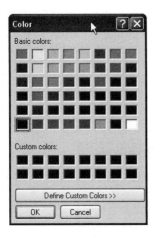

Figure 1-14. *Configuring a color property for a REALbasic control*

Now click the StaticText control. The Properties pane now displays properties associated with this control. Locate the Text property, which has a default value of Untitled. Replace this text with My First REALbasic Application. You can do this either by overtyping the current value entry or by clicking the ellipsis icon displayed alongside this value to open the Edit Value window, as Figure 1-15 shows. If necessary, increase the size of the control to see all the text.

Figure 1-15. *Adding a little descriptive text to your REALbasic application*

Next, scroll down and locate the TextAlign property. Click the drop-down list indicator to display the list of available options and select Center.

The last property you need to set is for the PushButton control. Select the control, and then locate its Caption property. Enter a value of Push me. At this point, your application should look like the example you see in Figure 1-16.

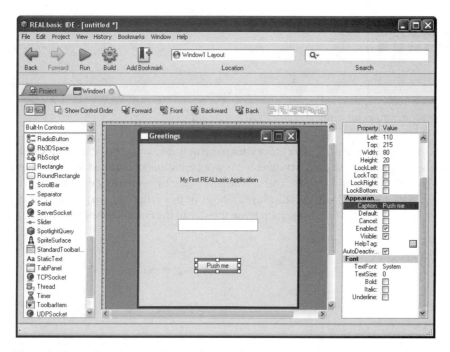

Figure 1-16. *By changing window and control properties, you can customize the appearance of your application's GUI.*

Adding a Little REALbasic Code

Now that your application has the proper look, its time to make it do something. You accomplish this by adding program code. In the case of the Hello World! application, all you need to do is add one line of code to the PushButton control to finish.

To associate programming code with a given control, locate the control in the Windows Editor and double-click it. This opens the Code Editor and provides you with a place to enter the code. Note, just to the left of the code editor you see a browser control that lists all the controls you added to your application. By default, the PushButton1 control's entry has been expanded and its Action event entry selected.

In REALbasic, actions such as the clicking or movement of the mouse cause events to trigger. You can set up your applications to respond to these events by supplying code statements you want to execute when a specific event is triggered (for example, when the user clicks the PushButton control).

The PushButton control's Action event executes whenever the user clicks it. Therefore, this makes the Action event the right event for controlling the display of text within the Hello World! application.

■**Tip** Visual Basic programmers should recognize the Action event as being equivalent to Visual Basic's Click event.

Enter the following text into the Code Editor, exactly as shown.

```
EditField1.Text = " Hello World! "
```

Once entered, the Code Editor should look exactly as Figure 1-17 shows. This code is formatted using a specific syntax required by REALbasic. If you do not follow REALbasic's syntax exactly, an error will result and your application won't run.

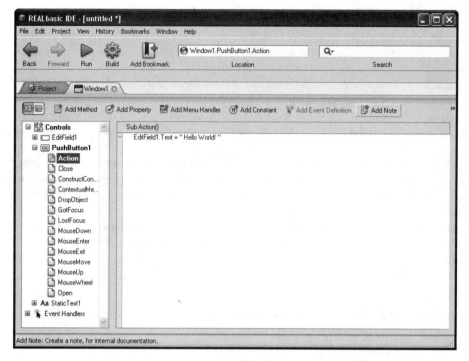

Figure 1-17. *The Code Editor color codes your code statements to make them easier to read.*

This code statement tells REALbasic to set or display the text string "Hello World!" as the EditField's Text property.

Testing Your Application

If you have not done so yet, now would be a good time to save your application. To do so, click the File menu and select Save. The Save As dialog appears. Type in the name for your application and specify the location where you want to save it, and then click OK. For this application, enter Hello World. In response, REALbasic creates a file named Hello World.rbp.

At this point, the Hello World! application is complete and should be ready to run. To test the application, click the green Run icon located in REALbasic's main toolbar. REALbasic will respond by compiling a development version of your application. Once the compilation is complete, REALbasic will run your application. Figure 1-18, Figure 1-19, and Figure 1-20 show how your application should look after you start it and click the PushButton labeled Push me, depending on your OS.

Figure 1-18. *The Hello World! application running on Windows*

Figure 1-19. *The Hello World! application running on Macintosh*

Figure 1-20. *The Hello World! application running on Linux*

Compiling Your Application for Macintosh, Windows, and Linux Execution

If you see an error message when you attempt to test your application, the odds are you mistyped the code statement associated with the PushButton's Action event. Go back and double-check your typing.

Once everything is working correctly, you are ready to create a stand-alone version—one that can execute outside of REALbasic IDE natively on the OS for which it was created—of your application.

By default, REALbasic compiles your application to run only for the OS you used to run the REALbasic IDE. For example, if you are using a Windows computer, then REALbasic, by default, compiles a stand-alone Windows application. To create a stand-alone application for your particular OS, click the Build icon, located just to the right of the Run icon on REALbasic's main toolbar. In response, REALbasic generates an executable version of your application stored in the same location where you installed REALbasic. You can run this application by double-clicking it. You can also make as many copies of the application as you want to give away or sell.

If you are using one of the Standard Editions of REALbasic, you may also generate a demo version of your application that will run for five minutes before halting its execution on other REALbasic-supported execution platforms. If you are using REALbasic Professional, then you can compile your application to run on Macintosh, Windows, and Linux.

Before you can use REALbasic to compile your application to run on other execution platforms, you must first tell it which execution platforms you want your application to run on. To do this, you specify which execution platforms you want to compile builds for. You do this by clicking the Project menu and selecting the Build Settings option. Figure 1-21 shows the Build Settings window.

Figure 1-21. *Specifying which execution platforms you want to create compiled copies of your application to run on*

By default, only the OS you are currently working with is selected. Select the desired target execution platforms, and then click OK. If you click the Build icon in REALbasic's main toolbar, REALbasic compiles your application for each specified target execution platform, giving each instance of your application the default name of My Application. This probably is not what you want, though. Instead, click the Project tab in the REALbasic IDE, and then click the App item. You can see the properties associated with the APP item are now displayed in the Properties pane. To provide REALbasic with a name for your application on each target execution platform, enter a name for the application in WindowsAppName, MacAppName, MacOSXAppName, MacClassicAppName, and LinuxAppName properties, as appropriate. Now, when you click the Build icon located in main toolbar, REALbasic compiles separate copies of your application, using the names you supplied for each execution platform you selected.

Each of these stand-alone copies of your application will run and look exactly as you saw in Figures 1-18 through 1-20.

Summary

REALbasic is a cross-platform software development tool that provides programmers with a rich and powerful set of features, which stack up against any programming language currently available on Macintosh, Windows, or Linux. With REALbasic, the name of the game is cross-platform portability. REALbasic provides you with all the tools you need to develop powerful applications that can be ported to all three of the major desktop OSs. REALbasic does this without reliance on frameworks or virtual machines, using a programming language that is both easy to learn and master.

CHAPTER 2

■ ■ ■

Navigating the REALbasic Integrated Development Environment

In Chapter 1, you were introduced to REALbasic and many of its capabilities. In this chapter, you build upon this knowledge by learning the ins and outs of working with the REALbasic IDE. This includes learning how to create and manage REALbasic projects, learning how to work with REALbasic Windows and Code Editors, and learning how to take advantage of REALbasic's integrated Help resources. In addition, you learn how to work with a number of other integrated development environment (IDE) features, including the REALbasic menus, the Bookmarks bar, the Tabs bar, the Editor toolbar, the Project Editor, the Controls and Properties Panes, and the Tips bar. You also learn how to create a custom web browser application. By the time you complete this chapter, you will learn how to

- Work with REALbasic editors, menus, and toolbars

- Customize REALbasic toolbars

- Organize and manage REALbasic projects

- Take advantage of REALbasic's integrated Help resources

Starting REALbasic

As you learned in Chapter 1, you interact with REALbasic by way of its IDE. This includes application development, testing, and compilation. REALbasic's IDE provides you with all the tools you need to create new applications. These software tools include

- Windows Editor

- Code Editor

- Menu Editor

- Compiler

- Debugger

Like most modern programming language's development environments, REALbasic's IDE is involved, consisting of an assortment of menus, toolbars, and screens. In short, this IDE is packed with features and functionality. As a result, when you first begin working with REALbasic's IDE, you can easily get lost or overwhelmed.

To help alleviate stress and to get you up and running as quickly as possible, a solid familiarity with the IDE is essential for any REALbasic programmer. The primary focus of this chapter is to help provide you with a thorough overview of the REALbasic IDE and to give you all the information you need.

Each time you start REALbasic, its main IDE appears, as Figure 2-1 shows. As you learned in Chapter 1, REALbasic's IDE looks and operates almost exactly the same, regardless of whether you are running it on Macintosh, Windows, or Linux. The IDE also looks and works almost exactly the same way for both the Standard and Professional editions of REALbasic.

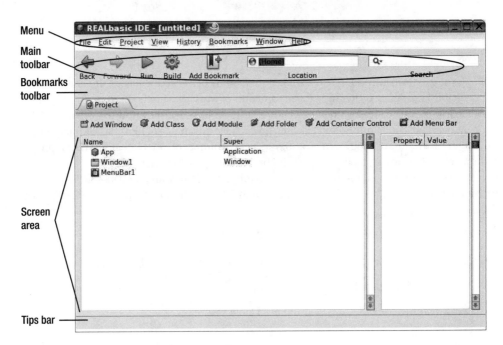

Figure 2-1. *REALbasic's IDE running on Linux*

■**Note** One difference between the REALbasic IDE on Macintosh, and the REALbasic IDE on Windows and Linux is the location of the main menu. As is the case for most Macintosh OS X applications, REALbasic's main application menu is not displayed on the application but is, instead, displayed at the top of the Mac OS X desktop.

The REALbasic Menu

REALbasic's menu is loaded with essential commands that provide convenient access to key REALbasic functionality. REALbasic's menu is organized into the following menus.

- **File**. Provides access to commands for opening, creating, and saving REALbasic projects.

- **Edit**. Provides access to commands for performing standard editing functions (copy, paste, and so forth), as well as to REALbasic specific commands that interact with the Window Editor and the Code Editor.

- **Project**. Provides access to commands for adding items to REALbasic projects, as well as for testing, debugging, and creating REALbasic applications.

- **View**. Provides access to commands that control the look and functionality of the REALbasic IDE.

- **History**. Provides access to commands that enable you to revisit REALbasic screens that you have already worked with when developing a project.

- **Bookmarks**. Provides access to commands for bookmarking REALbasic items and screens, as well as for accessing bookmarked items and screens.

- **Window**. Provides access to commands for minimizing and maximizing the REALbasic IDE, and for moving forward and backward between REALbasic screens.

- **Help**. Provides access to commands that access REALbasic documentation and online content.

■**Note**   On the Macintosh, REALbasic also provides an Apple menu and a REALbasic menu, as Figure 2-2 shows.

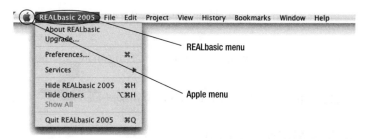

Figure 2-2. *On Macintosh, REALbasic also includes an Apple and a REALbasic menu.*

The *Apple menu* is a standard menu item for Macintosh applications. However, it does not contain any REALbasic specific commands. The REALbasic menu contains menu commands found on other menus in Windows and Linux, as Figure 2-2 shows.

The sheer number of available REALbasic menu commands makes it impossible to fully explore and review them all in this chapter. You learn more about many of these commands as you work your way through the rest of this book.

REALbasic's Main Toolbar

REALbasic's Main toolbar, shown in Figure 2-3, holds a collection of icons and edit fields that enable you to navigate between REALbasic screens, to test and build REALbasic applications, and to locate and search your program code.

Figure 2-3. *The default view of the REALbasic Main toolbar (Windows version)*

Default Main Toolbar Resources

Like many REALbasic toolbars and IDE features, the REALbasic Main toolbar is configurable. In its default configuration, this toolbar provides a number of key features. The major features found on the default REALbasic Main toolbar are outlined in the following list.

- **Forward**. Provides the capability to move forward to previously viewed screens.

- **Backward**. Provides the capability to move backward to previously viewed screens.

- **Run**. Provides the capability to compile and run a test version of your application from within the IDE. If an error is detected during compilation, REALbasic stops the build process and displays an error message.

- **Build**. Provides the capability to create a stand-alone version of your application based on the currently defined build settings that will run natively on target operating systems (OSs).

- **Add Bookmark**. Creates either a local or a global bookmark for the currently selected item or screen.

- **Location**. Provides the capability to locate project items by specifying an item name and pressing Enter.

- **Search**. Provides the capability to search for items within your program code.

Configuring REALbasic's Main Toolbar

The REALbasic Main toolbar is highly configurable. You can add and remove icons to control key functionality. You can change the order in which these icons are displayed. You can also define the size and appearance of the toolbar's icons. To configure the Main toolbar, click View ▶ Main Toolbar ▶ Customize. This opens the Customize Main Toolbar dialog, as Figure 2-4 shows.

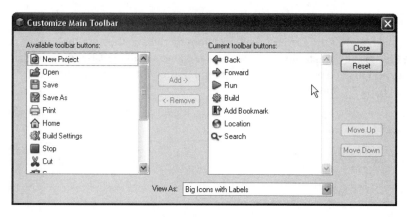

Figure 2-4. *The Customize Main Toolbar dialog when viewed from Microsoft Windows*

A list of optional icons is displayed on the left side of the Customize Main Toolbar dialog. On the right side of the dialog, a list of icons already defined on the toolbar is displayed. You can add new icons to the toolbar by selecting an icon from the available list and clicking the Add button. Similarly, you can remove an icon from the toolbar by selecting it in the list of currently defined icons, and then clicking the Remove button.

You can change the order in which icons are displayed on the Main toolbar by selecting an icon, and then clicking either the Move Up or Move Down button. You can also specify how REALbasic displays these icons by selecting one of the following options from the View As drop-down list:

- Big icons with labels

- Small icons with labels

- Big icons (no labels)

- Small icons (no labels)

- Labels only

Finally, if you want to restore REALbasic's default icon selection for the Main toolbar to its default configuration, you can do so by clicking the Reset button (or Reset Defaults on Macintosh).

REALbasic's Bookmarks Toolbar

Bookmarks are shortcuts to REALbasic items. By setting bookmarks, you provide yourself with shortcuts to items such as controls or REALbasic editors that you work with frequently. REALbasic supports two types of bookmarks: local and global. A *local bookmark* is one that is available only in the project in which it is set, whereas a *global bookmark* is available in all your REALbasic projects. Local bookmarks are displayed on the Bookmarks toolbar. Global bookmarks are accessed by opening the Bookmarks menu.

Adding New Bookmarks

You can add a new bookmark for the currently selected item by clicking the Add Bookmark icon located on the REALbasic Main toolbar. Or, you can add a new bookmark by selecting the Add Bookmark command located on the Bookmarks menu. Either option displays the Add Bookmark dialog, as Figure 2-5 shows.

Figure 2-5. *Adding a new bookmark when running REALbasic on the Mac OS X*

You can supply a custom name for your bookmark by replacing the default text shown in the Add Bookmark dialog's Name field. You can then specify whether the bookmark should be local or global.

Editing Your Bookmarks

REALbasic enables you to edit your bookmarks at any time from the Edit Bookmarks dialog, as Figure 2-6 shows.

Name	Project	Location
untitled:(Home)	untitled	(Home)
Window1.Open	untitled	Window1.Open
Window1.Close	untitled	Window1.Close
Window1 Layout	untitled	Window1 Layout

Edit Bookmarks

Bookmarks available in any project:

New Folder   Cancel   OK

Figure 2-6. *Editing your bookmarks when running REALbasic on the Mac OS X*

To open the Edit Bookmarks dialog on Windows or Linux, right-click the Bookmarks toolbar and choose the Customize option. On Macintosh, Control-click the Bookmarks toolbar to access the Customize option. Once opened, you can retype the name assigned to any bookmark by double-clicking it and overtyping its name.

REALbasic's Screen Area

The Screen area takes up the bulk of REALbasic's IDE workspace and is made up of multiple parts, as Figure 2-7 shows. These parts include

- Tabs bar

- Editor toolbar

- Screen(s)

Figure 2-7. *The Screen area, shown here running on Windows, is the work area in the REALbasic IDE.*

The Screen area is used to organize the different parts of your REALbasic application into screens. This is where you create your application's interface, menu system, and program code. Each screen is identified by its tab, which is displayed in the Tabs bar, located at the top of the Screen area.

Tabs Bar

The *Tabs bar* displays a tab for each screen opened in the Screen area. A tab for the Project Editor screen is always present, as this screen cannot be closed. All other screens have a Close box displayed on their tab. By clicking the Close box on a screen tab, you close it, but this has no effect on content you created on the screen (the user interface, application menu, or program code is simply removed from view).

The Tabs bar provides a convenient mechanism for quickly moving between major applications components, each of which is created and managed on its own screen.

Editor Toolbar

Each REALbasic screen provides access to an editor or viewer. Each editor has its own custom toolbar, which is referred to as the Editor toolbar. For example, the Code Editor has a different toolbar than the Menu Editor. Figure 2-7 shows the contents of the Project Editor screen, which provides access to icons you can use to add various components to your projects.

Most of the functionality found on the Editor toolbar is replicated on the Project menu's Add submenu. However, the Editor toolbar provides a much easier and more intuitive tool.

Screens

Each major component of your REALbasic projects is created and managed on its own screen. For example, each of the following IDE editors has a unique screen.

- **Project Editor**. Manages the items that make up your REALbasic projects.

- **Windows Editor**. Used to design Windows dialogs that make up your applications.

- **Menu Editor**. Used to develop menus for your application Window dialogs.

- **Code Editor**. Used to write and edit the code statements that make your applications work.

Each screen is organized into two or more panes. For example, the Project Editor screen is divided into two panes, as you saw in Figure 2-7. The left pane contains all the items that make up your REALbasic projects. On the right side of the screen is the Properties pane. Each pane is separated by a divider, which you can click and drag to the left or right to increase or decrease the amount of space provided to each pane on the screen.

■**Note** The REALbasic Properties pane looks and operates in almost exactly the same manner as the Visual Basic Properties Window. If you have a Visual Basic programming background, you probably only need to take a cursory look at the REALbasic Properties pane. Then, you can focus your attention on other IDE features in this chapter.

Because working space is limited within the IDE, REALbasic provides you with the capability to increase the amount of available space by temporarily hiding the display of toolbars. This is achieved by clicking the View menu and selecting the Editor Only menu item. This temporarily hides the following toolbars.

- Main toolbar

- Bookmarks bar

- Editor toolbar

The Project Editor

The *Project Editor* is your focal point for managing all the different items that make up your REALbasic projects. As Figure 2-8 shows, the Project Editor consists of two panes. The left pane displays a listing of all the items that make up your project. The right pane displays the properties associated with the currently selected item. If no item is selected, the Properties pane appears blank.

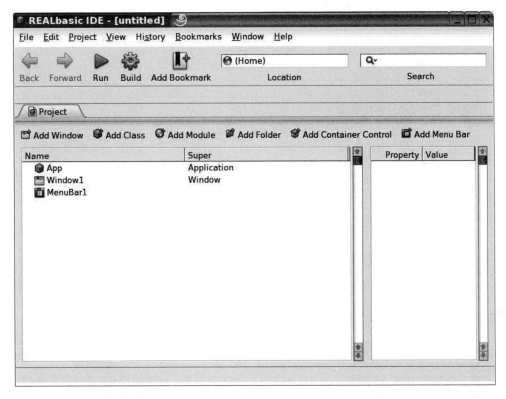

Figure 2-8. *The Project Editor, as seen here on Linux, is used to manage all the items that make up a REALbasic project.*

Each time you start REALbasic, it creates a new empty project. This project contains three items (App, Window1, and MenuBar1) and is your starting point for developing new desktop applications. However, REALbasic also supports the development of other types of applications. For example, if you click File and select the new Project menu item, REALbasic responds by displaying the New Project dialog, as Figure 2-9 shows.

CREATING CUSTOM PROJECT TEMPLATES

If you want, you can create custom templates and add them to REALbasic to facilitate the creation of certain types of applications. This can be a handy way to facilitate application development in situations where you create multiple projects that share common features and functionality. In this scenario, you'd create a base application that contains all the features commonly shared, and then use it as a template for the creation of new applications. To do so, all you must do is copy the project you want to use as templates into REALbasic's Project Templates folder, which you can find in the directory where you installed REALbasic.

Figure 2-9. *Selecting the type of application you want to create using REALbasic, as shown on Mac OS X*

As shown in Figure 2-9, you can also use REALbasic to create console applications. A *console application* is one that does not usually require user interaction and, instead, is run as a background program. Console applications do not have a graphical user interface (GUI). Therefore, the only item you find listed for a new Console application project is the App item.

Both the Desktop and Console applications entries displayed in the New Project dialog represent templates that REALbasic uses when creating a new project. When selected, REALbasic starts the project creation process by loading a copy of the selected template.

You can add new items to your project by clicking one of the Add icons located in the Editor toolbar or by opening the Project menu, selecting Add, and then clicking an item from the list of choices. You can also add items to your projects by dragging them from the desktop and dropping them onto the Project Editor. Deleting an item is even easier: simply select the item you want to remove from your project, and then press Delete.

■**Note** You can add and remove functionality from the Editor toolbar by opening the View menu, clicking Editor Toolbar, and then selecting Customize. This opens the Customize Project Toolbar dialog where you can Add and Remove toolbar buttons, as well as configure the look and feel of the toolbar.

■**Tip** As your projects grow in size, they may end up containing numerous items. If you choose, you can reorder your project's items by dragging them to a new location in the project list, as indicated by a vertical line that appears during the move process. In addition, you can further organize your project items by creating Folder items into which you can then move other project items. To do so, open the Project menu, click Add, and then select Folder. A new folder is added to the list of items in your project. The Folder item has a single property: its Name. Select the folder and change its name to something appropriate, and then drag-and-drop any project items you want into it.

The Project Editor also provides easy access to project items. Simply double-click an item and REALbasic responds by opening the appropriate editor and displaying the item in it. Or, if an item does not have an editor, REALbasic displays the item in a viewer.

As you learned when building the Hello World! application in Chapter 1, when you work in the Project Editor, you can assign a name to your application by selecting the App item and modifying the MacAppName, WindowsAppName, or LinuxAppName properties. You can also set properties belonging to menu bar items or any other item that is part of your project from the Properties pane.

■**Note** Some properties can be modified only during application development. Other properties can be modified during both application development and programmatically during application execution. In addition, some properties can only be set at run-time, so you will be unable to modify them via the REALbasic IDE.

The Window Editor

The *Window Editor* provides you with the tools needed to build your application's GUI and is organized into three panes. The left-hand pane provides access to a collection of predefined controls you can use to customize your application's GUI, as Figure 2-10 shows. The center pane provides a Windows editing area, where the windows you are working with are displayed. The right-hand pane displayed properties associated with the currently selected window or control.

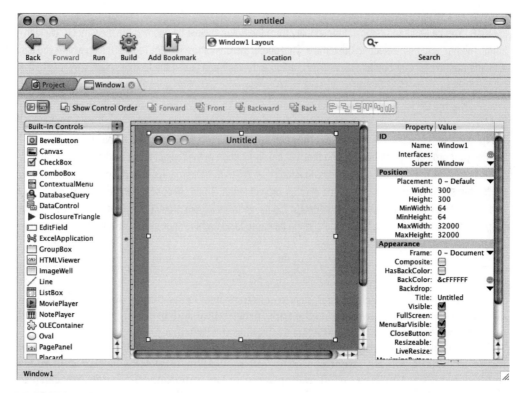

Figure 2-10. *REALbasic controls, seen here on Mac OS X, provide the basic building blocks for building your application's GUI.*

Controls are prebuilt interface-development elements that form the building blocks on which you design your application's windows. Each instance of a control you add to a window can be customized. For example, using its resizing handles, you can resize it. You can also move it to a different location within the window. Finally, you can select it to view and modify its properties, which will be visible in the Properties pane.

■**Note** Visual Basic programmers should see many similarities between the Visual Basic Control toolbar and the REALbasic Controls pane. In many cases, REALbasic provides exactly the same functionality in its controls as is found in Visual Basic Controls, just with different control names.

Note, at the top of the Controls pane is a drop-down list. This drop-down list provides access to any of the four Controls categories, as you can see in the following list.

- **Built-in**. The default collection of controls displayed by REALbasic.

- **Project**. Custom-built controls added to the project via the Project Editor.

- **Plug-in**. Third-party controls added to REALbasic by copying them into the REALbasic Plug-ins folder.

- **Favorite**. Controls you marked as favorites.

■**Note** You can add a control to a window by dragging-and-dropping it from the Controls pane onto the window in the Windows Editor. You can also add a Control by double-clicking it in the Controls pane.

You can use the Window Editor to modify any window you added to your project by double-clicking the window in the Projects Editor. REALbasic responds by opening the Window Editor and displaying the selected window. In addition, a new entry is added to the Tab bar for the Window Editor.

The name of the Default Window for any REALbasic project is Window1. You may add other windows as needed by your applications by clicking the Add Window icon on the Project Editor toolbar. When you finish editing the window's GUI, you can close it by clicking the Close box in the Tab bar associated with the window.

Because the space available to you when working with the Window Editor is limited, REALbasic has horizontal and vertical scroll bars on the top and right-hand side of the window editing area. This enables you to move the window you are working with without having to resize the REALbasic IDE or to hide its toolbars temporarily (via commands located on the View menu).

The Menu Editor

The REALbasic Menu Editor, shown in Figure 2-11, provides you with everything you need to create a robust menu system for your REALbasic applications. The Menu Editor consists of two panes. The left pane displays the contents of the menu being developed. The right pane displays the properties associated with the selected menu, submenu, or menu item.

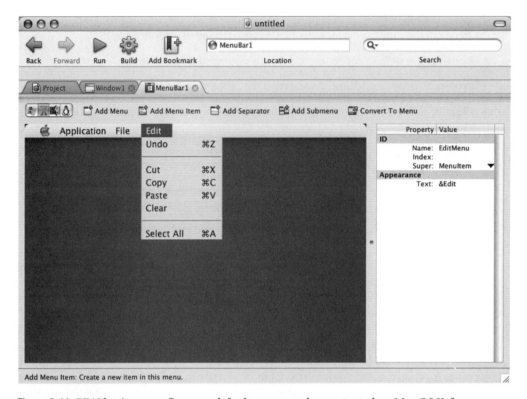

Figure 2-11. *REALbasic preconfigures a default menu, as demonstrated on Mac OS X, for every new application.*

■**Note** One area where REALbasic and Visual Basic differ somewhat is the manner in which application menus are developed. Programmers with a Visual Basic background may want to jump ahead to Chapter 4 to investigate how menu development works in REALbasic.

PREVIEWING OS-SPECIFIC VERSIONS OF YOUR MENU SYSTEM

REALbasic displays a set of four icons on the left-hand side of the Project toolbar whenever the Menu Editor is displayed. Each of these icons represents one of the OSs supported by REALbasic (Windows, Mac OS X, Classic MAC OS, and Linux). By clicking these icons, you can get a sneak peek at how your application's menu will look when it's run on different OSs.

By default, REALbasic automatically creates File and Edit menus for every new application. In addition, REALbasic automatically adds a number of menu items to these two menus, as shown in Table 2-1. As already noted, REALbasic also creates an Apple and REALbasic menu for REALbasic applications compiled to run on the Macintosh OS.

Table 2-1. *REALbasic Default Application Menu and Menu Items*

Menu	Menu Item
File	Exit
Edit	Undo
	Cut
	Copy
	Paste
	Delete
	Select All

For more detailed information on how to use the Menu Editor to create and work with REALbasic menus, read Chapter 4.

The Code Editor

You use the *Code Editor* to type in the program statements for your applications. The REALbasic Code Editor is divided into two panes. The left pane has a browser-like feature that lets you view and select the objects that make up your application. The right pane provides the workspace where you type in your application's programming statements.

In the Code Editor's browser area, shown in Figure 2-12, you see a listing of all the objects that make up your applications. Each object, be it a window or a control or any other object element, has a collection of events associated with it.

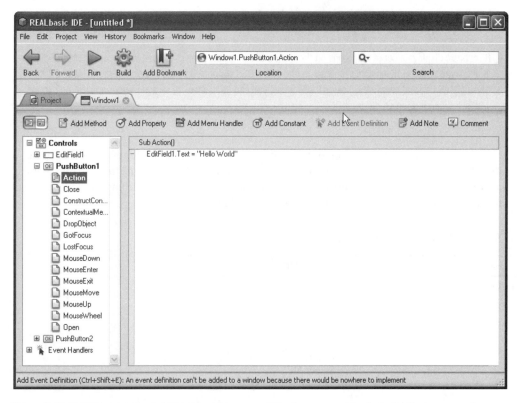

Figure 2-12. *REALbasic's Code Editor, as shown on Windows, provides helpful features, such as automatic code indentation and keyword color coding.*

■**Note** An *event* is an action initiated by the user or the application itself. REALbasic is able to detect the occurrence of these events and execute programming statements you associate with them. For example, if the user clicks a PushButton control you added to an application window, the Action event associated with that PushButton is executed. If you supplied any program code for that PushButton's Action event, it is automatically executed.

REALbasic's Tips Bar

One easily overlooked, but exceptionally helpful, feature of REALbasic is the Tips bar located at the bottom of the IDE. Each time you compile an application, REALbasic checks the syntax of your application's programming statements. If it detects an error, REALbasic displays a description of the error in the Tips bar. By looking for this error message, you may be able to quickly determine what went wrong without having to dig through your program code looking for the source of the problem.

REALbasic uses the *Tips bar* to provide you with all kinds of additional information. For example, REALbasic keeps an eye on what you are doing as you work within the IDE and, when appropriate, displays hints in the Tips bar. For example, as Figure 2-13 demonstrates, REALbasic uses the Tips bar to display information about menu and icons, as well as other items found in the IDE.

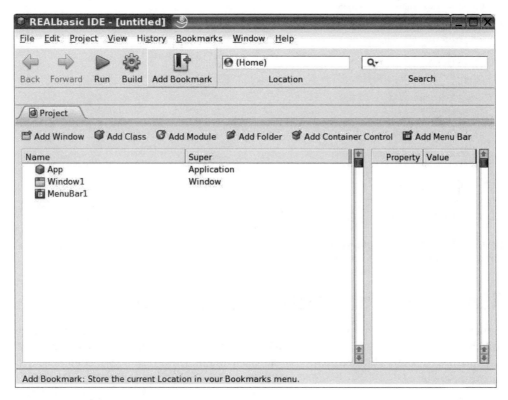

Figure 2-13. *REALbasic uses the Tips bar, as shown here on Linux, to provide you with helpful information as you work within the IDE.*

REALbasic also uses the Tips bar to display syntax information as you type in your code statements. For example, Figure 2-14 shows an example of how REALbasic displays the syntax required to format a particular programming statement.

Figure 2-14. *REALbasic displays command syntax, as shown here on Linux, to help you properly formulate statements as you enter your program code.*

REALbasic's Integrated Help Features

From time to time, even the most experienced programmer needs a little help. Fortunately, the REALbasic IDE provides easy access to all of REAL Software's REALbasic documentation. You can find these resources located on REALbasic's Help menu. These resources include access to electronic copies of REALbasic manuals and links to online resources at the REALbasic website, as well as access to REALbasic's Reference Manual.

DOWNLOADING REALBASIC'S DOCUMENTATION

Copies of the Getting Started, Tutorial, and User's Guide manuals are available as free downloads from the REALbasic website at http://www.realsoftware.com/download/windows/, http://www.realsoftware.com/download/mac/, and http://www.realsoftware.com/download/linux/. In addition, you can download a copy of the PDF version of REALbasic's Language Reference manual from each of these web pages.

■**Note** REALbasic's online documentation is provided in PDF format. You'll need a copy of the Adobe Acrobat Reader or a similar application installed on your computer before you can view this documentation.

Accessing REALbasic's Manuals

REALbasic provides access to three manuals. Each of these manuals is designed to serve a different purpose. These manuals include

- **Getting Started**. A small REALbasic manual designed as an introduction to REALbasic by guiding the reader through the creation of a sample application.

- **Tutorial**. A REALbasic manual designed to provide the reader with a thorough introduction by demonstrating how to create a word-processing application.

- **User's Guide**. A REALbasic manual designed to provide a complete overview of REALbasic programming.

■**Note** REALbasic's Tutorial and User's Guide are not installed with REALbasic. Instead, you are prompted to download them the first time you try to access them from the Help menu.

Accessing REALbasic Online Resources

REALbasic's Help menu also provides easy access to two useful online links available at the REALbasic website. These resources include

- **REALbasic on the Web**. Opens your default web browser and loads www.realbasic.com, REALbasic's official website.

- **REALbasic Feedback**. Opens your default web browser and loads http://www.realsoftware.com/feedback/, as Figure 2-15 shows. This web page enables you to report problems and submit enhancement requests.

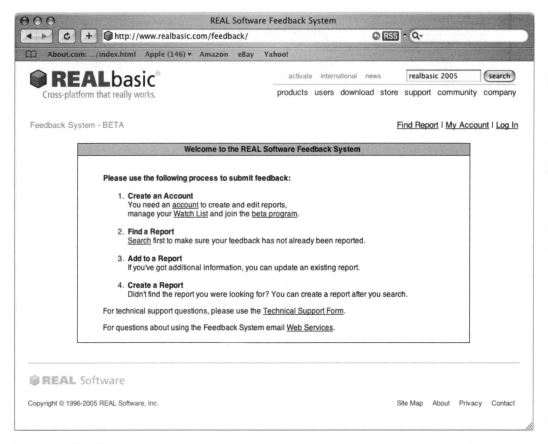

Figure 2-15. *REALbasic makes it easy to report errors or submit enhancement requests, as shown here on Mac OS X.*

Working with REALbasic's Electronic Language Reference

REALbasic's Help menu also provides you with access to an electronic copy of the REALbasic Language Reference, shown in Figure 2-16.

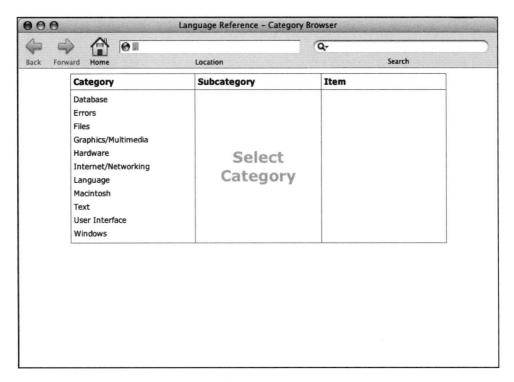

Figure 2-16. *The REALbasic Language Reference provides easy access to information about REALbasic programming language elements, as shown here on Mac OS X.*

■Tip In addition to accessing the Language Reference from the REALbasic Help menu, you can also open it by either pressing the F1 key or using CTRL-/ on Windows or Linux or by pressing the ⌘-? key on Macintosh.

The REALbasic Language Reference is organized into three panes. The left-most pane contains a listing of high-level categories where major programming language elements are logically grouped. When you select a category, a listing of available subcategories is displayed in the middle pane. When you select a subcategory entry, a list of topics is displayed in the right-most pane. To view the available information for any given topic, click its entry in the right pane. For example, Figure 2-17 shows an example of the reference information available for the If...Then...Else statement.

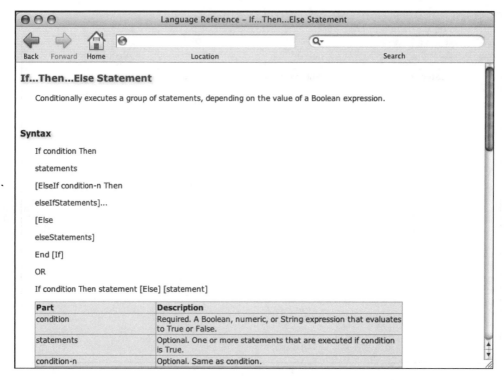

Figure 2-17. *Using the REALbasic Language Reference to learn about programming language keywords, as shown here on Mac OS X.*

At the top of the Language Reference dialog, you can see Forward and Back buttons that let you navigate through the data you've viewed while using this dialog. The Home button returns back to the listing of categories you see when the Language Reference first opens. Just to the left of the Home button is the Location area. The *Location area* is used to locate information about a REALbasic object, such as a PushButton or EditField. As you start to type in the name of an object, REALbasic attempts to help you by anticipating the name of the object you are typing and displaying this text in light gray. To accept the REALbasic suggestion, press Tab. If REALbasic has more than one suggestion, it displays three gray dots. To view REALbasic's suggestions, press Tab and a pop-up menu appears, enabling you to use your keyboard's up and down arrows, and Enter or Return to select the appropriate choice.

To the right of the Location area is the Search area, which you can use to perform a keyword search on any term. In response, REALbasic displays a list of matching topics from which you can select, as Figure 2-18 shows.

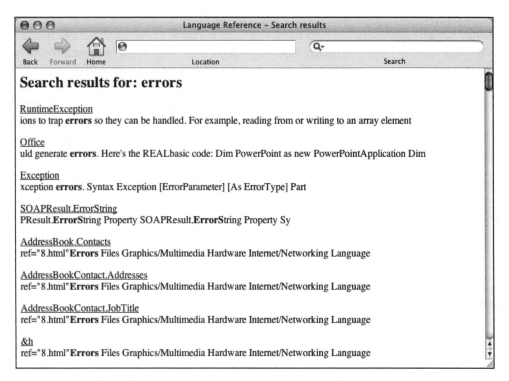

Figure 2-18. *Searching the REALbasic Language Reference for information on errors, as shown here on Mac OS X.*

Building a Custom Web Browser

One of the goals of this book is to ensure that you get the opportunity to create a new application in every chapter. So, before wrapping up your work on this chapter, take a few minutes to develop your next REALbasic application.

To help streamline presentation, the demonstration of how to build this application is done entirely using REALbasic for Windows. As a result, some minor tweaking may be required to ensure it will run on Macintosh and Linux. Specifically, you may need to resize and adjust the location of controls a bit to make sure they display correctly on other versions of REALbasic.

■**Note** This application uses REALbasic's HTMLViewer control to create a custom web browser. This control is different than most other REALbasic controls in that it depends on other software being installed to work correctly. For the RB Book Browser application to run on Windows, Internet Explorer (IE) must be installed. To run the RB Book Browser application on Mac OS X, the Apple WebKit must be installed. Mac OS X's default browser, Safari, also uses the Apple WebKit to run. To run on Linux OS, the Mozilla browser must be installed. While you can count on your Windows and Mac OS X users to have the required software already installed on their computers, you cannot count on all your Linux users having Mozilla installed. As you can see, cross-platform application development is a challenge.

The RBBookFinder Browser

The *RBBookFinder Browser,* shown in Figure 2-19, is a custom-designed web browser designed to assist the user in locating computer and Information Technology (IT) books on the Internet.

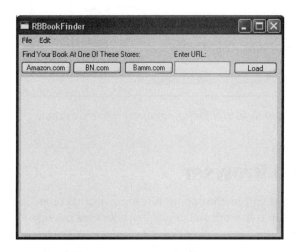

Figure 2-19. *A look at the finished RBBookFinder browser application*

As you learned in Chapter 1, you typically follow a distinct series of steps in the development of a new REALbasic application. These steps include developing the application's interface, modifying window and control properties, adding program code, and application testing. You follow this same basic design process as you work your way through the creation of the RBBookFinder Browser.

■**Note** As you work your way through the development of the RBBookFinder browser application, focus on your interaction with the IDE and its various components. The development of the RBBookFinder Browser involves little program code and, for now, you should simply type in program statements as instructed.

Designing the User Interface

The first step in creating the RBBookFinder browser application is to create its GUI. You begin this process by double-clicking on the Window1 item on the Project screen tab. This opens the Window Editor, which you will use to design your application's GUI.

For starters, click the Window1 window and use the resizing handles to reposition and increase the window's size until it takes up most of the space in the window area, as Figure 2-20 shows.

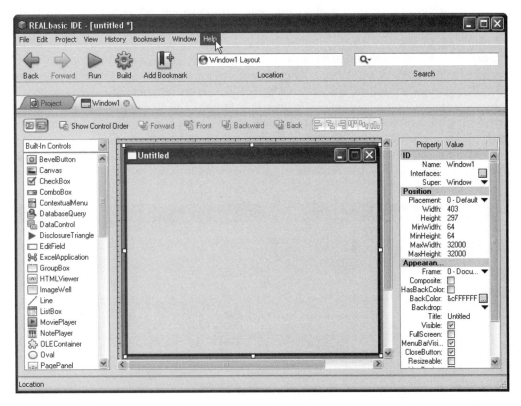

Figure 2-20. *Increasing the size of a window in the IDE can make it easier to work with and modify.*

Just to the left of the Window Editor is the Controls pane. To build the RBBookFinder browser application's GUI, you need to drag-and-drop the appropriate controls on to Window1. Begin by dragging-and-dropping an instance of the HTMLViewer control on to Window1, and then resize it, so it takes most of the available window space, as seen in Figure 2-20. Note, by default, the name assigned to this control is HTMLViewer1. This control is used to display web pages. In the IDE, the HTMLViewer control does not look exactly like the display area for a web browser. Once completed, however, the control's appearance changes and displays as you would expect.

■**Note**   An *HTMLViewer control* is a control that functions as the display area in a web browser.

Add three PushButtons controls to Window1, placing them side by side, just above the upper left-hand corner of the HTMLViewer1 control. Note, by default, the names REALbasic assigned to each of these controls are PushButton1, PushButton2, and PushButton3. These three buttons are used to load the URLs of specific online book retailers.

Now, add an EditField control just to the right of the PushButton3 control. Note that REALbasic assigns it a default name of EditField1. This control is used to provide users with the capability to specify any URL they want to visit. Then, add another PushButton control to the right of the EditField, which REALbasic automatically names PushButton4. This control is used to initiate the loading of a URL that is manually entered into the EditField1 control by the user.

Finally, to help make the application a little more user-friendly, add two StaticText controls, placing the first one over the set of three PushButton controls and the second one over the EditField1 control. In the next section, you will add descriptive text into these controls to provide the user with instructions on how to work with the RBBookFinder browser application.

At this point, the basic design of the user interface for the RBBookFinder browser application is complete and should look something like the example in Figure 2-21.

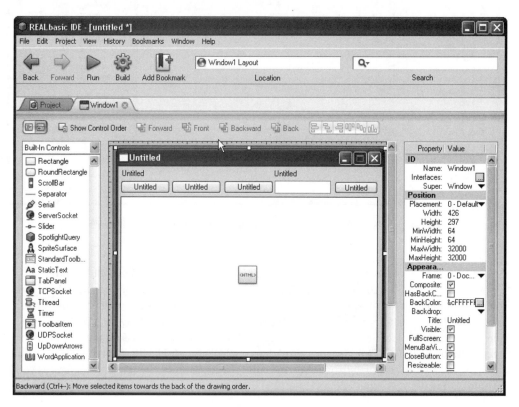

Figure 2-21. *Finishing the development of the RBBookFinder browser application's GUI*

Go ahead and give the application a test run by clicking the Run icon located on REALbasic's Main toolbar. As you can see, the application doesn't do anything yet. You can fix that a little later by adding a little program code to the window and various controls. Also note, the application's window is too small to effectively display the content presented at most websites and it currently lacks the capability to provide the user with the capability to increase its size.

Changing Windows and Control Properties

The next step in creating the RBBookFinder browser application is to modify properties associated with Window1 and the controls you placed on it. As you learned when you created the Hello World! application in Chapter 1, you modify the properties belonging to any window or control by selecting it, and then entering a new property value into the appropriate property field in the Properties pane. Table 2-2 provides a list of property changes that need to be made to Window1 and controls that make up the RBBookFinder browser.

Table 2-2. *Property Modification for the RBBookFinder Browser Application*

Object	Property	Value
Window1	Title	RBBookFinder
	Resizable	Enabled
	MaximizeButton	Enabled
HTMLViewer	LockLeft	Enabled
	LockTop	Enabled
	LockRight	Enabled
	LockBottom	Enabled
PushButton1	Caption	Amazon.com
PushButton2	Caption	BN.com
PushButton3	Caption	Bamm.com
EditField1	LockLeft	Enabled
	LockRight	Enabled
PushButton4	Caption	Load
	LockRight	Enabled
StaticText1	Text	Find Your Book At One Of These Stores:
StaticText2	Text	Enter URL:

By setting, or enabling, the Resizable property for Window1, you give the user the capability to resize the RBBookFinder browser application to any size they want. By selecting the MaximizeButton, you tell REALbasic to add a corresponding maximize control to your application.

By default, the HTMLViewer1 control retains its size when the user resizes the RBBookFinder browser application. In other words, while the application's user interface may get larger or smaller, the size of the HTMLViewer1 control does not change. This is not what you want. Instead, what should happen is this: the size of the HTMLViewer1 control should increase or decrease as the user resizes the application. Setting the LockLeft, LockTop, LockRight, and LockBottom properties of the HTMLViewer1 control accomplishes this by telling REALbasic to lock the four corners of the HTMLViewer1 control in relation to their current location to each side of the window that contains them. So, if Window1 is resized, the HTMLViewer1 control is proportionally resized as well. Similarly, you also need to set the LockLeft and LockRight properties for the EditField1 control, and the LockRight property of PushButton4.

Changing the Caption property for each of the application's PushButton controls labels each control, so the user will know what they represent. In the case of the RBBookFinder browser application, they are links to various online bookstores. Note, you need to resize the PushButton controls and the StaticText controls as you modify them to ensure everything fits together and the controls do not overlap one another. Once you finish modifying property settings and making any adjustments to the size of controls, the end result should be that your application's user interface looks like the example you saw in Figure 2-19.

Adding a Little REALbasic Code

Now that you have designed the GUI for the RBBookFinder browser application, it is time to add the programming logic to make it do something, specifically to make it work like a web browser.

The first thing the RBBookFinder browser application should do is display a default website when it starts up. For this application, the default website is www.apress.com. To accomplish this action, you need to set up a code statement that will execute when the application initially opens. This is done by double-clicking Window1. In response, REALbasic opens the Code Editor. As you can see, REALbasic automatically expands the tree shown in the browser pane to show the Open event for the window. Any code associated with the Open event executes the moment the application opens. Now, enter the following code statement:

```
HTMLViewer1 LoadURL "http://www.apress.com"
```

This statement tells REALbasic to execute the LoadURL method belonging to the HTMLViewer class. In short, this statement loads the specified URL into the HTMLViewer1 control.

Next, you need to add program statements for each PushButton control. Begin by drilling down in the tree shown in the browser pane by expanding the Controls branch, followed by the PushButton1 control. Locate the Action event, and then enter the following code statement:

```
HTMLViewer1.LoadURL "http://www.amazon.com"
```

This statement tells REALbasic to load the URL specified in the HTMLViewer1 control. Next, locate the Action event for PushButton2 and enter the following code statement:

```
HTMLViewer1.LoadURL "http://www.bn.com"
```

Locate the Action event for PushButton2 and enter the following code statement:

```
HTMLViewer1.LoadURL "http://www.bamm.com"
```

Next, you need to add a programming statement that executes when the user clicks the PushButton with the Load caption. To do this, locate the Action event for PushButton4 and enter the following code statement:

```
If Instr(EditField1.Text, "http://") = 0 Then
  HTMLViewer1.LoadURL "http://" + EditField1.Text
Else
  HTMLViewer1.LoadURL EditField1.Text
End If
```

These statements tell REALbasic to load the URL entered into the EditField1 control (for example, the control's Text). If the user does not begin the URL with http://, these statements automatically add it to the beginning of the URL string.

Testing Your Application

If you have not done so, go ahead and save your application by clicking the File menu and selecting Save. Type **RBBookFinder** as the name of your application, specify the location where you want to save it, and then click OK.

The application is now ready to run. Click the green Run icon located in REALbasic's main toolbar. REALbasic compiles a development version of your application, and then runs your application. Figure 2-22 shows how your applications should look after you start it. You can load any of the three predefined online bookstore websites by clicking the appropriate PushButton. Or, you can enter any other URL you want by typing its address into the EditField control and clicking the PushButton with the Load caption.

Figure 2-22. *A look at the RBBookFinder browser application in action*

If an error occurs when REALbasic attempts to compile your application, the odds are you made a typo when keying in the application's code statements. If this is the case, go back and review each of the programming statements you added and fix any typos you find.

When you finish, click the Project tab to display the Project Editor. Next, click the App item and assign a value of "RBBookFinder" to the WindowsAppName property. You are now ready to compile a stand-alone version of the RBBookFinder browser application.

Summary

Having a solid understanding of how to work with IDE is a requirement for developing REAL-basic applications. In this chapter, you learned the basic steps involved in working with the REALbasic IDE. This included learning how to interact with the Project, Windows, and Code Editors. It also included a review of the Controls and Properties panes. You learned how to access and use REALbasic's integrated Help system. In addition to all this, you learned how to work with and configure REALbasic menus and toolbars, including the Bookmarks bar, Tabs bar, and Editor toolbar. This chapter also provided you with various tips for working more effi-ciently within the REALbasic IDE, such as using Folder items to improve the organization of project items.

PART 2

Learning How to
Program with REALbasic

■ ■ ■

CHAPTER 3

Creating an Application's User Interface

In Chapter 2, you learned the basics of working with REALbasic's IDE. This information helps prepare you to create and work with new REALbasic projects. The first step in creating a new REALbasic application is usually interface design. In this chapter, you receive a thorough introduction to user interface development, including a look at every type of window and control supported by REALbasic. In addition, you develop another REALbasic application, the REALbasic Clock. By the time you complete this chapter, you will have learned

- How to decide which of REALbasic's 11 windows to use when creating your application's windows

- How to add, configure, and align REALbasic controls

- How to use the functionality provided by each of REALbasic's built-in controls

- How to extend REALbasic functionality by adding plug-ins and ActiveX controls to your applications

Building Application Windows

A good user interface is critical to any application. If users do not find your application's user interface intuitive and easy to learn, they may give up and move on to another application without ever giving your application a fair chance. Therefore, it is important that your application's user interface be visually appealing, well-organized, and easy to work with. In most cases, your desktop application's user interface is created using one or more windows. A large application may consist of dozens of custom windows, whereas a small application may consist of a single window.

By default, REALbasic creates a new blank window, named Window1, as part of each new desktop application. If necessary, you can add as many additional windows as you need. REALbasic supports 11 different types of windows, each of which is designed to fulfill a slightly different purpose.

■**Tip** REALbasic provides you with all the building blocks you need to create graphical user interfaces (GUIs) that comply with design standards for Macintosh, Windows, and Linux applications. If you are interested in learning about design standards for the Macintosh, you can do so by reading "Introduction to Apple Human Interface Guidelines" at `http://developer.apple.com/documentation/UserExperience/Conceptual/ OSXHIGuidelines`. And, you can learn about Windows GUI development standards by reading "Microsoft's Official Guidelines for User Interface Developers and Designers" at `http://msdn.microsoft.com/ library/default.asp?url=/library/en-us/dnwue/html/welcome.asp`. You can also learn about Linux development standards by reading "KDE User Interface Guidelines" at `http://developer.kde.org/ documentation/standards/kde/style/basics`.

You can add a new window to your application by clicking the Add Window button found on the Project Editor's toolbar or by clicking Project ➤ Add ➤ Windows. REALbasic responds by adding a new Document window to your project. To specify a different type of window, you change the window's Frame property to one of the following values:

- Document
- Movable
- Modal
- Floating
- Plain Box
- Shadowed Box
- Rounded
- Global Floating
- Sheet
- Metal
- Drawer

■**Tip** You can also add a new window to your application within the Project Editor by right-clicking (control-clicking on Macintosh), selecting Add (from the contextual menu that appears), and then selecting window.

Each of these different types of windows is examined in the following sections. Except where noted, the functionality provided by each type of window is cross-platform.

Document

The *Document Window*, shown in Figure 3-1, is the default window that REALbasic automatically adds to every new REALbasic desktop application The Document Window is typically used in situations where you want a window to remain open until the user closes it. With the Document Window, the user can click other windows, pushing the Document Window to the background.

Figure 3-1. *The Document Window, as shown on Windows*

A Document Window can have a close box, as well as minimize and maximize buttons. On Windows and Linux, a Document Window has a menu bar by default. However, you have the option of removing the menu bar or substituting a different one. On Mac OS X, the Document Window has the standard set of red, yellow, and green (close, minimize, and maximize) buttons in its title bar.

Movable Modal

The *Movable Modal Window*, which Figure 3-2 shows, is used in situations where you want the window to remain in front of all the other windows in your application until the user closes it. Because this window is moveable, the user can reposition it, if necessary, to see information displayed in windows underneath it.

On Windows and Linux, a Movable Modal Window can have minimize, maximize, and close buttons. On Max OS X, the Movable Modal Window does not have a close box, leaving it up to you to provide a button (or other means) for closing the window.

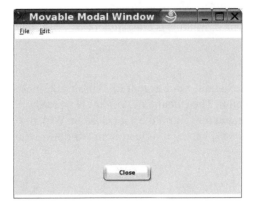

Figure 3-2. *The Movable Modal Window, as shown on Linux*

Modal Window

The *Modal Window,* shown in Figure 3-3, is similar to the Movable Modal Window, except the user cannot move it. This type of window is used to force the user to respond to it before getting access to the rest of the application. Except when opened on Linux, the Modal Window does not have a title bar. On Linux, the Modal Window has minimize and close buttons.

Figure 3-3. *The Modal Window, as shown on Mac OS X*

Floating Window

The *Floating Window,* as Figure 3-4 shows, floats on top of other windows and can be moved like Movable Modal Windows. However, Floating Windows do not prevent users from being able to access and work with other parts of the application. Floating Windows can even float on top of Modal and Movable Modal Windows.

Figure 3-4. *The Floating Window, as shown in Linux*

Floating Windows can display a Close button. In addition, on Linux, a Floating Window can also have minimize and maximize buttons.

Plain Box Window

The *Plain Box Window* works just like a Modal Window. As Figure 3-5 shows, Plain Box Windows do not have title bars, not even on Linux. The Plain Box Window is sometimes used to hide the desktop (when it is maximized) or to create About dialogs found on Help menus.

Figure 3-5. *The Plain Box Window, as shown on Mac OS X*

Shadowed Box Window

The *Shadowed Box Window*, shown in Figure 3-6, operates exactly like a Modal Window. Like the Plain Box Window, the Shadowed Box Window is often used to create About windows. Unlike Shadowed Box Windows on Windows and Linux, which do not have title bars, the Mac OS X Shadowed Box Window has a title bar and includes a minimize button.

Figure 3-6. *The Shadowed Box Window, as shown on Windows*

Rounded Window

The *Rounded Window* looks like the Document Window, as you see in Figure 3-7. One small difference is, on Mac OS X, the Rounded Window cannot be resized. The Rounded Window is considered obsolete and is seldom used because all its functionality is duplicated in the Document Window.

Figure 3-7. *The Rounded Window, as shown on Mac OS X*

Global Floating Window

A *Global Floating Window,* shown in Figure 3-8, looks like Floating Window. The only difference is in addition to being able to float in front of windows belonging to its own applications, a Global Floating Window can also float in front of other applications' windows.

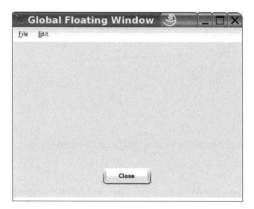

Figure 3-8. *The Global Floating Window, as shown on Linux*

Sheet Window

The *Sheet Window,* which acts like a Modal Window, is a drop-down dialog you can add to a parent window. Sheet Windows are only supported on Mac OS X. Figure 3-9 shows a Document Window to which a Sheet Window had been associated. As you can see in Figure 3-10, the Sheet Window is designed to appear as if it drops down from the top portion of its parent window.

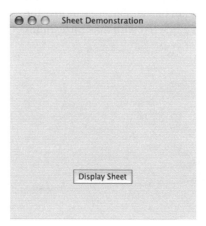

Figure 3-9. *A window to which a Sheet Window has been added, as shown on Mac OS X*

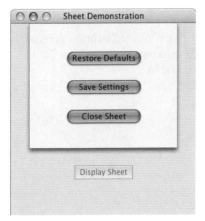

Figure 3-10. *Once exposed, a Sheet Window provides the capability to significantly enhance its parent window, as shown on Mac OS X.*

Once displayed, the Sheet Window is modal and cannot be moved. The user must respond to it to gain access to the rest of the application.

■**Note** If you use the Sheet Window on Windows or Linux, REALbasic displays it as a regular Modal Window.

Metal Window

The *Metal Window,* which Figure 3-11 shows, is available only on Mac OS X 10.2 or above. It displays a window with a metallic-like background. Other than its metallic appearance, the Metal Window works like a Document Window. It includes a title bar with maximize, mini-mize, and close buttons.

Figure 3-11. *The Metal Window, as shown on Mac OS X*

■**Note** If you use the Metal Window on Windows or Linux, REALbasic displays it as a regular Document Window. The Metal Window is not supported on Mac Classic either and, instead, looks and operates like a Document Window.

Drawer Window

The *Drawer Window*, as Figure 3-12 shows, is only supported on Mac OS X 10.2 or above. A Drawer Window appears as a hidden window that slides out from underneath another window, much like a drawer slides out of a dresser. The Drawer Window is useful for displaying optional functionality in a manner that is intuitively friendly by allowing it to be tucked away and pulled out only when needed.

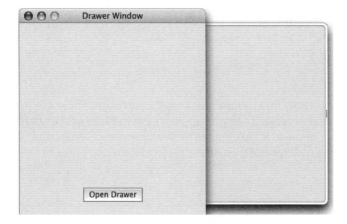

Figure 3-12. *The Drawer Window, as shown on Mac OS X*

You can specify whether the Drawer Window slides out of the top, bottom, or either side of the parent window. Optionally, you can let REALbasic determine, on its own, the best side on which to display the Drawer Window.

■**Note** If you use the Drawer Window on Windows or Linux, REALbasic displays it as a separate floating window.

Changing the Default Window

As you add additional windows to your application, you may decide to make a different window the application's default opening window. You specify an application's opening window by selecting the App item in the Project Editor, and then picking one of the windows you added to your application from the DefaultWindow property's drop-down list.

USING PREBUILT POP-UP WINDOWS

At times, all your application needs to do is display a brief message for the user to read or collect a Yes/No type response to a simple question. Rather than creating, and then customizing, a new window to serve this purpose, you can, instead, use either of two REALbasic options for displaying pop-up styled dialog boxes. One of these options is the *MsgBox function,* which is best suited to displaying informational messages. The MsgBox function is also included in REALbasic to help facilitate the conversion of Visual Basic applications that use a similarly named Visual Basic function.

Your other option for creating pop-up styled dialog boxes is the *MessageDialog class,* which gives you more control over how text is displayed and how dialog buttons look. Information on how to work with the MsgBox function is provided in Chapter 8. Information and examples of how to use the MessageDialog class are also available in Chapter 8.

You learn from examples in upcoming chapters how to set up your application to call on and display other windows you may add.

Deleting Windows

As you work on your applications, you may find you no longer need a particular window anymore. In addition, as you are adding new windows to your applications, you may accidentally add an extra window when you did not mean to. In either of these circumstances, you can delete any unwanted windows either by selecting them in the Project Editor and pressing Delete or by clicking Edit ➤ Delete.

■**Tip**   You can also delete a window from your application by right-clicking (control-clicking on Macintosh) on the window and selecting Delete from the contextual menu that appears.

Encrypting and Decrypting Windows

If you plan on sharing or selling the source code for your applications with other REALbasic programmers, you may want to consider encrypting one or more of the windows that make up your application. For example, if you developed a particular piece of code you consider proprietary, you may want to protect it from the view by other programmers, while still sharing the rest of the code that makes up the application.

You can achieve this by encrypting the window with which the code to be protected is associated. When you encrypt a window, you do so by supplying a password. Anyone who later attempts to open the window is prompted to supply the password, without which the window and its associated code will not be displayed.

To encrypt a window, you must first select it in the Project Editor, and then click Edit ➤ Encrypt. This opens the Encrypt Window dialog, as Figure 3-13 shows. You must supply the required password two times, and then click the Encrypt button.

Figure 3-13. *Encrypting a window to protect its contents from being viewed*

■**Tip** You can also encrypt a window by right-clicking it (control-clicking on Macintosh) and selecting Encrypt from the contextual menu that appears.

Once encrypted, a window can only be viewed and modified by decrypting it. To do this, select the window, and then click Edit ➤ Decrypt. This opens the Decrypt Window, shown in Figure 3-14, where you are prompted to supply the window's associated password.

Figure 3-14. *You must supply a password to decrypt and view an encrypted window.*

■**Tip** You can also decrypt an encrypted window by selecting it in the Project Editor and right-clicking it (control-clicking on Macintosh) and selecting Decrypt from the contextual menu that appears.

Working with Controls

Users interact with desktop applications by working with controls that you place on top of their windows. REALbasic makes controls available to you on the Controls pane, located on the Windows Editor.

In most cases, REALbasic controls are visible to the end user, who must interact with them to work with your application. However, some controls, such as the *StaticText control,* are "display only," meaning that although the user sees them, no actual interaction occurs. Still other controls are completely invisible to the user. These controls are visible to you as icons residing on your windows within REALbasic's IDE, but they will not be visible when your application runs. Adding these types of controls to your applications makes available specific functionality provided by the control. For example, the *Timer control* provides you with the capability to execute code on a schedule basis and the *TCPSocket control* provides you with the capability to create applications that can communicate over networks and the Internet.

Adding Controls to Windows

As you already saw in previous examples, you can add controls to application windows by dragging-and-dropping them. You can also add controls by double-clicking them. When you do this, REALbasic adds a copy of the control to the window, leaving it up to you to change its location and size, as appropriate.

■**Tip**   You can also add controls to your REALbasic applications by right-clicking the background of a window, and then selecting the Add option from the contextual menu that appears. REALbasic responds by displaying a list of objects you can add to the window.

You can also add a control to your application windows by clicking the control to select it, and then using the pointer to draw the area where you want the control placed. The advantage of using this technique is this: it not only places the control where you want it, but it also resizes the control to fit the area you drew.

■**Tip**   If you need to add more than one instance of the same control to a window, such as when adding multiple CheckBox or RadioButton controls, you can add each type of control one time, and then duplicate each control as many times as necessary. You do this by selecting a control, and then selecting Edit ➤ Duplicate.

Finding Lost Controls

As you design your windows by adding and modifying controls, controls can sometimes disappear. This can happen if you place one control over the top of another. This can also happen if you add a control to a window, and then accidentally modify its Top and Left properties with a negative value, causing the control to be removed from view.

You can view a listing of all the controls that were added to a window by right-clicking the window where the control resides and clicking Select, followed by the control you are looking for. Once selected, you can modify the control's properties as necessary to bring it back into view.

Modifying Control Properties

You can modify control properties in several ways. One is to programmatically modify them from within program code. Another is to physically move or resize the control within a window. A third option is to modify control properties displayed within the Properties pane after the control is selected.

In addition to modifying the properties for one control at a time, as demonstrated in previous chapters, you can also select two or more controls and modify their properties at the same time. You can select more than one control by using the pointer to draw a selection area around them. You can also select more than one control by pressing Control, while clicking on multiple controls. When more than one control is selected, REALbasic responds by displaying properties common to all selected controls. When modifying a property in this manner, the result is a change to the same property for each selected control.

Deleting Controls

If you accidentally add more controls to a window than you need, you can easily remove them. To do so, open the window where the control resides and select the control. Next, click Edit ➤ Cut or Edit ➤ Delete to remove the control. By cutting the control instead of deleting it, you paste a copy of the control on the clipboard of the operating system (OS), enabling you to paste it into other windows.

■**Tip** You can also remove controls from a window by right-clicking the control (control-clicking on Macintosh) and selecting Cut or Delete from the contextual menu displayed.

A REALbasic Control Overview

REALbasic includes dozens of built-in controls, each of which is designed to provide a specific type of functionality to your REALbasic applications. In the following sections, you get an overview of each of these controls and their functionality. As you progress through the rest of the chapters in this book, you have the opportunity to see many of these controls in action.

The BevelButton Control

The *BevelButton control*, as Figure 3-15 shows, is similar to the PushButton control you already worked with in the first two chapters of this book. The only difference is that, with the BevelButton control, you can add both text and an image to the BevelButton control and specify their positioning within the control.

Figure 3-15. *Examples of the BevelButton, as shown on Windows*

The Canvas Control

The *Canvas control,* seen in Figure 3-16, is used to display pictures or to draw a picture using REALbasic's programming statements. The Canvas control can also be used as a foundation for building a custom control.

Figure 3-16. *An example of the Canvas control, as shown on Windows*

■Tip Another special type of control you might want to look into is the *Container control,* which provides you with the capability to group together other controls to create reuseable interface components. The creation of custom controls using the Canvas and Container controls is an advanced programming topic, and is out of the scope of this book. However, programmers with a strong Visual Basic background may want to explore these controls further in REALbasic's Reference manual. Using these controls as a starting point, Visual Basic programmers can create custom controls to re-create any Visual Basic controls for which REALbasic does not provide an equivalent control.

The CheckBox Control

The *CheckBox control,* which Figure 3-17 shows, is used to provide users with choices that have two options or states. You can use check boxes to perform tasks, such as collecting user preferences or enabling and disabling specific application features.

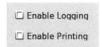

Figure 3-17. *An example of Checkbox controls, as shown on Linux*

The ComboBox Control

The *ComboBox control,* as you see in Figure 3-18, provides features found in both the EditField and PopupMenu controls. You can use it to enable users either to type input or select an item from a list of items.

Figure 3-18. *An example of the ComboBox control, as shown on Linux*

Once a ComboBox is selected, users can use the up and down arrows to locate an item, and then press Enter or Return to select it, or press Escape to close the pop-up list without making a selection.

The ContextualMenu Control

The *ContextualMenu control,* as shown in Figure 3-19, is used to display a pop-up list of choices for any control that supports it. Once created, one ContextualMenu can be associated with any number of controls and is accessed by right-clicking (control-clicking on Macintosh) on an associated control. More information on how to work with this control is in Chapter 4.

Figure 3-19. *An example of the ContextualMenu control, as shown on Linux*

The DatabaseQuery Control

When added to a window, the *DatabaseQuery control* provides your application with the capability to submit a SQL query to a database when the window to which it was added loads. Note, while this control provides the capability to query a database, it is invisible to the user. For more information on how to work with the DatabaseQuery, read Chapter 10.

The DataControl Control

The *DataControl control,* seen in Figure 3-20, provides your application with the capability to create a database front end, enabling users to navigate the database by moving forward or backward, or by jumping to the database's first or last records.

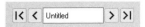

Figure 3-20. *An example of the DataControl control, as shown on Windows*

Typically, you use this control to control the display of database data in EditFields and other controls. For more information on how to work with the DataControl, see Chapter 10.

The DisclosureTriangle Control

The *DisclosureTriangle control,* shown in Figure 3-21, is used to build an interface that can display a hierarchical listing of files and folders. REALbasic enables you to control the direction in which the DisclosureTriangle points (left or right), as well as whether it is in a disclosed (down) or undisclosed (up) state.

Figure 3-21. *An example of a DisclosureTriangle control, as shown on Mac OS X*

The EditField Control

The *EditField control,* as seen in Figure 3-22, is used to enable the user to enter and to display text. The EditField supports single line and multiline text input. With *single-line input,* the EditField control provides the capability to display or collect small amount of user input.

With *multiline input,* the EditField provides the capability to accept and display text using features commonly associated with Word processors. These multiline EditField control features include the capability to display text in

- Different fonts

- Different colors

- Different sizes

The EditField control's multiline features also include the capability to display scrollbars and to format paragraphs.

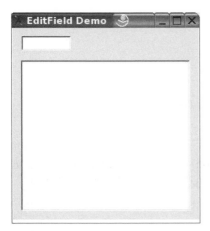

Figure 3-22. *Two examples of the EditField control, as shown on Linux*

The ExcelApplication Control

The *ExcelApplication control* is one of three REALbasic controls that provide you with the capability to develop applications that incorporate Microsoft Office functionality into your applications, provided Microsoft Office is installed on the computer where the applications executes. This control is used to integrate Microsoft Excel functionality into REALbasic applications. This control is invisible to the user.

The ExcelApplication control works with Microsoft Office 2000 and 2003 on computers running Windows and Office 98, and Office 2001 on Macintosh. Also, Microsoft Office *X* is supported on Mac OS X. Microsoft Office Applications do not run on Linux, so this control is not supported on that OS.

■**Note** To effectively use this control, you must have some familiarity with Microsoft VBA, which you can find published in numerous books, including *Definitive Guide to Excel VBA, Second Edition* (ISBN: 1590591038), published by Apress.

The GroupBox Control

The *GroupBox control,* which you can see in Figure 3-23, is typically used to group together related controls on a window. The GroupBox control is particularly useful for grouping RadioButton controls, which allow different groups of RadioButton controls to operate independently of each other.

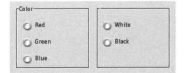

Figure 3-23. *Examples of the GroupBox control, as shown on Linux*

The HTMLViewer Control

The *HTMLViewer control*, seen in Figure 3-24, provides your applications with the capability to function like a web browser. The HTMLViewer control can display any URL or even render HTML code that is passed to it.

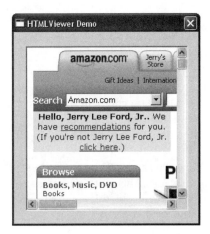

Figure 3-24. *An example of the HTMLViewer control, as shown on Windows*

The ImageWell Control

Like the Canvas control, the *ImageWell control,* as shown in Figure 3-25, provides you with the capability to display BMP and PNG images on Windows and Linux, and PICT images on Macintosh. However, unlike the Canvas control, which can be used as the basis for building custom controls, the ImageWell control is limited to only displaying graphic images.

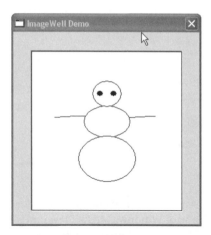

Figure 3-25. *An example of the ImageWell control, as shown on Windows*

The Line Control

The *Line control,* which you see in Figure 3-26, provides you with the capability to draw a line on an application window. The line can be any length and thickness. The default width of a line is 1 pixel, drawn horizontally in black.

Figure 3-26. *An example of the Line control, as shown on Linux*

■ **Note** A *pixel* is the smallest addressable area on a picture or screen that you can write to.

The ListBox Control

The *ListBox control,* shown in Figure 3-27, provides the capability to display a list of choices. This list can be made up of one or more columns and can even display headings. Once selected, the user can navigate the contents of the ListBox control using the up and down keys, and selecting a choice by pressing Enter or Return.

Figure 3-27. *An example of the ListBox control, as shown on Mac OS X*

The MoviePlayer Control

The *MoviePlayer control*, which Figure 3-28 shows, provides you with the capability to create applications that can play movies. To do so, Apple QuickTime or Windows Media Player must be installed on the computer where the application is run. As a result, this control does not work on Linux applications.

Figure 3-28. *An example of the MoviePlayer control, as shown on Windows*

The NotePlayer Control

The *NotePlayer control* provides you with the capability to play music using Apple QuickTime musical instruments. While this control does provide your applications with functionality, it is invisible to the user.

The OLEContainer Control

The *OLEContainer control* is a Windows-specific feature that provides you with the capability to integrate ActiveX controls into your REALbasic applications. While this control does provide your applications with functionality, it is invisible to the user.

The Oval Control

The *Oval control*, as Figure 3-29 shows, provides the capability to draw oval shapes on windows. Oval drawings are, by default, 1 pixel thick, and they are black with a white center. However, you can change line thickness, as well as line and fill colors.

Figure 3-29. *An example of the Oval control, as shown on Linux*

The PagePanel Control

The *PagePanel control* provides the capability to define and display different panels on a window, where only one panel is visible at a time. The PagePanel control does not provide a visual navigation feature that enables the user to switch between panels. Instead, providing this capability is up to the user. Figure 3-30 shows a typical Document Window. The content for this window is stored on two pages.

Figure 3-30. *A Document Window to which a PagePanel Window has been added*

Figure 3-31 shows the contents displayed on the second page of the PagePanel control. In this example, the user is able to switch between pages by clicking a PushButton control that was added to each page.

Figure 3-31. *An example of the PagePanel control, as shown on Windows*

The Placard Control

The *Placard control,* which you see in Figure 3-32, provides the capability to add a placard to your REALbasic applications. Placards are typically used to help provide emphasis to controls or text placed on them. As Figure 3-32 shows, placards can have background colors, and they can be displayed in normal, pressed, and disabled states.

Figure 3-32. *Examples of the Placard control, as shown on Windows, in pressed, disabled, and normal states.*

The PopupArrow Control

The *PopupArrow control,* shown in Figure 3-33, enables you to display an arrow in any of four directions (north, south, east, and west). The PopupArrow control is often used as a building block for creating custom controls.

Figure 3-33. *An example of the PopupArrow control, as shown on Mac OS X*

The PopupMenu Control

The *PopupMenu control,* seen in Figure 3-34, is a space-saving feature that let's you display a list of choices to the user. Once selected, the user can use the up and down keys to navigate the list, and Enter or Return to make a selection.

Figure 3-34. *An example of the PopupMenu control, as shown on Windows*

The PowerPointApplication Control

The *PowerPointApplication control* is one of three REALbasic controls that provide you with the capability to develop applications that incorporate Microsoft Office functionality into your applications, provided Microsoft Office is installed on the computer where the applications execute. This control is used to integrate Microsoft PowerPoint functionality into REALbasic applications. The PowerPointApplication control is invisible to the user.

The PowerPointApplication control works with Microsoft Office 2000 and 2003 on computers running Windows, and Office 98, and Office 2001 on Macintosh. Also, Microsoft Office X is supported on Mac OS X. Microsoft Office Applications do not run on Linux, so this control is not supported on that OS.

■**Note** To effectively use this control, you must have some familiarity with Microsoft VBA, which you can find published in numerous books, including *Office 2003 Programming: Real World Applications* (ISBN: 1590591399), published by Apress.

The ProgressBar Control

The *ProgressBar control,* shown in Figure 3-35, provides you with the capability to display an indicator that shows some sort of progress as your applications process a particular task. The ProgressBar control only has a horizontal orientation.

Figure 3-35. *An example of the ProgressBar control, as shown on Mac OS X*

The ProgressWheel Control

The *ProgressWheel control,* seen in Figure 3-36, provides you with the capability to visually indicate when a time-consuming operation is taking place.

Figure 3-36. *An example of the ProgressWheel control, as shown on Linux*

The PushButton Control

As you saw in previous chapters, the *PushButton control*, shown in Figure 3-37, is used to display buttons that users can click to initiate specific actions.

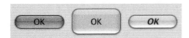

Figure 3-37. *Examples of PushButton controls, as shown on Mac OS X*

The RadioButton Control

The *RadioButton control*, which you can see in Figure 3-38, is used to present users with a choice between one or more values. RadioButton controls operate in groups, where only one RadioButton in the group can be selected at a time. In situations where you want to create distinct sets of RadioButton controls on the same window, you can use the GroupBox control to separate and organize the RadioButton controls.

Figure 3-38. *Examples of RadioButton controls, as shown on Windows*

The Rb3Dspace Control

The *Rb3Dspace control* provides you with the capability to display animation in a predefined three-dimensional space.

The RbScript Control

The *RbScript control* provides you with the capability to let users submit REALbasic code, and then executes it from your compiled application. While this control does provide your application with functionality, it is invisible to the user.

The Rectangle Control

The *Rectangle control,* seen in Figure 3-39, provides the capability to draw rectangle and square shapes on windows. Rectangle drawings are, by default, 1 pixel thin and they are black with a white center. However, you can change line thickness, as well as line and fill colors.

Figure 3-39. *An example of the Rectangle control, as shown on Linux*

The RoundRectangle Control

The *RoundRectangle control*, as shown in Figure 3-40, provides the capability to draw rectangle-like and square-like shapes (with rounded corners) on windows. RoundRectangle drawings are by default, 1 pixel thick and black with a white center. However, you can change the line thickness, as well as line and fill colors.

Figure 3-40. *An example of the RoundRectangle control, as shown on Linux*

The ScrollBar Control

The *Scrollbar control*, which you see in Figure 3-41, is used to add vertical and horizontal scrollbars to your applications. By default, ScrollBar controls are vertical, but, by reshaping them, you can make them horizontal.

Figure 3-41. *An example of the ScrollBar control, as shown on Mac OS X*

You can resize your ScrollBar controls as required by your application. However, be careful not to make them less than 16 pixels thick or they will not look right.

The Separator Control

The *Separator control*, shown in Figure 3-42, is used to visually divide or organize a window into different parts. Otherwise, the Separator control has no effect on the operations within an application.

Figure 3-42. *An example of the Separator control, as shown on Linux*

The Serial Control

The *Serial control* provides you with the capability to create applications that can communicate with other applications or devices by sending and receiving messages over the computer's serial port. While the Serial control does provide your applications with functionality, it is invisible to the user.

The ServerSocket Control

The *ServerSocket control* provides you with the capability to create web server applications capable of handling thousand of simultaneous incoming TCP/IP connections over a single port. While the ServerSocket control does provide your applications with functionality, it is invisible to the user.

The Slider Control

The *Slider control,* as seen in Figure 3-43, provides you with the capability to accept user input provided when the user drags the slider and moves it to a new location on the slider bar. You can display the Slider control horizontally or vertically.

Figure 3-43. *An example of the Slider control, as shown on Mac OS X*

The SpotlightQuery Control

The *SpotlightQuery control* is a Mac OS X-specific (Mac OS X 10.4 or higher) control that provides you with the capability to accept and pass on user queries to Spotlight, and then display any returned results. While the SpotlightQuery control does provide your applications with functionality, it is invisible to the user.

■**Note** *Spotlight* is a Mac OS X feature that uses metadata to assist users in performing searches.

The SpriteSurface Control

The *SpriteSurface control* provides you with the capability to produce animated effects using sprites. A *sprite* is an object with a picture that can be moved around the screen via program code. The SpriteSurface control is responsible for handling all drawing operations and for informing your application code when collisions occur.

The StandardToolbarItem Control

The *StandardToolbarItem control* is a Macintosh-specific control that provides you with the capability to add toolbars, complete with graphic icons, to Macintosh applications.

The StaticText Control

As you saw in previous chapters, the *StaticText control,* as Figure 3-44 shows, provides the capability to display text on windows. The StaticText control is typically used to display labels for other controls.

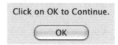

Figure 3-44. *An example of the StaticText control, as shown on Mac OS X*

The TabPanel Control

The *TabPanel control,* shown in Figure 3-45, provides the capability to organize content on two or more tabs that share space on the same window. This control is often used to conserve space and logically organize related controls. Users navigate between panels by clicking their associated tabs. By default, REALbasic sets up a TabPanel control with two tabs, but you can add as many additional tabs as you require.

Figure 3-45. *An example of the TabPanel control, as shown on Linux*

The TCPSocket Control

The *TCPSocket control* provides you with the capability to create applications that can communication with other TCP/IP-based programs on computer networks and the Internet. While the TCPSocket control does provide your applications with functionality, it is invisible to the user. Its functionality differs from that provided by the ServerSocket control, which is designed to support the development of web server applications.

The Thread Control

The *Thread control* provides you with the capability to develop applications that run in the background without any user interaction. Threads also run in parallel with one another, enabling you to develop applications that can do a number of things at the same time. While the Thread control does provide your applications with functionality, it is invisible to the user.

The Timer Control

The *Timer control* is used to execute program code at specific time intervals. For example, if you develop a REALbasic game, you might use the time control to limit how long a player's turn lasts. While the Timer control does provide your applications with functionality, it is invisible to the user.

The ToolbarItem Control

The *ToolbarItem control* is a Macintosh-specific control that provides you with the capability to add toolbars, complete with graphic icons, to Macintosh applications.

The UDPSocket Control

The *UDPSocket control* provides you with the capability to create applications that can communicate with other TCP/IP-based programs using the UDP protocol on computer networks and the Internet. While the UDPSocket control does provide your applications with functionality, it is invisible to the user.

The UpDownArrows Control

The *UpDownArrows control,* shown in Figure 3-46, is typically used to control interface scrolling.

Figure 3-46. *An example of the UpDownArrows control, as shown on Windows*

The WordApplication Control

The *WordApplication control* is one of three REALbasic controls that provide you with the capability to develop applications that incorporate Microsoft Office functionality into your applications, provided Microsoft Office is installed on the computer where the application executes. This control is used to integrate Microsoft Word functionality into REALbasic applications. The WordApplication control is invisible to the user.

The WordApplication control works with Microsoft Office 2000 and 2003 on computers running Windows and Office 98, and Office 2001 on Macintosh. Also, Microsoft Office X is supported on Mac OS X. Microsoft Office Applications do not run on Linux, so this control is not supported on that OS.

■Note To effectively use this control, you must have some familiarity with Microsoft VBA, which you can find published in numerous books, including *Microsoft Office Programming: A Guide for Experienced Developers* (ISBN: 1590591216), published by Apress.

Extending REALbasic Functionality by Adding New Controls

Sometimes, you may find yourself in need of functionality not provided by REALbasic's built-in collection of controls. In these situations, you have several choices. For starters, you can use REALbasic to create a solution yourself, but chances are good that if you have come up with a need or an idea for a new control, someone has already invented it. You may want to do a little surfing on the Internet to see if you can find a plug-in that provides the required functionality.

Some plug-ins are free, while others are for sale. To use these plug-ins, all you have to do is download them and add them to the REALbasic plug-ins folder, which you can find in the same directory where you installed REALbasic.

Plug-Ins

One source of free plug-ins is the REALbasic website, where you can find database plug-ins in the download area. One way to find other sources of REALbasic plug-ins is to search the Internet for REALbasic Plug-ins. In addition, you might want to check out the REALbasic Plugins Web ring at `http://w.webring.com/hub?ring=rbplugins`.

Other sources of REALbasic plug-ins include Van Hoek Software REALbasic Plugins at `http://homepage.mac.com/vanhoek/` and Mile 23 (`http://www.mile23.com/plugins.html`) and Monkeybread plugins at `http://www.monkeybreadsoftware.de`.

ActiveX

If you are developing applications specifically for Windows, you can take advantage of Microsoft ActiveX controls, which are available on most users' home computers. By adding these controls to REALbasic, you can programmatically work with them just as if they were built-in REALbasic controls.

■Note *ActiveX* is a collection of technologies that provide information for sharing between Windows applications.

The following procedure outlines the steps involved in adding ActiveX controls to REALbasic.

1. Open the REALbasic Project Editor screen.

2. Click the Add ActiveX Component button or select Project ➤ ActiveX Components. The COM Components dialog appears, displaying a list of installed ActiveX controls and programmable objects, as Figure 3-47 shows.

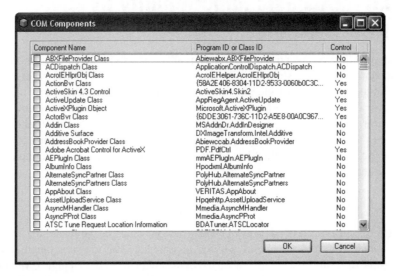

Figure 3-47. *Viewing a list of ActiveX controls installed on a computer running Windows XP*

3. Select any controls you want to add to REALbasic, and then click OK. The controls you select are displayed in the Project Editor.

Note To work with an ActiveX control, you need some documentation explaining how the control works. The first place to look is `http://msdn.microsoft.com/library/`.

Control Alignment

Once placed on a window, you can change any control's size and position by dragging its handles using the mouse. You can also select a control and move it one pixel at a time using the up and down keys. In addition, you can move and resize a control by setting its Top and Left properties, along with the control's Height and Width properties.

As you have already seen, when you use the mouse to resize or move controls, REALbasic's Interface Assistant displays temporary vertical and horizontal alignment indicators to help you align them. In addition, REALbasic provides four properties (LockLeft, LockRight, LockTop, and LockBottom) for each control, which you can use to lock the side of each control into place in relation to its distance from the horizontal and vertical edges of the window. This way, the control maintains its distance from the specified window edge when the user increases or decreases the size of the window. You saw each of these properties in use through your development of the RBBookFinder application in Chapter 2.

In addition to all these alignment tools, REALbasic also provides you with tools for evenly aligning the space between groups of controls. These tools are represented by six icons located on the Windows Editor toolbar, as Figure 3-48 shows.

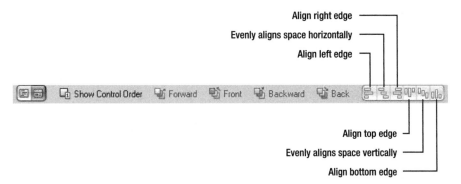

Figure 3-48. *Alignment controls are located on the right-hand side of the Windows Editor toolbar.*

To align two or more controls, begin by selecting a control that is properly positioned, and then click the Back icon on the Windows Editor toolbar to mark it as an anchor around which the other controls will be aligned. Then, you select it and the other controls you want to align, and then click the appropriate alignment icon.

In similar fashion, you can evenly assign the space between selected controls by selecting two or more controls, and then clicking either of the two space alignment icons.

Changing Tab Order

When your applications run, the user can use Tab to jump from control to control. The currently selected control is the control that has focus. In other words, the currently selected control is the control that will receive any keyboard input.

Not all controls can receive focus and the controls that can receive focus vary from OS to OS, as Table 3-1 shows.

Table 3-1. *REALbasic Controls That Are Capable of Receiving Focus*

Control	Macintosh	Windows	Linux
EditField	Yes	Yes	Yes
ComboBox	Yes	Yes	Yes
Canvas	Yes	Yes	Yes
PushButton	Yes	Yes	Yes
			Continued

Table 3-1. *Continued*

Control	Macintosh	Windows	Linux
ListBox	Yes	Yes	Yes
PopupMenu	No	Yes	Yes
CheckBox	No	Yes	Yes
Slider	No	Yes	Yes

By default, the order in which the focus is transferred between controls depends on the order in which the controls were added to the window. The first control added to the window gets the initial focus and, when Tab is pressed, focus is passed off to the control that was added second, and so on.

You can change the default Tab order using the icons found on the Windows Editor toolbar. The first step is to get REALbasic to display a visual indication of each control's Tab order by clicking the Show Control Order button on the Windows Editor toolbar. The result is a number displayed in the button's right-hand corner of each control showing its Tab order. The control with the lowest number gets focus first. You can change a given control's order by selecting it, and then clicking one of the following Windows Editor toolbar buttons:

- **Forward**. Moves the selected control ahead one position in the Tab order.

- **Front**. Moves the selected control to the end of the Tab order.

- **Backward**. Moves the selected control backward one position in the Tab order.

- **Back**. Moves the selected control to the beginning of the Tab order.

■**Tip** You can also change the default Tab order by changing the value of each control's ControlOrder property.

Building a Desktop Clock

In keeping with this book's promise to show you how to create a new application in every chapter, the rest of this chapter is dedicated to guiding you through the creation of the RBClock desktop clock application. For this example, REALbasic for Macintosh is used. However, you should be able to cross-compile this application into a Windows or Linux application with minimal tweaking to the user interface.

The RBClock application, shown in Figure 3-49, is designed to provide the user with a small desktop clock that can easily be tucked away in the corner of the screen.

Figure 3-49. *A look at the RBClock application running on Mac OS X*

Designing the User Interface

The first step in creating the RBClock application is to assemble its user interface. Begin by double-clicking the Window1 item on the Projects screen to open the Windows Editor. Next, click the Window1 window and, using its resizing handles, reduce the size of the window. Figure 3-49 shows the appearance and size of the window in the completed application.

As you can see, the RBClock application has a simple interface. To build it, start by dragging-and-dropping an instance of the EditField control onto Window1. Note, by default, the name assigned to this control is EditField1. This control is used to display the current time.

Next, add a PushButton control to the form and place it just under the EditField control. To help make the RBClock application a little more user-friendly, add a StaticText control just above the EditField. Finally, open the Project Editor, and then select and remove MenuBar1. This simple desktop application does not need a MenuBar.

■**Note** Removing the MenuBar control may not seem to have much of an impact on the Macintosh version of this application, because of the manner in which the Macintosh separates the display of the MenuBar from the application itself. However, it does have a much greater visual effect on Windows and Linux.

At this point, the basic design of the user interface for the RBClock application is complete and should resemble the example you see in Figure 3-49.

Even though the design of the appearance of the user interface is complete, you still must complete one more step before you move on. For the clock to operate as expected, your application needs the capability to update the display of the time every second. To provide your application with this capability, you must add an instance of the Timer control.

When you add an instance of the Timer control to the window, you can see a small icon, as Figure 3-50 shows, representing the control. By default, the Timer control is set up to automatically execute every second once the window that contains it is opened. While visible in REALbasic's IDE, this icon is invisible to the user when your application is running.

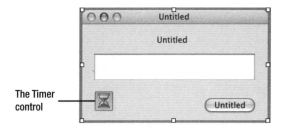

The Timer control

Figure 3-50. *The Timer control provides the RBClock application with much needed functionality.*

Changing Window and Control Properties

The next step in creating the RBClock application is to modify properties associated with
Window1 and the controls you placed on it. Table 3-2 provides a list of property changes you
need to make.

Table 3-2. *Property Modifications for the RBClock Application*

Object	Property	Value
Window1	Title	RBClock
	Frame	Rounded
	CloseButton	Disabled
	MinimizeButton	Enabled
PushButton1	Caption	Close
StaticText1	Text	REALbasic Clock
EditField1	TextFont	Courier
	TextSize	36
	Alignment	Center
	ReadOnly	Enabled

By disabling the CloseButton, you force the user to use the PushButton control you added
to the window. By enabling the MinimizeButton, you let the user minimize the application
and, later, restore it, without having to close, and then reopen the application.

Also, note, the ReadOnly property of the EditField1 control is enabled. This enables the
user to view the current time, but it prevents the user from entering any text into this field.
Note, too, you may have to resize the EditField1 control a bit once you change the TextSize
property to make sure the control is big enough to display everything.

Adding a Little REALbasic Code

Only three lines of code are required to bring the RBClock application to life. The first program-ming statement, shown in the following, is assigned to the PushButton1 control's Action event.

```
Quit
```

This statement tells REALbasic to close the RBClock application when the user clicks the PushButton control. The other two lines of code, shown in the following, are needed to make the application display the current time in the application's EditField.

```
Dim d as New Date
EditField1.Text = d.LongTime
```

To apply this code, double-click the icon representing Timer1. This opens the Code Editor and displays the control's Action event, where the code should be entered. For now, key in these two statements exactly as shown.

■**Note** The first line of code defines an object variable of type Date. The second line of code displays the current time by setting the EditField control's Text property to a value retrieved using the Data object's LongTime property.

Testing Your Application

If you have not done so already, save your application. Name your application RBClock. Your application is now ready to run. If an error occurs during compilation, then you probably made a typo when keying in the code statements. Go back and review each statement, and then fix any typos you find.

Summary

In this chapter, you learned about each of the windows supported by REALbasic. You also learned how to change the default window, and to encrypt and decrypt a window and its con-tents. You received a overview of each of REALbasic's built-in controls. You then learned how to expand REALbasic's capabilities by adding plug-in and ActiveX controls. In addition, you learned how to create the REALbasic Clock application.

■ ■ ■

CHAPTER 4

Working with REALbasic Menus

In Chapter 3, you learned the fundamentals of creating graphical user interfaces for your REALbasic applications. In this chapter, you learn how to finish your application's user interface by adding professional-looking menus. This includes the development of menus, submenus, and menu items, and the configuration of these resources using features such as shortcuts. On top of all this, you learn how to enable and disable menu items, and to associate program statements with each menu item. Specifically, you learn how to

- Customize a menu system for your application windows

- Add shortcuts and accelerator keys to your application menus

- Control access to application menus and menu items

- Add additional menu bars to your applications

Working with REALbasic Menu Bars

Today, most users expect their desktop applications to come equipped with a menu system that provides access to application commands. A *menu system* provides you with a means for organizing commands that make your REALbasic applications work. A menu system is also a great space saver, taking up minimal space while also enabling you to remove PushButtons and other controls you would otherwise have to add to your applications.

If you want your applications to be well-received by the people who will use them, you must develop menu systems for your REALbasic applications. Fortunately, REALbasic makes this easy to do.

■**Note** In the context of this book, the term "menu system" refers to the collection of menus, submenus, and menu items for any given window in a REALbasic application. Different windows can have different menu systems, each of which is customized to meet a specific set of needs.

REALbasic provides you with a built-in Menu Editor, which provides all the tools you need to add menus, menu items, and submenus to your application's menu system. REALbasic implements menus through MenuBar items managed in the Project Editor and configured using REALbasic's built-in Menu Editor.

The usefulness of a well-designed menu system is especially apparent on Windows and Linux applications, where each menu is displayed directly on application windows, as Figure 4-1 and Figure 4-2 show.

Figure 4-1. *All the functionality provided by the Windows Notepad applications is made available through its menu system.*

Figure 4-2. *Programs, such as the Textfile application, found on SuSe Linux, provide access to key application commands via their menu systems.*

On Macintosh, menus are displayed at the top on the screen, as opposed to directly on application windows, as Figure 4-3 shows.

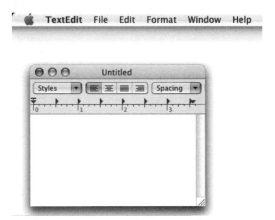

Figure 4-3. *Macintosh applications display their menu systems at the top of the desktop display area, instead of directly on top of application windows.*

Examining Menu Components

A typical application's menu system is made up of a number of different parts, including the high-level menu headings you see displayed on menu bars. In addition, under each menu, you can find different menu elements, including submenus and menu items. REALbasic provides you with all the tools you need to create professional-looking menus. This includes providing you with the capability to define shortcuts and to visually organize menu contents using separator bars. The following list provides a complete overview of the options REALbasic provides for you when developing a menu system for your applications:

- **Menus**. High-level headers displayed on the menu bar (File, Edit, Help, and so forth).

- **Menu Items**. Text items located under menus that represent commands users can select.

- **Submenus**. Collections of menu items grouped together and accessed through a parent menu (for example, a submenu).

- **Shortcuts**. Keyboard characters, or character sequences, that provide the capability to access menu items directly from the keyboard.

- **Accelerator Keys**. Keyboard keys that activate a menu or menu item when pressed in conjunction with the Alt key.

- **Separator Bars**. Horizontal lines you can use to visually group and separate submenus and menu items into logical groups.

Figure 4-4 provides a demonstration of how each of these menu components can be used in building an application's menu system.

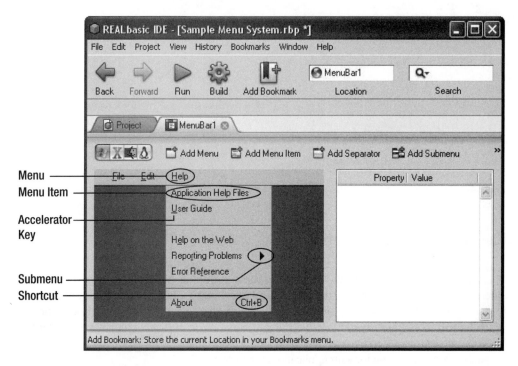

Figure 4-4. *An example of a Help menu as viewed using REALbasic's built-in menu preview option*

The Default MenuBar

By default, REALbasic provides every new desktop application with a new menu bar, as Figure 4-5 shows. By default, this menu bar is named MenuBar1.

By default, this menu bar is assigned to the application's default window (Window1). In addition, you have the option of assigning this menu to any other windows you add to your application, making it a shared menu bar.

■**Note** Programmers with a Visual Basic background immediately notice that REALbasic approaches menu design a little differently than they are used to. Instead of adding toolbars to windows using the Visual Basic MenuStrip control, REALbasic menu bars are added to REALbasic projects as items managed on the Project Editor. In addition, REALbasic makes it easy for windows to share access to the same menu bar. Visual Basic programmers will be happy to find out, however, that the process of adding menus, menu items, and submenus is nearly the same in REALbasic as it is in Visual Basic.

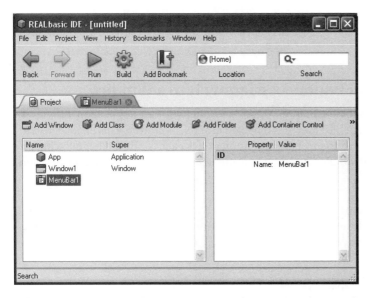

Figure 4-5. *Every new REALbasic dekstop application starts out with a default menu bar.*

By default, the default menu bar and every menu bar you add to a REALbasic application contains a File menu and an Edit menu. Table 4-1 outlines the menu items REALbasic automatically adds to these menus.

Table 4-1. *REALbasic Default Menus and Menu Items*

Menu	Command	Description
File	Exit or Quit*	Close the application
Edit	Undo	Undo a previous operation or command
	Cut	Remove selected data and place on clipboard
	Copy	Copy selected data and place on clipboard
	Paste	Copy data from clipboard to insertion point
	Delete	Delete selected data
	Select All	Select all data in the file

* Use of the Exit or Quit command depends on which operating system an application is running on (for example, Exit on Windows and Linux, and Quit on Macintosh).

On Mac OS X, REALbasic also automatically adds the Apple and Applications menus. You learn more about these menus and how to configure them in the section "Customizing the Apple and Macintosh Menus."

■Tip If your application does not use the Edit menu, you can delete it by selecting Edit menu and clicking Delete.

Adding a New Menu Bar and Assigning It to a Window

While you can use the default menu bar on windows throughout your application, often is it necessary to create and assign different menu bars to different windows. This enables you to customize a different menu bar to meet the requirements for each window. The following procedure outlines the steps involved in adding a new menu bar to a REALbasic application and assigning it to a window.

1. Open the Project Editor and click the Add Menu Bar button or click Project ➤ Add ➤ Menu Bar. REALbasic responds by adding a new menu bar to your application with a default name of MenuBar2, as Figure 4-6 shows.

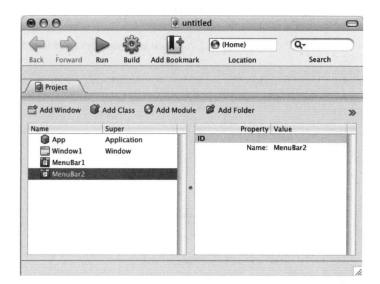

Figure 4-6. *Adding a new menu bar to a REALbasic application*

2. Select the window to which you want to add the new menu bar and modify its MenuBar property by selecting the new menu bar from the property's drop-down list, as Figure 4-7 shows.

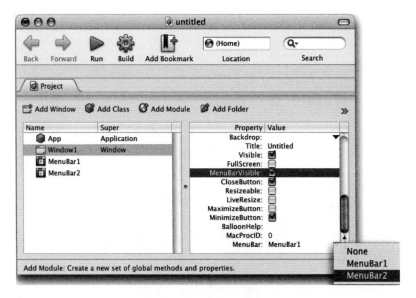

Figure 4-7. *Assigning the new menu bar to a window*

Adding Menus, Submenus, and Menu Items

One of the strengths of REALbasic is the ease with which it assists you in creating menu systems for your application windows. Using the REALbasic Menu Editor, you can create a professional menu system for any application in a matter of minutes.

Adding a New Menu

The first step in customizing a menu bar is usually to add additional menus to it. Menus do not do anything within your applications, other than provide access to menu items and submenus.

The menu items provide access to application commands. The following procedure outlines the steps involved in adding a new menu to a menu system.

1. Double-click the new menu bar item in the Project Editor that you want to modify. REALbasic responds by opening the menu bar to the REALbasic Menu Editor, as Figure 4-8 shows.

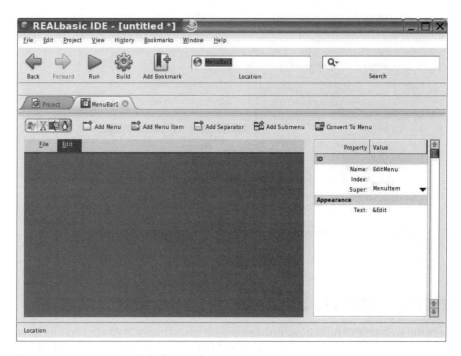

Figure 4-8. *A new, unmodified menu bar as shown on Linux*

2. Click the Add Menu button located on the Menu Editor toolbar or click Project ➤ Add ➤ Menu. REALbasic responds by adding a new menu, as Figure 4-9 shows.

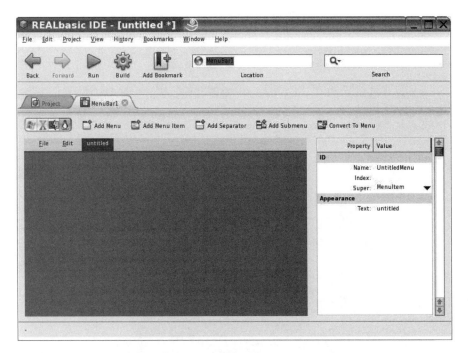

Figure 4-9. *A newly added menu, as shown on Linux*

■**Note** By default, REALbasic adds a new menu just to the right of the currently selected menu. If you do not select a menu prior to adding a new one, REALbasic adds the new menu to the end of the menu (on the far right-hand side).

3. If necessary, click the new menu and drag, and then drop it to the desired position on the menu bar.

4. Assign a name to the new menu by selecting it, and then modifying the value of the Name property in the Property pane. The name you assign to the new menu will be the name you use when you programmatically refer to the menu from within your program code.

5. Assign the text to be displayed on the menu by modifying the value of the Text property in the Property pane. Figure 4-10 shows how the new menu will look once its properties have been modified.

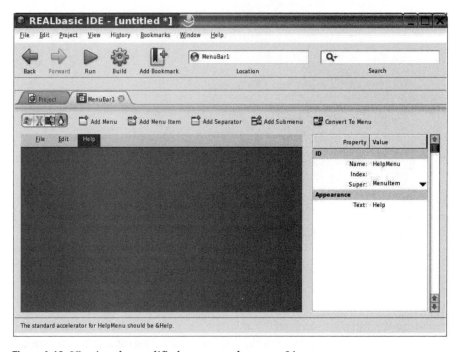

Figure 4-10. *Viewing the modified menu, as shown on Linux*

Repeat this procedure as many times as necessary to add additional menus to the menu bar. Once you finish adding menus, you are ready to customize them by adding menu items and submenus.

■**Tip** It's important for you to be consistent when assigning text to menus, submenus, and menu items. Always make sure you capitalize the first letter of each word that makes up your menu, submenu, and menu item text properties.

Adding Menu Items

To make your applications useful, you need to provide users with access to application commands. One way to do this is by adding PushButtons and other types of controls to your application windows. If your application provides access to many commands, you may find not enough room is available on your application window to comfortably display a control representing each available command.

Too many controls make your applications seem cluttered and difficult to work with. Instead, you will probably want to organize and group related commands together, and display them as menu items located under the menus on your application's menu bars. The following procedure outlines the steps involved in adding new menu items to your menus.

1. Double-click the menu bar in the Project Editor whose menus you want to modify. REALbasic responds by opening the menu bar in the REALbasic Menu Editor. Select the menu to be modified.

2. Click the Add Menu Item button located on the Menu Editor toolbar or click Project ➤ Add ➤ Menu Item. REALbasic responds by adding a new menu item to the selected menu, as Figure 4-11 shows.

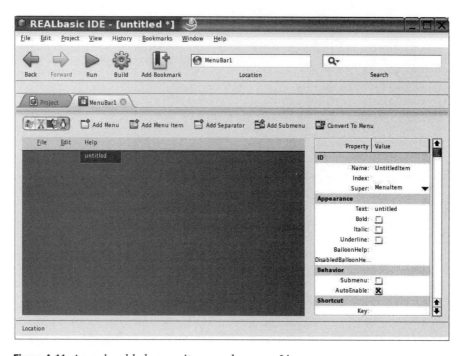

Figure 4-11. *A newly added menu item, as shown on Linux*

3. If necessary, click the new menu item and drag, and then drop it to the desired position on the menu.

4. Assign a name to the new menu item by selecting it, and then modifying the value of its Name property in the Property pane. The name you assign to the new menu item is the name you use when you programmatically refer to the menu from within your program code.

5. Assign the text to be displayed on the menu item by modifying the value of the Text property in the Property pane. Figure 4-12 shows how the new menu will look once its properties have been modified.

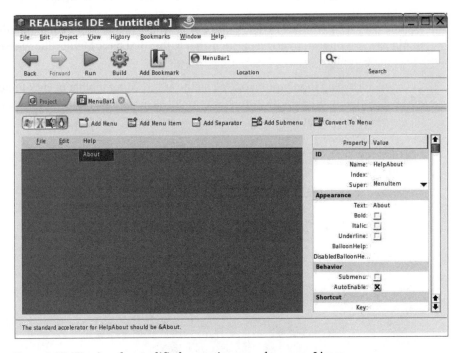

Figure 4-12. *Viewing the modified menu item, as shown on Linux*

6. If desired, modify the Bold, Italic, or Underline properties for the menu items by enabling the corresponding properties in the Property pane.

Repeat this procedure as many times as necessary to add an additional menu item to the selected menu. Once you finish adding menu items, you are ready to set them up to execute program code, as explained in the section "Using Menu Items to Trigger Command and Code Execution."

■Note REALbasic also provides you with the capability to populate a menu with a list of menu items using menu item arrays. Information on how to use arrays is available in Chapter 5.

Creating a Submenu

If you find your menus are becoming too crowded with menu items, you may want to improve how things are organized by grouping together related menu items and making them accessible through a submenu. A *submenu* is a menu item that displays a list of menu items when it's clicked.

The following procedure outlines the steps involved in adding a new submenu to a menu by converting an existing menu item to a submenu.

1. Double-click the menu bar item in the Project Editor where you want to define the submenu. REALbasic responds by opening the menu bar in the REALbasic Menu Editor.

2. Select the menu item to be turned into a submenu.

3. Enable the menu item's Submenu property by selecting it in the Property pane. REALbasic responds by displaying an indicator to the right of the menu item to identify it as a submenu, as Figure 4-13 shows.

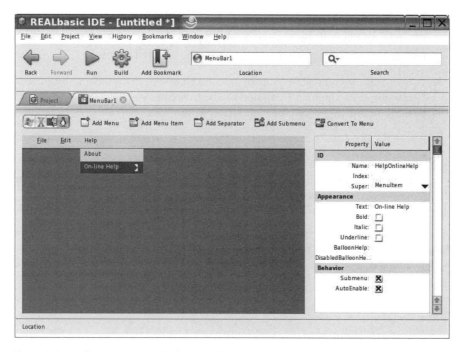

Figure 4-13. *Submenus provide the capability to reduce the size of menus by organizing and temporarily hiding the display of menu items.*

USE SUBMENUS PRUDENTLY

Submenus are a useful organizational tool, which you can use to significantly improve the overall organization of your applications. In fact, you can even add submenus to your submenus to further organize how your menu items are organized and presented. However, submenus also have a downside, especially for inexperienced users. While intermediate to advanced users should not have problems working with them, less-experienced users may not realize that additional functionality has been tucked away in submenus. Depending on the target audience for your applications, you may either want to reorganize menu items by creating additional menus under which to store them or you may decide to create a menu item that displays a new window in place of a submenu. You could then customize the new window by adding whatever controls are necessary to enable the user to select the appropriate command.

Once you create a submenu, you can add menu items to it by following the steps outlined in the next procedure.

1. Select the submenu to which you want to add menu items.

2. Click the Add Menu Item button or select Project ➤ Add ➤ Menu Item. REALbasic will respond by adding a new menu item under the selected submenu.

3. Give the new menu item a name by selecting it and then modifying the value of its Name property. The name assigned will be the name you have to use when you programmatically refer to the menu from within your program code.

4. Assign the text you want displayed on the menu item by changing the value assigned to the Text property.

5. Repeat steps 2 through 4 to add as many additional menu items as necessary to the submenu.

Note You can also add a new submenu directly to a menu by clicking the Add Submenu button located on the Menu Editor toolbar.

Previewing Your REALbasic Menus

When you design and create a menu system for REALbasic applications, which you plan on compiling for multiple operating systems (OSs), visualizing exactly how the menu system you develop will look when executed on other OSs can be difficult. Obviously, you can stop midway through the development process and compile a temporary copy of your new application to test it on target OSs to see how your menu system will look.

Fortunately, REALbasic negates this process by providing you with the capability to get a sneak peek at how your menu system will look. This functionality is provided by four buttons located on the far left-hand side of the Menu Editor toolbar, as shown in Figure 4-14.

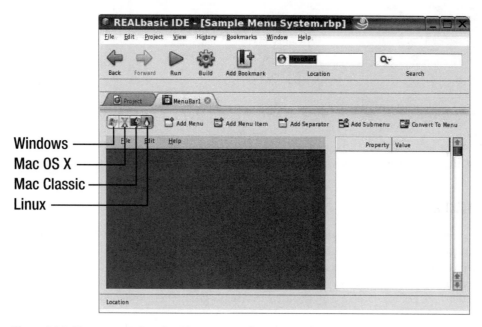

Figure 4-14. *You can preview the appearance of your REALbasic menu system for any supported OS from within the Menu Editor.*

By clicking one of these buttons, you can see how your menu system will look on different OSs. For example, Figure 4-15 shows a preview of how a menu system will look on Windows, even though the application is currently being developed on Linux.

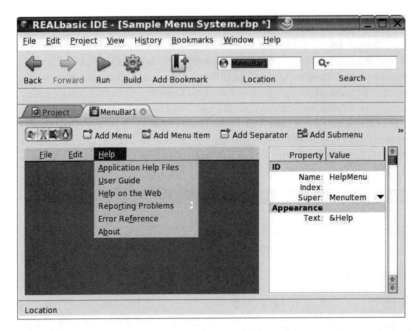

Figure 4-15. *Previewing the Windows version of an application's menu system*

Enhancing Menu Systems

Building effective application menu systems is more than simply creating menus, menu items, and submenus. To meet user expectations and to provide a fully functional menu system, you also need to think about other menu system features. For example, as you add more and more functionality to your application's menus, they can grow considerably. You can add separator bars in between groups of related menu items to visually group them and make your menu systems more intuitive.

You might also want to consider providing your users with the capability to access the menu system or to execute menu item functionality directly from the keyword, instead of limiting menu access strictly to the mouse. Options for providing menu-item access to the keyboard include the following:

- **Shortcuts**. Provide users with the capability to access a menu item's functionality directly from the keyboard by pressing keystrokes associated with each menu item.

- **Accelerator Keys**. Provides Windows and Linux users with the capability to access menus, menu items, and submenus directly from the keyboard by pressing the Alt key and a designated accelerator key.

- **Keyboard Equivalents**. Provides Windows XP users with the capability to execute menu-item functionality directly from the keyboard by pressing a predefined combination of keys.

Using Separator Bars to Organize Menu Items

To make your application's menu system easier and more intuitive to work with, make sure to group menu items and submenus together in a logical manner. For example, on the File menu of most Windows and Linux applications, the customary presentation is to have menu items related to creating, opening, or closing documents first, followed by menu items for saving or printing. The last menu item should be an Exit or Quit option.

Once you organize your menu items into related groups, visually separating these groups by inserting a horizontal separator bar in between them is often helpful. The following procedures outlines the steps required to insert a separator bar in between your menu items.

1. Finish building the menu system for your REALbasic application, making sure your group-related menu items are together in a logical order.

2. Select a menu where you want to insert a separator bar.

3. Click the menu item, and then insert the separator bar.

4. Click the Add Separator button located in the Menu Editor's toolbar or click Project ➤ Add ➤ Separator. The separator bar is immediately visible, as Figure 4-16 shows.

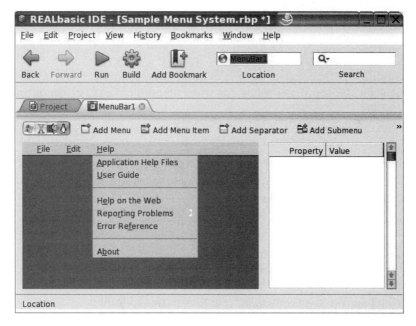

Figure 4-16. *Visually improving the organization of menu items using separator bars*

5. Repeat steps 2 through 4 to add additional separator bars to other menus, as needed.

■**Tip** REALbasic automatically inserts separator bars just beneath the currently selected menu item. If, after adding the separator bar, you decide it needs to be moved to a different location within the menu, you can do so by selecting the separator bar, and then dragging-and-dropping it at the appropriate spot.

Setting Up Shortcut Keys

Shortcuts are designed to provide users with easy access to menu item functionality via the keyboard. For example, in most Macintosh applications, users can save their work by pressing Command+S. Likewise, users can save their work on Windows and Linux applications by pressing Ctrl+S.

While not required, most users today have become savvy enough to look for and expect to find application shortcuts, so it is important that you provide them. Otherwise, you run the risk of disappointing your users and, perhaps, making them think your applications are not yet ready for prime time. Fortunately, REALbasic makes the process of assigning shortcuts to your menu items a snap. Given how easy defining shortcuts is, it is important that you add them to your applications to make your applications look as professional as possible.

To specify shortcuts, you need to modify the following properties for each menu or menu items:

- **Key**. A single letter pressed in conjunction with a modifier keys to trigger a menu event handler.

- **MenuModifier**. When enabled, the user must press and hold Control on Windows (or Command on Macintosh) in conjunction with the specified key to trigger the menu's event handler.

■**Note** Macintosh, Windows, and Linux all begin looking for shortcuts starting with the left-most menu. Therefore, if you assign the same shortcut to a menu item located on two separate menus, only the first instance (the left-most instance) will work as expected.

For example, the following procedure demonstrates how to assign a shortcut of Command+I or Ctrl+I to a menu item named Properties on a File menu.

1. Finish building the menu system for your REALbasic application.

2. Select the File menu to expand and see its contents.

3. Select the Properties menu item.

4. Specify *I* as the value of the Properties menu item's Key property.

5. Enable the MenuModifier property by selecting it. The new shortcut is immediately displayed just to the right of the menu item, as Figure 4-17 shows.

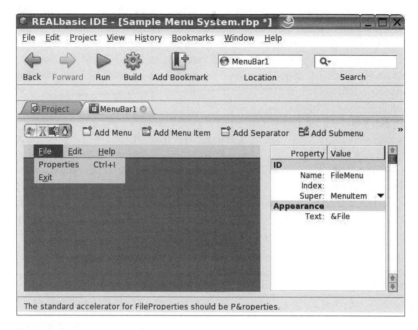

Figure 4-17. *Assigning a shortcut to a menu item, as shown on Linux*

REALbasic provides additional options for specifying more complex forms of shortcuts. For example, you might want to set up a shortcut that is accessed as Ctrl+Shift+A (on Windows and Linux) or Command+Shift+A (on Macintosh). To set up this type of shortcut, you must specify a value for the Key property, and then enable both the MenuModifier and Alternate-MenuModifier properties.

If you are developing applications only for Windows or Linux, you also have the option of enabling the PCAltKey property, which requires the Alt key also be pressed to access a shortcut. For example, to set up a shortcut on Windows or Linux as Ctrl+Alt+H, you need to specify *H* has the value of the Key property and enable both the MenuModifier and PCAltKey properties.

REALbasic also provides two Macintosh-only modifier keys, which you can use to create additional shortcut variations on those OSs. For starters, when you select the MacControlKey property, it requires you to hold down Control in addition to any other specified keys. And, when you enable the MacOptionKey, it requires you also to press Option.

Defining Accelerator Keys on Windows and Linux Menus

Another important menu system feature to implement when you are developing applications for Windows and Linux is accelerator keys. *Accelerator keys* provide you with the capability to activate menus and menu items using only the keyboard. A menu or menu item's accelerator key is activated by pressing the Alt key, and then pressing the appropriate key.

FOLLOW ACCEPTED DESIGN CONVENTIONS

Today's computer users have become sophisticated and demanding, so it's critical that your applications measure up to their expectations. One expectation most users have is that their applications follow a predictable design pattern. This means, among other things, that an application's menu system presents its menus in the manner they expect. For example, menu headings should be labeled File, Edit, and Help, not Document, Modify, and Assistance. In addition, users expect to see certain features on certain menus. For example, the File menu should contain menu items for opening and closing files. Putting these menu items under a different menu can frustrate and confuse users.

Also important is that your menus and menu items include shortcuts, where appropriate, and that you follow standards appropriate for naming your shortcuts as appropriate for each OS where your applications will run. For example, if your application provides users with the capability to select and copy data, then your users will expect to see a Copy menu item located under an Edit menu. In addition, Macintosh users will expect your application to provide a Command+C shortcut. Likewise, Windows and Linux users will expect to see a Ctrl+C shortcut. If you fail to provide a shortcut or you assign a different shortcut key, you run the risk of missing your users' expectations. To help provide you with some guidance, Table 4-2 provides a listing of shortcut key definitions that represent common application-shortcut standards.

Table 4-2. *Recommended Reserved Operating System Shortcut Keys*

Menu	Macintosh	Windows	Linux	Command	Description
File	⌘-N	Ctrl+N	Ctrl+N	New	Create a new file
	⌘-O	Ctrl+O	Ctrl+O	Open	Open an existing file
	⌘-W	Ctrl+W	Ctrl+W	Close	Close a file
	⌘-S	Ctrl+S	Ctrl+S	Save	Save a file
	⌘-P	Ctrl+P	Ctrl+P	Print	Print a file
	⌘-Q	Ctrl+Q	Ctrl+Q	Quit	Close the application
Edit	⌘-Z	Ctrl+Z	Ctrl+Z	Undo	Undo a previous operation or command
	⌘-X	Ctrl+X	Ctrl+X	Cut	Remove selected data; place on clipboard
	⌘-C	Ctrl+C	Ctrl+C	Copy	Copy selected data; place on clipboard
	⌘-V	Ctrl+V	Ctrl+V	Paste	Copy data from clipboard to insertion point
	⌘-A	Ctrl+A	Ctrl+A	Select All	Select all data
	⌘-Period	Esc	Esc	Terminate	Terminate the current operation
	⌘-M	Ctrl+M	Ctrl+M	Minimize	Minimize the window

Accelerator keys are identified by the presence of an underscore character somewhere in the text of the menu, submenu, or menu item. For example, the letter *F* is generally used as the accelerator key for the File menu and is displayed as File. When the user presses the Alt key, and then presses the *F* key, an application displays the contents of its File menu. Once displayed, the user can access any of the submenus of menu items located under that menu by continuing to press the Alt key, and then press the accelerator key assigned to the submenu or menu item. Using accelerator keys, a user may access any part of an application's menu system without ever touching their mouse. Figure 4-18, shows how accelerator keys are implemented in a typical Windows application.

Figure 4-18. *Examining the accelerator key provided on the File menu of Microsoft's Notepad application*

Accelerator keys are specified by placing an ampersand (&) character in the Text property belonging to a menu, submenu, or menu item. For example, to assign an accelerator key of *B* for a menu item that has a Text value of Background, you would place the ampersand character just at the beginning of the word, as the following shows.

1. Finish building the menu system for your REALbasic application.

2. Select the menu where the menu items reside.

3. Select the menu item and locate its Text property.

4. Add the ampersand (&) character to the beginning of the specified value.

5. Press Enter or Return. The results should be immediately visible.

Using Menu Items to Trigger Command and Code Execution

Once you finish putting together your application's menu system, you need to associate program code statements with each menu item to make the menu functional. Users can then activate menus and execute associated programming statements by clicking the appropriate menu item.

The process of associating program code with individual menu items is relatively straight-forward, as the following shows.

1. Finish building the menu system for your REALbasic application.

2. Open the Project Editor and assign the menu bar to a window by selecting the window, and then selecting the name of the appropriate menu bar from the drop-down list of property values associated with the MenuBar property.

3. Double-click the specified window in the Project Editor to open it.

4. Click the Code View icon located on the far left-hand side of the Windows Editor toolbar.

5. To add code to your application for each menu item, add a menu event handler. This enables you to associate specific code statements with specific menu items. Click the Add Menu Handler button located on the Windows Editor toolbar.

Note   A *menu handler* is a collection of code statements executed whenever you click an enabled menu item.

---

6. The entry of a menu handler is displayed in the left-hand browser area, with a single entry underneath it. By default, this entry is selected and the right-hand side of the Windows Editor displays a new procedure, as Figure 4-19 shows.

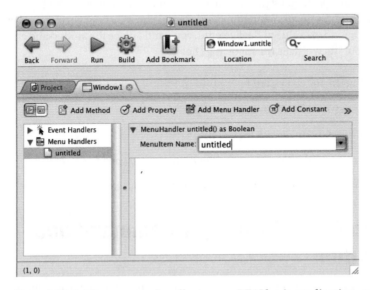

Figure 4-19. *Adding a menu handler to your REALbasic application, as shown on Macintosh*

7. Select the name of a menu item from the drop-down list for the MenuItem Name field, as you see in Figure 4-20.

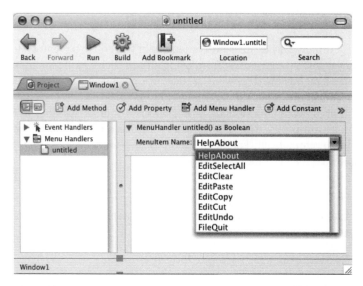

Figure 4-20. *Specify the menu for which you want to add code statements, as shown on Macintosh.*

8. Enter the code statements to be executed when the user clicks the menu item in the text edit area, as Figure 4-21 shows.

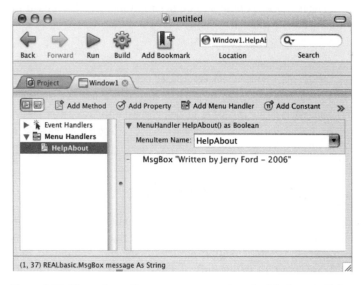

Figure 4-21. *Enter the code statements associated with the specifed menu item, as shown on Macintosh.*

9. Repeat steps 5 through 8 as many times as necessary to provide program code for each remaining menu item.

Controlling Access to Menu Items

By default, REALbasic automatically enables every menu item you add to a menu system. At times, though, you may want to prevent users from being able to click a particular menu item. You may want to disable a menu item to prevent the user from being able to click it at certain times during the execution of the application. For example, you may want to disable a menu item that enables the user to save a file as long as no file has been opened or as long as the user has not made any changes to an opened file. Later on, once the user has opened a file and made changes to it, you can programmatically enable the menu item. Note, a disabled menu item is still visible, but it is grayed out and cannot be selected.

■**Note** For a menu item to perform an action, you must associate program code with it. Until you do so, the menu item remains grayed out and the user is unable to select it.

If a menu item should not be enabled when the application first starts, you should deselect its AutoEnable property. Later, at the appropriate time, you can programmatically enable the menu item, using a statement similar to the following:

```
MenuHandlerName.AutoEnable = True
```

In this statement, MenuHandlerName is a placeholder representing the name of the menu item you want to enable. The remainder of the statement simply instructs REALbasic to enable the menu item, enabling the user to select it.

■**Tip** When deselected (or set to False), a menu remains disabled until the user clicks the menu that contains it, at which time you can programmatically determine if it is appropriate to enable the menu item. For example, the Cut and Copy menu items on the Edit menu are only enabled when a selection has been made within an application. Enabling these menu items when nothing has been selected does not make sense.

Reconfiguring Menu Organization

REALbasic is extremely flexible in the manner in which it lets you build menus, and create submenus and menu items. REALbasic adds new menus just to the right of the currently selected menu and it adds new menu items just beneath the currently selected menu item. At times, though, you might decide you want to change the order in which your menus or menu items are presented. REALbasic makes it easy to move things around the want you want them.

Moving Menus and Menu Items

If, after you add a new menu, you decide you don't like its current location, you can move it. One way to accomplish this is to delete the menu and add it back at the desired location. You can also drag-and-drop the menu to a new location without having to delete and re-create it by using the following procedure.

1. Open the appropriate menu bar in the MenuBar Editor.

2. Select the menu you want to move and drag it to a different location.

3. A vertical bar appears, indicating the current insertion point. Drop the menu at the desired location.

REALbasic also enables you to move menu items to different locations within the menu system. For example, the following procedure outlines the steps involved in moving a menu item from one location to another within the same menu.

1. Open the appropriate menu bar into the MenuBar Editor.

2. Select the menu where the menu item to be moved resides.

3. Select the menu item you want to move and drag it to a different location.

4. A horizontal bar appears, indicating the current insertion point. Drop the menu at the desired location.

Converting Menu Items to Menus

REALbasic also lets you convert a menu item into a new menu. This can come in handy when you make an enhancement to an application where you plan to expand on the capabilities provided by a given command. The following procedure outlines the steps involved in converting a menu item to a menu.

1. Open the appropriate menu bar in the MenuBar Editor.

2. Select the menu where the menu item currently resides.

3. Select the menu item, and then click the Convert to Menu button located on the Menubar Editor toolbar or click Project ➤ Modify ➤ Convert to Menu.

4. The menu item disappears and reappears as a new menu. Drag-and-drop the menu to the appropriate location.

Removing Menu and Menu Items

If a menu or menu item is no longer needed, you can remove it from your application by selecting it and pressing Delete or by clicking Edit ➤ Delete. Take care when deleting a menu because you also delete any submenus and menu items defined under it. Also, REALbasic does not delete any menu handler associated with a deleted menu item, so it's up to you to remember both to select and delete it.

Customizing the Apple and Macintosh Menus

As you already saw, application menus work a little differently on the Macintosh than they do on Windows and Linux. For starters, menus are not displayed on application windows on the Macintosh. Instead, menus are displayed at the top of the display area for the currently selected application.

Differences also exist between the ways that menus look and operate on Macintosh Classic and Mac OS X. Specifically, on Macintosh Classic, an Apple menu is added to the left of the File menu. On Mac OS X, though, an application menu is added to the left of the File menu, but just to the right of the Apple menu.

■**Note** REALbasic displays the name of the application as the text value for the Application menu (for example, the name you specified as the application's name in the Mac Settings section of the APP item on the Project Editor.

To add an menu item in the Application menu on Mac OS X, you begin by placing the menu item in the menu where you want it to appear on Windows, Linux, and Macintosh Classic (if you're going to compile the application for these OSs). You then change the Super property from the default value of MenuItem to PrefsMenuItem. The result is this: the new menu item appears in the menu where it was defined on Windows, Linux, and Macintosh Classic, but it is displayed on the Application menu on Mac OS X.

You cannot add a menu item to the Apple menu on Mac OS X, but you can add it to the Macintosh Classic Apple menu. To do so, add the menu item where you want it to appear on Windows and Linux, and then change the Super property from the default value of MenuItem to AppleMenuItem. This results in the display of the menu item on the Macintosh Classic menu and the display of the menu item on the Application menu for Mac OS X. The menu item displays on the menu where you added it on Windows and Linux.

Creating a StickyPad Application

To help solidify your understanding of how to create menu systems for your REALbasic applications, this section demonstrates how to create a new application called RBQuickNote. *RBQuickNote* is a small application that enables you to create and save small, sticky note-like files on your computer.

For demonstration purposes, this application is created using the Linux version of REALbasic. However, you can use its source code to create a functional version of the application on both Macintosh and Windows. All the functionality of the RBQuickNote application is provided via its menu system, which consists of menu items located on File, Edit, and Help menus, as Figure 4-22 shows.

Figure 4-22. *The RBQuickNote application provides users with the capability to create and retrieve reminder notes and text documents.*

■**Note** Starting in the next chapter and continuing throughout the rest of this book, you will begin learning the ins and outs of writing REALbasic code. For now, continue to key in code statements as instructed and take note of the brief explanations provided with each batch of code statements. As you progress through the remainder of this book, you may want to return and reexamine the program code included in this application.

Designing the User Interface

The RBQuickNote application is a little different from the applications you previously created in that other than the menu bar, it has no interface controls except for a single EditField control, which provides the application with a multiline entry field for collecting user input.

For the purpose of this application, the default window size of the Window1 window is fine and needn't be changed. Begin by adding an EditField control to Window1 and resize it, so it takes up the entire window. Next, change the following properties for the window and the EditField controls, as Table 4-3 shows.

Table 4-3. *Property Modifications for the RBQuickNote Application*

Object	Property	Value
Window1	Title	RBQuickNote
	Resizable	Enabled
	MaximizeButton	Enabled
EditField1	LockLeft	Enabled
	LockTop	Enabled
	LockRight	Enabled
	LockBottom	Enabled
	Multiline	Enabled
	TextColor	&c0000FF

The next step in creating the RBQuickNote is to create its menu system. Begin by double-clicking the menu bar item located on the Projects screen to open the Menubar Editor. At this point, you should see File and View menu. Modify the menu system for Menubar1 by adding the menu items you see in Table 4-4.

Table 4-4. *Menus and Menu Items for the RBQuickNote Application*

Menu	Menu Item	Text Property
File	FileOpen	&Open
	FileSave	&Save
	FileClear	C&lear
	FileQuit	E&xit
Edit	EditUndo	&Undo
	EditCut	Cu&t
	EditCopy	&Copy
	EditPaste	&Paste
	EditClear	&Delete

Menu	Menu Item	Text Property
	EditSelectAll	Select &All
Help	HelpAbout	&About

You do not have to add the FileQuit menu item on the File menu or any of the menu items for the Edit menu. REALbasic already added these menu items for you. In addition, you do not have to add any program code for these menu items as REALbasic has already provided everything these menu items need to do their job.

At this point, the menu system for the RBQuickNote application is complete and should look like the example Figure 4-23 shows.

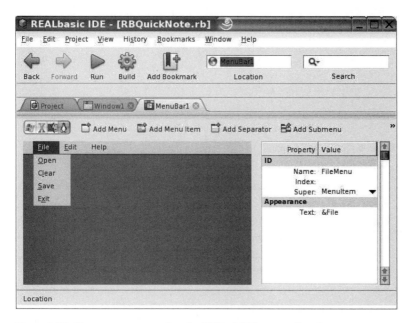

Figure 4-23. *The menu system for the RBQuickNote application*

Supplying Application Code

All code for the RBQuickNote application is placed in four event handlers, one for each menu item you added to the File and Help menus. Begin by opening the MenuBar1 in the REALbasic MenuBar Editor and switching over to Code view. Next, click the Add a Menu Event Handler button located on the MenuBar Editor toolbar. A Menu Handler's entry is added to the left-hand browser area in the Menubar Editor; a single entry is displayed beneath it with a text property of untitled. By default, this entry is selected and the right-hand side of the Windows Editor is set up to accept the code statements you want to associate with this menu item.

Select the entry for the FileClear menu item from the drop-down list for the MenuItem Name field and enter the following program statements.

```
Window1.EditField1.Text = ""
```

When executed, this statement tells REALbasic to clear out any currently displayed text in the application EditField control. Next, click the Add Menu Handler button again to add a new menu handler. Select the entry for the FileOpen menu item from the drop-down list for the MenuItem Name field and enter the following program statements.

```
Dim f as FolderItem
Dim TextInput as TextInputStream

Window1.EditField1.Text= ""

f = GetOpenFolderItem("Application/Text")

If f <> nil Then

  TextInput = f.OpenAsTextFile

  Window1.EditField1.Text = TextInput.ReadAll

End If
```

Note To learn more about the basic file operations implemented in the RBQuickNote applications, see Chapter 9.

These statements are responsible for creating a new empty file the user can use to create a new note. Next, click the Add Menu Handler button again to add another new menu handler. This time, select the entry for the FileSave menu item from the drop-down list for the MenuItem Name field and enter the following program statements.

```
Dim f as FolderItem
Dim TextStream As TextOutputStream

f=GetSaveFolderItem("Application/text","TextFile")

If f <> nil Then

  TextStream=f.CreateTextFile
  TextStream.WriteLine Window1.EditField1.Text
  TextStream.Close
End If
```

These statements are responsible for saving the note created by the user as a text file in whatever folder the user chooses to save them. Finally, click the Add Menu Handler button to add one last new menu handler. This time, select the entry for the HelpAbout menu item from the drop-down list for the MenuItem Name field and enter the following program statements.

```
MsgBox"RBQuickNote Version 1.0 - 2006"
```

This statement uses a built-in REALbasic function called MsgBox to display a text message in a preformatted pop-up dialog window.

Figure 4-24 demonstrates how the RBQuickNote looks when it's running. As you can see, it functions much like a simple text-entry application. Any text entered into it is displayed in blue and it can be minimized or maximized. By default, any files created by the application are assigned a file extension of .1st, which is a default file extension assigned by REALbasic.

Figure 4-24. *A demonstraton of the RBQuickNote application in action*

Testing RBQuickNote

If you have not done so, go ahead and save your application. Name your application RBQuickNote. The application is now ready to compile. If any errors are flagged during compilation, then you probably made one or more typos entering code statements. Take a few moments to review the code statements and fix any typos you find.

Summary

In this chapter, you learned how to complete the development of your REALbasic application's user interface by adding menus, submenus, and menu items. You learned how to configure menus, submenus, and menu items by defining shortcuts. In addition, you learned how to define accelerator keys for applications that run on Windows and Linux. On top of all this, you learned how to visually organize menu items using separator bars, and how to reorganize menus and menu items using drag-and-drop. You also learned how to change menu items into menus. Finally, you learned how to trigger the execution of program code based on the selection of menu items.

CHAPTER 5

■ ■ ■

Storing and Retrieving Application Data

As you develop more and more complex REALbasic applications, you will find yourself needing to collect, store, and process data during program execution. This chapter shows you a number of different ways that REALbasic enables you to store and manipulate application data. This includes learning how to work with variables, arrays, dictionaries, and constants. You also learn how to enhance your applications using a number of different techniques for embedding comments.

Specifically, you learn how to

- Store and retrieve data in variables and arrays

- Work with different data types and convert data between them

- Set variable scope

Adding Comments to Your Code

Up to this point in the book, the sample applications you developed were relatively small and straightforward. However, as your applications grow, they will become more complex and more difficult to understand. One way to cope with this is by embedding comments and notes in your applications. This will be greatly appreciated by those who come along behind you to provide support and to modify your program code.

REALbasic provides you with a number of different ways of embedding documentation within your applications, including comments, notes, and property comments.

Comments

Comments are text statements embedded within your applications that document your programming statements and logic. While visible to the programmer, comments are not compiled into REALbasic applications and have no impact on application performance. REALbasic provides you with a number of different ways to add comments to your applications, including single quotes ('), forward slashes (//), and the *REM keyword*.

All three comment statements are functionally equivalent. There is no advantage to using one type of comment over another. You can embed comments within your REALbasic applications using any of these options, as the following demonstrates.

```
'Define a variable name blnAnswer with a data type of Boolean
Dim blnAnswer As Boolean
```

```
//Define a variable name blnAnswer with a data type of Boolean
Dim blnAnswer As Boolean
```

```
REM Define a variable name blnAnswer with a data ttype of Boolean
Dim blnAnswer As Boolean
```

REALbasic enables you to add comments to the end of statements, as the following shows.

```
Dim blnAnswer As Boolean    'Define a variable to store the user's choice
```

▪**Note**   If you have a number of consecutive code statements that you want to comment, you can do so by selecting these statements, and then clicking the Comment Command button located on the Code Editor toolbar or by clicking Edit ➤ Comment. When you do so, REALbasic responds by adding a single-quote comment character to the beginning of each statement and changing the Comment Command button into the Uncomment Command button (Edit ➤ Uncomment).

Notes

Another option of embedding comments directly into your applications is to add notes. A *note* is an item you can add in the browser window located in the Code Editor. Like regular comments, notes are not compiled and have no effect on application performance. The following procedure outlines the steps involved in adding a note to applications.

1. Open the Code Editor for the resource for which you want to add the note.

2. Click the Add Note button located on the Code Editor toolbar or click Project ➤ Add ➤ Note.

3. Enter a name for the Note in the Note Name field.

4. Enter your comments into the data entry area, as Figure 5-1 shows.

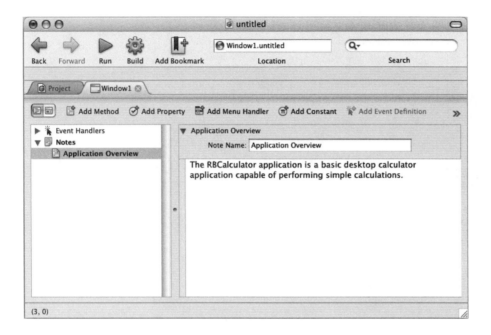

Figure 5-1. *Embedding a note in a REALbasic application, as shown on Macintosh*

Property Comments

REALbasic also provides you with the capability to document any properties you add to windows, classes, and modules. Properties are added by clicking the Add Property button or by clicking Project ➤ Add ➤ Property. As Figure 5-2 shows, you can add comments beneath any property by entering text in the data entry area beneath the property declaration data.

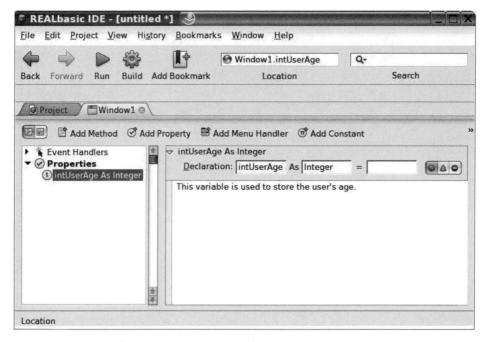

Figure 5-2. *Embedding comments into Property declarations, as shown on Linux.*

Information on classes and modules is provided in Chapter 8.

Storing and Retrieving Data

Like other programming languages, REALbasic provides the capability to store and retrieve data in memory while applications are running. *Data* is the information applications collect, process, and store when running. REALbasic provides you with two primary means of storing and retrieving data that changes during program execution: variables and arrays.

A *variable* provides your application with the capability to store data that may change while the application executes. Variables are logical pointers to locations in memory where data is stored. An *array* is an indexed list of related data. By providing the capability to store related data in collections, REALbasic equips you with a tool for storing and processing large amounts of data with relatively few programming statements, which makes for more efficient program code.

REALbasic provides other options for working with data, including constants, dictionaries, and classes. Dictionaries and constants are covered in the sections "Working with Dictionaries" and "Constants." To learn about classes, see Chapter 8.

Working with Variables

Variables are used to store and process individual pieces of data, such as values in an equation or the number of turns left in a game. Unlike constants, variables are meant to store data that changes during application execution. REALbasic variables are capable of working with many different types of data, such as text strings and different types of numbers. Table 5-1 provides a listing of the different data types that REALbasic supports.

Table 5-1. *REALbasic Data Types*

Category	Data	Type
String	CFString	Stores a string reference (Mac only)
	CString	A null-terminated string
	PString	A Pascal string used on Macintosh with a limit of 255 characters
	String	Text consisting of alphanumeric characters whose size is limited only by the amount of available memory
	WString	A null-terminated string used on Windows NT
Numeric	Byte	An integer between -128 and 127
	Double	A number that supports decimals between 2.2250738585072013 e-308 and 1.7976931348623157 e+308
	Integer	A whole number between -2,147,483,648 and 2,147,483,647
	OSType	A 4-byte integer used on Macintosh when declaring into QuickTime
	Short	A 16-bit integer capable of storing values between -32,768 and 32,767
	Single	A number capable of storing a decimal that stores values between $-1.175494E-38$ and $-3.402823E+38$
	Ubyte	An 8-bit unsigned integer with a value between 0 and 255
	UShort	A 16-bit unsigned integer with a value between 0 and 65,535
	WindowPtr	A 4-byte integer used to store a link or pointer to a window
Special	Boolean	An intrinsic data type of either True or False
	Color	A set using RGB, HSV, CMY color models, or the &c literal
	Ptr	A 4-byte link or pointer to a location in memory
	Variant	A special data type that can be used to store data of any type

SPECIFYING THE CORRECT DATA TYPE

By specifying the correct data type for each piece of data processed by your application, you optimize your application to run as efficiently as possible by conserving the amount of memory required to store data. A trade off exists, however, between your development time and the savings in time your applications may, ultimately, realize if you tweak memory usage to perfection. In more cases, you won't see any tangible improvement in performance no matter how carefully you specify variable data types. As such, you'll probably be best served in 99 percent of all cases by using the following commonly used data types: Boolean, Color, Double, Integer, Single, String, and Variant.

As shown in Table 5-1, REALbasic provides support for a wide variety of data types, each of which is designed to store a different type of data. When you instruct REALbasic as to what data type to associate with a particular variable, you tell it what types of actions are permissible when working with the variable. For example, numeric data types, such as an integers, can be added together, but they cannot exceed a maximum value of 2,147,483,647. On the other hand, a special data type, such as a Boolean value, can only be set equal to True or False.

Working with Properties

Variables directly related to REALbasic objects, such as a window, PushButton, or menu, are referred to as properties of objects. *Properties* are accessed by name and have specific data types. For example, the Caption property of a PushButton control has a data type of string.

Assigning Values to Properties

Many properties are available for modification at design time. However, you can also modify most properties programmatically during program execution. The following outlines the syntax for property assignment.

```
ObjectName.PropertyName = Value
```

As you can see, to assign a value to a property, you must identify the name of the owning object, the name of the property, and the value you want to assign to the property. Take note of the dot that separates the ObjectName and PropertyName in the previous example. This is an example of dot notation or dot syntax and is the standard means by which you refer to object attributes like properties.

The following shows an example of how to assign a value to a property.

```
PushButton1.Caption = "Cancel"
```

■**Note** Similar dot notation was used back in Chapter 4 to enable access to menu items. Likewise, when you supply the program code required to build the RBCalculator application, which you read about in the section "Supplying Application Code," you'll see additional examples of how to programmatically control access to interface elements by modifying control properties.

In this example, the Caption property associated with an instance of a PushButton control named the PushButton1 is assigned a value of Cancel. Note, this example assumes the code for this statement was placed within the method belonging to the window where the PushButton1 control was added or within one of the methods belonging to a control on that window. If, on the other hand, the PushButton1 control resides on another window, you must specify the full path to the control using the following syntax to refer to it.

```
WindowName.ObjectName.PropertyName = Value
```

Note Up to this point in the book, you have been keying in code statements associated with either a window or one of its controls. The collection of code statements associated with either of these types of resources is referred to as a method within REALbasic programming. You learn more about methods later in Chapter 8.

For example, if the PushButton1 control you wanted to modify resided on a window named Window2, you would need to modify this example as the following shows.

```
Window2.Pushbutton1.Caption = "Cancel"
```

ME AND SELF

REALbasic provides a pair of useful programming shortcuts you may want to use to streamline your program statements. *Me* is a keyword that refers to the control in which program code is placed. By referring to Me in place of a control's name, you can reduce the amount of keystrokes required to complete your code statements. For example, you could rewrite

```
PushButton1.Caption = "Cancel"
```

as

```
Me.Caption = "Cancel"
```

This example assumes the code for this statement is located within the method associated with the PushButton1 control. Another advantage of using the Me keyword in place of a specific control's name is this: because the Me keyword is generic, you can reuse it by copying-and-pasting it into the method of another PushButton control without then having to modify the ObjectName part of the statement.

Self is a keyword that refers to a control's parent object. For example, the parent object of a PushButton control would be the window on which it was placed. Thus, instead of programmatically referring to a window's Title property from within one of its controls as

```
Window1.Title = "My test Application"
```

You could, instead, generically reference the property using the Self pronoun as the following shows.

```
Self.Title = "My test Application"
```

Retrieving Property Values

In addition to assigning a value to a property, you can also retrieve it using the following syntax.

```
Result = ObjectName.PropertyName
```

Here, the value assigned to the PropertyName is assigned to a variable named Result. For example, the following statement retrieves the value assigned to the Caption Property of the PushButton1 control

```
x = PushButton1.Caption
```

If the Property resides on a different window, you would have to modify this statement, as the following shows.

```
x = Window2.PushButton1.Caption
```

Creating and Working with Variables

When you need to store and retrieve individual pieces of data that are not directly associated with an object, such as a control, you will want to store them in regular variables. REALbasic enables you to create variable names of any length. Variables names are not case-sensitive, so as far as REALbasic is concerned, TEMP, tEMP, and TeMp are all the same. REALbasic does impose a few rules on the creation of variable names, as shown in the following list:

- Variable names must begin with a letter.
- Variable names can only contain uppercase and lowercase alphabetic characters and numbers.
- Variable names cannot contain blank spaces.
- Reserved words cannot be used as variable names.

Defining Variables and Assigning Data

Two steps are involved in creating a variable. For starters, you must declare the variable using the Dim statement. In declaring a variable, you give it a name and specify the type of data it will store. The following shows the syntax of the Dim statement.

```
Dim VariableName As DataType
```

For example, the following statement declares a variable named strUserName that will hold string data.

```
Dim strUserName As String
```

Once you declare a variable, you can assign data to it, as the following shows.

```
strUserName = "Alexander Ford"
```

■Tip Always be sure to assign a value to your variables. If you forget, REALbasic will substitute a default value, which can create unpredictable results in your applications. For example, if you fail to assign a value to a variable with a numeric data type, REALbasic assigns a default value of 0. Similarly, if you fail to assign a value to a variable that stores string data, REALbasic automatically assigns an empty string ("") as the variable's default value.

REALbasic is flexible in the manner in which it enables you to declare variables. For example, it lets you declare more than one variable of the same data type at a time using a single Dim statement, as the following shows.

```
Dim strFirstName, strLastname As String
```

REALbasic lets you mix and match data types in declaration statements, as you see here.

```
Dim strUserName As String, strUserAge as Integer
```

REALbasic also enables you to assign a value to a variable at the same time you declare it, as the following shows.

```
Dim strPlayAgain As Boolean = False
```

■Note One thing REALbasic does not do, and this may surprise Visual Basic programmers, is let you implicitly create variables simply by referencing them, without first declaring them.

CREATING MORE USEFUL VARIABLE NAMES

To help make your REALbasic code statements easier to understand, use a variable-naming scheme. For example, going forward, the examples in this book use variables whose names begin with a three-character prefix that identifies their data type. In addition, the names assigned to all variables attempt to describe their use or contents. Examples of common prefix characters include

- Boolean - bln
- Color - clr
- Double - dbl
- Integer - int
- Single - sng
- String - str
- Variant - var

Determining Variable Scope

A key concept you should be aware of when working with variables is scope. A variable's *scope* determines which parts of your REALbasic application can access a variable. Variables declared using the Dim statement are local in scope, which means the variables can only be accessed within the method where they were defined.

For example, if you declare a variable named strUserName in a method belonging to a PushButton control, that variable can only be accessible by other programming statements associated with that method. You can declare a variable anywhere you want within a method, just as long as you declare it before other code statements that reference it.

You can further refine variable scope with methods by declaring variables within If...Then statements and looping statements. These types of statements, and any code stored within them, represent a block of code. Any variable declared within a code block is local only to that code block. For example, the following example shows a declaration statement located inside an If...Then code block. Any other code statements in the method where this If...Then code block resides will be unable to access the variable. Information on how to work with If...Then and looping statements is available in Chapters 6 and 7.

```
If intUserAge > 21 Then
    Dim blnAccessFiles As Boolean
    blnAccessFiles = True
End If
```

If, on the other hand, you need to set up a variable with a broader scope, you can add a module to your application and define the variable within the module. This gives the variable a global scope, meaning it can be accessed from any part of the application. Modules are discussed in Chapter 8.

■**Tip** In addition to being considered a good programming practice, limiting the scope of variables help to prevent the code in one part of your application from accidentally changing a similarly named variable's value in another part of your application.

Converting Between Data Types

As you work with variables in your REALbasic applications, at times, you might need to convert the data type of values stored in properties and variables. For example, any time you use an EditField control to collect numeric data from users, you need to convert that data from string to a numeric format because REALbasic treats anything entered into an EditField control as a string.

Built-In Conversion Functions

To help make things easier for you, REALbasic provides a number of built-in functions you can use to convert data from one data type to another. These functions include the following:

- **CDbl**. Converts a string value into a numeric value with a Double data type. This function is typically used to convert data supplied by the user.

- **CStr**. Converts any data type into a string value.

- **Str**. Converts a numeric value into a string value.

- **Val**. Converts a string value into a numeric value with a Double data type. This function is typically used to convert data generated by code within your application.

The following statement demonstrates how to work with the CDbl conversion function.

```
Dim dblUserAge As Double
dblUserAge = CDbl(EditField1.Text)
```

In this example, a variable named dblUserAge capable of storing double data is declared. Then, a value is retrieved from an EditField control and is converted to a double and assigned to dblUserAge. You can just as easily convert a integer to a string data type, as the following shows.

```
Dim intUserAge As Integer = 30
EditField1.text = CStr(strUserAge)
```

In this example, the integer value stored in the intUserAge variable is converted to a data type of string, and then displayed in an EditField control.

String Manipulation Functions

Another common programming technique you need to know when developing REALbasic applications is how to manipulate and extract the contents of strings. In fact, string manipulation is such a commonly performed task that REALbasic provides a number of built-in string handling functions to assist you, as the following list shows.:

- **InStr**. Searches for a string within another string.

- **Len**. Returns a string's length.

- **Lowercase**. Converts a string to lowercase characters.

- **Ltrim**. Removes leading spaces from the left-hand side of a string.

- **Mid**. Extracts a portion of a string.

- **Replace**. Replaces one string with another string.

- **Rtrim**. Removes trailing spaces from the right-hand side of a string.

- **Trim**. Removes both leading and trailing spaces from a string.

- **Uppercase**. Converts a string to uppercase characters.

The following statement demonstrates how to work with string manipulation functions.

```
Dim strSampleMsg As String = "   A long time ago in a galaxy far, far away    "
MsgBox(Replace(strSampleMsg, "galaxy", "universe"))
MsgBox(Uppercase(strSampleMsg))
MsgBox(Trim(strSampleMsg) + " where no one boldly dared go before!")
```

■**Note**   In the section "Supplying Application Code," where you'll supply the program code required to create the RBCalculator application, you have the opportunity to use both the Mid and InStr functions.

The first statement declares a variable name strSampleMsg and assigns it a text string. The second statement uses the Replace function to replace the first occurrence of the string "galaxy" with the string "universe," found in strSampleMsg before displaying the resulting value of the string in a pop-up dialog. The third statement uses the Uppercase function to convert the value stored in strSampleMsg to all uppercase characters before displaying the resulting string in a pop-up dialog. The last statement uses the Trim function to remove any leading and trailing blank spaces from the value stored in strSamplemsg before appending the variable's value to another string.

■**Note**   When used with two strings, the + character adds together or concatenates the strings to create a new string. Visual Basic programmers should note that, in REALbasic, the + character is used instead of the & character to perform concatenation.

Storing Data in Arrays

The more variables your REALbasic applications have to manage, the more complicated your code becomes. In many cases, data managed by your applications may be closely related. For example, an application might need to collect customer names or IDs. In these cases, you can simplify things by storing data in an array.

An *array* is an indexed collection of data that can be processed as a unit. Individual pieces of data stored in an array are referred to as *elements*. The first element in an array is assigned an index number of zero. As each additional piece of data is added to an array, it is assigned an incremental index number. Once loaded, you can reference any piece of data in the array by specifying its index number.

■**Tip**   When creating an array name, try to find a name that describes the array's purpose or contents. For example, an array whose purpose is to hold user names might be named strNamesArray. Note, in this example, a three-letter prefix was added to the beginning of the array name to identify the type of data stored. Also, note, the word "Array" was added to the end of the array name to identify it as an array.

REALbasic supports single dimensional and multidimensional arrays. A *single dimensional array* is a single list of data, such as a list of grocery items you might write down before visiting the supermarket. A *multidimensional array* is like a table made up of rows and columns that can be likened to an Excel spreadsheet. Just like variables, you use the Dim keyword to declare arrays. The syntax for declaring an array is outlined in the following.

```
Dim ArrayName(dimensions) As DataType
```

ArrayName represents the name of the array. *Dimensions* is a comma-separated list of numbers that specifies the number of dimensions the array has and the highest-defined element in the array. DataType tells REALbasic what type of data will be stored in the array. For example, the following statement declares a single dimension array that can hold ten elements.

```
Dim strNamesArray(9) As String
```

Because the first element in a REALbasic array has an index of 0, the previous examples can store elements using index numbers 0 through 9. The following statement demonstrates how to declare a two-dimensional array.

```
Dim strNamesArray(4,9) As String
```

In this example, an array named strNamesArray, which is made up of five rows (0 through 4) and ten columns (0 through 9), was defined.

■Tip REALbasic also provides a built-in function called Array, which you can use to quickly set up small arrays. The Array function takes a list of comma-separated values and turns them into an array. For example, the following statements are all that is necessary to define an array named strNamesArray and populate it with five elements.

```
Dim strNamesArray() As String
strNamesArray = Array("Molly", "William", "Alexander", "Jerry", "Mary")
```

Loading Data into Arrays

Once an array is defined, you can load data into it. To do so, you specify the index location for each element assigned to the array, as shown here.

```
Dim strNamesArray(4) As String

strNamesArray(0) = "Molly"
strNamesArray(1) = "William"
strNamesArray(2) = "Alexander"
strNamesArray(3) = "Jerry"
strNamesArray(4) = "Mary"
```

Retrieving Data from Arrays

Once an array is populated with data, you can refer to any element in the array by specifying its index position. For example, the following statement retrieves the value assigned to the third element in the strNamesArray and assigns it to a variable.

```
Dim strCurrentName As String
StrCurrentName = strNamesArray(2)
```

Rather than accessing individual array elements one at a time, you can set up a loop that enables you to programmatically process every element in an array. In this way, you can process an array containing dozens, hundreds, or many thousands of elements using a relatively small amount of code, as the following shows.

```
Dim strNamesArray(4) As String
Dim intCounter As Integer

strNamesArray(0) = "Molly"
strNamesArray(1) = "William"
strNamesArray(2) = "Alexander"
strNamesArray(3) = "Jerry"
strNamesArray(4) = "Mary"

For intCounter = 0 To Ubound(strNamesArray)
     MsgBox("Now processing " + strNamesArray (intCounter))
Next intCounter
```

When this example runs, the For...Next loop will read and display the name of each array element one at a time in a series of pop-up dialog windows. Note the use of the Ubound function in the previous example. This function returns the index number of the last element stored in the specified array, which in this example would be 4. The Ubound function is designed to help set up loops that process arrays whose length may not be known in advance. Loops provide the capability to iterate through collections of data-like arrays. More information on the For...Next loop is available in Chapter 7.

Changing the Size of Your Arrays

You may not always know in advance exactly how many elements you need to store in an array. In these circumstances, declaring your array as a null array (or an empty array) is best. You can do this either by specifying a –1 as the array's index number or by simply not specifying anything at all. For example, both of the following statements are functionally equivalent.

```
Dim strNamesArray(-1)
Dim strNamesArray()
```

When defined in this manner, you can wait until later in your application to redefine the array when you know how big it needs to be. You do this using the Redim statement, as the following shows.

```
Redim strNamesArray(9)
```

In this example, the strNamesArray is resized to allow it to hold up to ten elements. Once an array is resized, you can begin assigning new elements to it.

■**Note** Visual Basic programmers should take note that in REALbasic, the Redim statement behaves differently than it does in Visual Basic. Unlike Visual Basic, redimensioning an array in REALbasic does not cause the loss of all the elements already defined in it.

Incrementing an Array Size an Element at a Time

In addition to redimensioning an array, REALbasic also lets you dynamically append data to the end of an array without first changing its size. This is accomplished through the Append method, as shown in the following.

```
strNamesArray.Append "Dolly"
```

This statement automatically increases the size of the strNamesArray by one and adds a new element to the end of the array. The Append method only works with single-dimension arrays.

Inserting Data into the Middle of an Array

REALbasic also enables you to insert new elements into any index position you choose within an array. This is accomplished by using the Insert method, as the following shows.

```
strNamesArray.Insert 2, "Dolly"
```

In this example, a new array element is inserted into the third index position of the array. The previously stored data in the array's third index position is reassigned to the fourth index position. Likewise, all other data stored above index position 3 automatically have their index number shifted up by one. The Insert method only works with single-dimension arrays.

Deleting Array Elements

REALbasic also provides the capability to selectively remove individual array elements using the Remove method. The *Remove method* works by deleting the data stored in the specified index position. The following statement demonstrates how to remove the third element from an array.

```
strNamesArray.Remove 2
```

Once an element is deleted, all remaining array elements have their index position shifted down by one position. The Remove method only works with single-dimension arrays.

Working with Dictionaries

One drawback of working with arrays is you are limited to accessing array elements only by their index position within the array. REALbasic provides an alternative to arrays in the form of dictionaries. A *dictionary* is an object made up of key-value pairs. What this means is, in addition to retrieving items using an index position number, you can also retrieve an item using its associated key. The best way to learn about the dictionary object is to see one in action. The following statements define a dictionary object named strNamesDictionary, and then populate it with data.

```
Dim strNamesDictionary As New Dictionary
strNamesDictionary.Value("Molly") = "Mollisa Lee Ford"
strNamesDictionary.Value("William") = "William Lee Ford"
strNamesDictionary.Value("Alexander") = "Alexander Lee Ford"
```

Look at the first statement in the previous list. It uses the Dim keyword to declare the new dictionary object. Notice it also uses the New keyword. The New keyword is required whenever you are creating a new instance of an object. More information about working with objects is available in Chapter 8. The last three statements populate the dictionary object using its Value method. The first argument passed to the Value method is a key, which is followed by the equals sign and the data to be associated with that key. Note, unlike arrays, you needn't worry about defining the size of your dictionary objects in advance.

Once loaded with data, you can use any of the dictionary object's properties and methods to access and modify its contents. For example, the following statement uses the dictionary object's Count property to display the number of items currently stored in the strNamesDictionary dictionary, as Figure 5-3 shows.

```
MsgBox "There are " + Str(strNamesDictionary.Count) + " key-value pairs in the
dictionary"
```

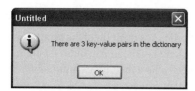

Figure 5-3. *Counting the number of items stored in a dictionary, as shown on Windows*

If you want, you can retrieve the value of any element in the dictionary by specifying its index location, as the following shows.

```
MsgBoxstrNamesDictionary.Value(strNamesDictionary.Key(0))
```

In this example, the first element stored in the dictionary object is displayed. The real power and convenience of working with a dictionary object is you can work with its data without having to specify index numbers. Instead, you can, for example, retrieve a value from the dictionary by specifying its key, as the following shows.

```
MsgBox strNamesDictionary.Value("Alexander")
```

The dictionary object provides a number other helpful methods that you can use to manage its contents. For example, you can use its Remove method to delete a specified element from the dictionary, as the following shows.

```
strNamesDictionary.Remove("Molly")
```

Similarly, you could delete all the elements stored in a dictionary using the Clear method, as shown here.

```
strNamesDictionary.Clear
```

■**Note** Compared to working with arrays, dictionaries provide a more efficient means of storing large amounts of data. Just as important, if your applications need to process large amounts of data, such as thousands of customer records, the dictionary object provides significantly faster lookup and retrieval when compared to arrays.

Constants

As useful as variables may be for storing individual pieces of data that don't belong to a specific object, at times, you may want to consider using constants instead. A constant is a known value that does not change during the execution of your application. For example, the value of pi is a perfect example of such a value.

Placing data that does not change in a constant instead of a variable provides you with several advantages. REALbasic can compile your application more efficiently because constants require less memory than variables. In addition, by storing data in a constant instead of a variable, you eliminate the possibility of accidentally changing the value of the data when your application runs.

REALbasic's Built-In Constants

REALbasic provides your application with access to all sorts of constants. One such constant is DebugBuild. *DebugBuild* returns a Boolean value of True or False, depending on whether your application is being tested within REALbasic's IDE or running as a standalone application. By checking the value returned by DebugBuild, you can add code to your applications that executes conditionally based on the current execution environment, as the following shows.

```
If DebugBuild = True Then  //The application is running in the IDE
   ...
End If
```

Another constant you may find useful is RBVersion, which returns a number indicating the major and minor version number of REALbasic. This information comes in handy if you are working with REALbasic functionality tied to a specific version of REALbasic. This might be the case if you previously developed REALbasic programs for a previous release of REALbasic that used features no longer supported by the current version of REALbasic. For example, the following statements can be used to display a warning message if you attempt to run a REALbasic application running REALbasic version 5 or later.

```
If RBVersion > 5 Then
    MsgBox "This application uses features not supported after REALbasic 5."
End If
```

Defining Your Own Constants

Like variables, REALbasic constants have different scopes depending on how and where they are defined. Specifically, a constant defined within application code stored in an application's window has a local scope, whereas a constant stored in windows or classes can have any of the following scopes, depending on how it is defined:

- **Protected**. Accessible only within the window in which it is defined.

- **Private**. Accessible only within the window in which it is defined, but not by any windows subclassed from the window.

- **Public**. Available throughout your application.

■**Note** Classes and subclasses are discussed later in Chapter 8.

In addition, constants defined within a module are global in their scope, allowing them to be accessed throughout an application. More information on modules and classes is available in Chapter 8.

Working with Local Constants

To declare a local constant, you need to use the CONST keyword, which has the following syntax.

```
Const ConstName = Value
```

For example, to define the value of pi as a local constant, you could add the following statement to the code belonging to a window or one of its controls.

```
Const PI = 3.141592
```

The following provides another example of how to use local constants within your applications.

```
Dim intResults As Integer
Const cAppName = "The Happy Holiday Calendar"

intResults = MsgBox("Welcome. Click on OK to Continue", 64, cAppName)
```

■**Note** In the previous example, the name of the constant was preceded with the letter *c* to label it as a constant. This makes the constant stand out better in your code.

Here, a constant named cAppName is defined and assigned a string of text. The constant is then used to display the name of the application in a pop-up dialog box generated by the MsgBox function, as Figure 5-4 shows. Once defined, a constant can be referred to over and over again.

Figure 5-4. *Constants provide a way to define data within your applications that cannot be changed during program execution, as shown on Windows.*

Adding a Constant to a Window

Constants defined within a window can have a public, protected, or private scope. The following procedure outlines the steps involved in adding a constant to a window.

Note The procedure you follow to declare a constant within a module and a class is practically identical to the procedure used to declare one within a window. The only difference is this: with modules, your choices for scope are Global, Public, and Protected, instead of Public, Protected, and Private.

---

1. Open the Code Editor for the appropriate window.

2. Click the Add Constant button or click Project ➤ Add ➤ Constant. The Add Constant declaration field is displayed.

3. Enter a name, data type, and value for the constant.

4. Click one of the three scope buttons located to the right of the Declaration field, as shown in Figure 5-5.

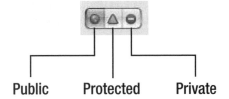

Public   Protected   Private

Figure 5-5. *REALbasic lets you select a scope by clicking the Public, Protected, or Private buttons, as shown on Linux.*

Reserved Keywords

REALbasic reserves a collection of keyword terms that makes up its programming language. You cannot use these keywords when naming variables, arrays, modules, constants, and so on within your applications. Table 5-2 provides a complete listing of REALbasic's reserved keywords.

Table 5-2. *REALbasic Reserved Keywords*

And	Array	As	Boolean	ByRef	ByVal
Call	Case	Catch	Class	Color	Const
DebugPrint	Declare	Dim	Do	Double	Downto
Each	Else	ElseIf	End	Event	Exception
Exit	False	Finally	For	Function	GoTo
Handles	If	Implements	In	Loop	Me
Mod	Module	Namespace	New	Next	Nil
Not	Object	Of	Or	Private	Protected
Public	Raise	ReDim	REM	Return	Select
Self	Shared	Single	Static	Step	String
Sub	Then	To	True	Try	Until
Wend					

Creating a Starter Desktop Calculator

To help further reinforce the information you learned in this chapter, this section shows you how to create a new desktop application called *RBCalculator,* which is a relatively simple implementation of a desktop calculator. The programming logic required to create a full-featured calculator application is too extensive to replicate here. Instead, the programming logic implemented in this application is limited to solving basic addition, subtraction, multi-plication, and division, and equations consisting of two numbers.

As a desktop calculator, all key functionality is provided via PushButton controls and an EditField located on the application window. In addition, the application has a small menu system made up of File and Help menus, as Figure 5-6 shows.

Figure 5-6. *RBCalculator is a basic desktop calculator application, as shown on Macintosh.*

■**Note** As you work your way through the creation of this application, you should be able to follow along and understand the interaction that occurs when the application accesses properties and variables. For pieces of code that have not yet been explained, go ahead and enter them exactly as shown. Once you finish reading Chapter 6, you may want to revisit this example. By that time, you should be ready to take another look at how this application works.

Designing the User Interface

Users interact with the RBCalculator application through PushButton controls placed on the main application window. Calculations and their results are displayed in an EditField control placed at the top of the window. In addition, a small menu system is available that enables the user to close the application or display additional information about it.

To begin the development of this application, open a new project in REALbasic, add the controls listed in Table 5-3, and then modify the window and control properties as shown.

Table 5-3. *Window and Property Modifications for the RBCalculator Application*

Object	Property	Value
Window1	Name	MainWindow
	Title	RBCalculator
EditField1	Name	OutputField
	ReadOnly	Enabled
	Alignment	Right
	Bold	Enabled

Next, add 19 button controls to the window, as shown in Table 5-4, and modify the Name property for each control.

Table 5-4. *Property Modifications RBCalculator PushButton Controls*

Object	Property	Value
PushButton1	Name	Button1
	Caption	1
PushButton2	Name	Button2
	Caption	2
PushButton3	Name	Button3
	Caption	3
PushButton4	Name	Button4
	Caption	4
PushButton5	Name	Button5
	Caption	5
PushButton6	Name	Button6
	Caption	6
PushButton7	Name	Button7
	Caption	7
PushButton8	Name	Button8
	Caption	8
PushButton9	Name	Button9
	Caption	9
PushButton10	Name	Button0
	Caption	0
PushButton11	Name	DecimalButton
	Caption	.
PushButton12	Name	NegativeButton
	Caption	-
PushButton13	Name	PlusButton
	Caption	+
PushButton14	Name	MinusButton
	Caption	-
PushButton15	Name	MulitiplicationButton
	Caption	*

Object	Property	Value
PushButton16	Name	DivisionButton
	Caption	/
PushButton17	Name	EqualsButton
	Caption	=
PushButton18	Name	OffButton
	Caption	Off
PushButton19	Name	ClearButton
	Caption	Clear

The next step in creating the RBCalculator application is to design its menu system. Double-click the menu bar item located on the Projects screen to open the MenuBar Editor. Delete the Edit menu. Then, modify the menu system for Menubar1 by adding a Help menu, and then add an About menu item beneath it. Assign &Help and &About as the value of the Text properties for each respective control.

At this point, the user interface for the RBCalculator application is finished. Now, you are ready to begin writing the code statements required to make the application work.

Supplying Application Code

Let's start adding the code statements associated with the Help menu's About menu item. To do so, open the application's window in the REALbasic Code Editor and switch over to code view. Click the Add Menu Event Handler button located on the Window Editor toolbar. A menu handler entry is added to the left-hand browser area in the Code Editor. Select the entry for the HelpAbout menu item from the drop-down list for the MenuItem Name field and enter the following program statement.

```
MsgBox("RBCalculator - Written By Jerry Ford - 2006")
```

This statement uses the MsgBox function to display information about the application's author in a preformatted pop-up dialog window. Now that the application's menu system is ready to go, it's time to provide the code associated with each of the application's PushButton controls.

For starters, add the following code statement to the method belonging to each of the PushButton controls that represents a numeric calculator button, as well as to the button representing a toggle value (for example, the PushButtons labeled 0–9 and -).

```
OutputField.Text = OutputField.Text + Me.Caption
```

This statement, when executed, adds the number of the appropriate PushButton control to the EditField control. For example, if the user clicks the PushButton control representing the number 5, this statement takes the value of that PushButton control's Caption (for example 5), which it gets from Me.Caption, and appends it to whatever text is currently displayed in the EditField control.

Next, add the following statements to the method belonging to the DecimalButton control.

```
Dim intResult As Integer

If intResult = Instr(OutputField.Text, ".") Then

  OutputField.Text = OutputField.Text + Me.Caption

End If
```

The first statement defines a local variable named intResult. The If…Then block that follows uses the Instr function to determine whether a decimal has already been entered before appending a decimal character to whatever text is stored in the EditField control. In other words, because a number can only have a maximum of 1 decimal, the If…Then statement prevents the user from accidentally entering a second decimal when keying in a number.

Likewise, add the following code to the PushButton controls representing plus, minus, multiplication, and division buttons.

```
OutputField.Text = OutputField.Text + " " + Me.Caption + " "
PlusButton.Enabled = False
MinusButton.Enabled = False
DivisionButton.Enabled = False
MultiplicationButton.Enabled = False
```

The first statement adds a plus (+) character to the string displayed in the EditField control. Note, this statement also adds a blank space before and after the plus character. The next four statements disabled the buttons representing the plus, minus, division, and multiplication buttons. Remember, the RBCalculator only supports one calculation at a time, which is enforced by disabling these buttons as soon as the user clicks one of them. These buttons are reenabled later when the user clicks the Clear button to allow a new equation to be entered. Another limitation of the RBCalculator is that is only lets you work with one decimal number as a time.

Next, add the following code statements to the PushButton control representing the equals button.

```
Dim dblResult  As Double

If InStr(OutputField.Text, "+") > 0 Then
  dblResult = Val(OutputField.Text.Left(Instr(OutputField.Text, _
    " + "))) + Val(OutputField.Text.Mid(Instr(OutputField.Text, _
    "+") + 2))
End If
```

```
If InStr(OutputField.Text, " - ") > 0 Then
  dblResult = Val(OutputField.Text.Left(Instr(OutputField.Text, _
    " - "))) - Val(OutputField.Text.Mid(Instr(OutputField.Text, _
    " - ") + 2))
End If

If InStr(OutputField.Text, " * ") > 0 Then
  dblResult = Val(OutputField.Text.Left(Instr(OutputField.Text, _
    " * "))) * Val(OutputField.Text.Mid(Instr(OutputField.Text, _
    " * ") + 2))
End If

If InStr(OutputField.Text, " / ") > 0 Then
  dblResult  = Val(OutputField.Text.Left(Instr(OutputField.Text, _
    " / "))) / Val(OutputField.Text.Mid(Instr(OutputField.Text, _
    " / ") + 2))
End If

OutputField.Text = Str(dblResult)

Button1.Enabled = False
Button2.Enabled = False
Button3.Enabled = False
Button4.Enabled = False
Button5.Enabled = False
Button6.Enabled = False
Button7.Enabled = False
Button8.Enabled = False
Button9.Enabled = False
Button0.Enabled = False
DecimalButton.Enabled = False
NegativeButton.Enabled = False
```

The first statement declares a variable named intResult with a data type of Double to ensure the calculator can handle nearly any number the user might enter. The next four sets of statements are If…Then blocks, each of which is designed to handle a particular operation.

The first If…Then block is set up to look for the presence of a + character in the equation entered by the user. If present, then the following statement is executed.

```
dblResult  = Val(OutputField.Text.Left(Instr(OutputField.Text, " + "))) +
  Val(OutputField.Text.Mid(Instr(OutputField.Text, "+") + 2))
```

This statement uses a series of REALbasic functions to process the equation the user enters. Here is a step-by-step breakdown of what happens when this statement executes.

1. The Instr function is used to locate the position of the + character in the equation.

2. This information is then fed to the Left function, which uses it to extract all the characters from the beginning of the text string to the + character.

3. The Val function is used to convert the remaining value to a number.

4. The Instr function is again used to locate the position of the + character in the equation.

5. The Mid function is then used to extract the remainder of the text in the EditField, starting two character positions to the right of the + character.

6. The Val function is then used to convert the remaining value to a number.

7. Finally, the numeric value extracted from step 3 is added to the numeric value extracted in step 6 and assigned to the intResult variable.

■**Note**   Refer to REALbasic's online reference (Help ➤ Language Reference) for detailed explanations of the syntax for various REALbasic functions.

The remaining If...Then blocks are designed to perform a similar set of steps for the subtraction, multiplication, and division operations. The first statement following the last If...Then block converts the value of intResult to a String and displays the results in the EditField control (named OutputField). The remaining statements disable all the PushButton controls on the application, except for the PushButtons representing the Equals, Off, and Clear operations.

Now, add the following statement to the PushButton control representing the Off button.

```
Quit
```

As you can see, this statement simply terminates the application when this PushButton control is clicked. Finally, add the following statements to the PushButton control representing the Clear button.

```
OutputField.Text = ""

PlusButton.Enabled = True
MinusButton.Enabled = True
DivisionButton.Enabled = True
MultiplicationButton.Enabled = True
```

```
Button1.Enabled = True
Button2.Enabled = True
Button3.Enabled = True
Button4.Enabled = True
Button5.Enabled = True
Button6.Enabled = True
Button7.Enabled = True
Button8.Enabled = True
Button9.Enabled = True
Button0.Enabled = True
DecimalButton.Enabled = True
NegativeButton.Enabled = True
```

These statements reenable the application's PushButton controls to let the user enter a new equation.

Testing RBCalculator

If you have not done so yet, go ahead and save your application, and then compile it and see how it operates. Double-check your typing if any errors are flagged. Once everything is working properly, compile a standalone copy of your application, pass it on to your friends, and ask them to test it as well.

Summary

In this chapter, you learned the fundamentals of storing and retrieving data in REALbasic applications. This included learning how to work with variables, arrays, dictionaries, and constants. You were introduced to the concept of variable scope. You learned how to document your applications by adding comments and notes. On top of all this, you learned about different data types and how to convert data from one data type to another.

CHAPTER 6

■ ■ ■

Making Decisions with Conditional Logic

To create truly useful applications, you need to provide your programs with the capability to analyze data, and then make logical decisions based on the results of that analysis. This is achieved through the execution of conditional statements that work with mathematical, comparison and logical operators to define conditional tests and the courses of action to take, based on the results of the test. By applying conditional programming techniques demonstrated in this chapter, you can develop REALbasic applications that react dynamically to different data and provide users with an interactive experience.

Specifically, you learn how to

- Test between two or more conditions

- Alter the logical flow of your program code

- Generate random numbers

- Apply operating system-specific conditional logic

Implementing Conditional Logic

By default, REALbasic executes code statements in a sequential order. For example, if you specified a set of ten code statements to be executed when the user clicks a PushButton control, REALbasic executes each statement, one at a time, in the order the statements were written. This type of execution works just fine much of the time.

In some situations, though, you might want to conditionally execute a block of statements. For example, suppose you wrote an application that continually writes text to a log file. Before writing to the log file, you would want to add logic to your program to make sure the log file exists. If the log file does not exist, then you would want to tell REALbasic to create the file first. In this scenario, the code statement that checks for and creates a new log file only runs when the application determines that a log file does not already exist. Otherwise, these statements are skipped. Adding this type of conditional check to your application can help prevent errors by ensuring the application always has a log file to write to.

Conditional logic within a computer program is only a matter of determining whether a condition evaluates to either True or False and specifying what actions to take based on the results of the test. REALbasic provides you with three sets of programming statements that you can use to implement conditional logic, each of which is designed to handle different situations. These statements include the following:

- **If...Then**. Tests a specific condition and conditionally executions code statements based on the results of the test.

- **Select...Case**. Tests different conditions against a specific value, and then executes code statements for the first matching condition.

- **#If...#EndIf**. Conditionally executes code statements based on the operating system (OS) on which the application is executing.

Working with the If...Then Statement

The If...Then statement provides you with the capability to test a single condition, and then evaluate the results to conditionally execute code statements based on the results of the test. The If...Then statement is so important, it is almost impossible to develop an application of any complexity without it.

The following outlines the syntax of the If...Then statement.

```
If Condition Then
    statements
ElseIf condition Then
    statements
Else
    statements
End If
```

Condition is a placeholder that represents a condition that evaluates to either True of False. *Statements* are placeholders representing executed code statements based on the results of the tests. The If...Then statement is extremely flexible and supports numerous variations, including the following:

- Single line If...Then statements

- Multiple line If...Then blocks

- The If...Then...Else Blocks

- The If...Then...ElseIf blocks

■**Note** If...Then, Select...Case, and #If...#EndIf statements, and any programming statement you embed within them, are sometimes referred to as *code blocks.*

Single Line If...Then Statements

In many cases, all you need to set up a conditional test is a single line If...Then statement. For example, each of the following statements is a single line If...Then statement.

```
If strUserName = "Molly" Then MsgBox("Hello Molly")
If strUserName = "Molly" MsgBox("Hello Molly")
If strUserName = "Molly" Then MsgBox("Hello Molly") Else MsgBox("Hello")
```

In the first example, the value of strUserName is tested to see if it is equal to "Molly" and if it is (for example, if the test result evaluates to True), the MsgBox function that follows the Then keyword is executed. However, if the result of the text is False, the MsgBox function is not processed. The second statement shown in the previous code is almost identical to the first statement, except the Then keyword is omitted. The Then keyword is optional on single line If...Then statements.

The third example shown in the previous code demonstrates how to provide an alternate course of action in case the test result is False. In this example, if strUserName equals "Molly", then MsgBox("Hello Molly") is executed and the rest of the statement is skipped. However, if strUserName does not equal "Molly", then the first instance of the MsgBox function is skipped and the second instance is executed (for example, MsgBox("Hello")).

Note When using the single line form of the If...Then statement, the closing End If statement, which normally follows an If...Then statement, is omitted.

Multiple Line If...Then Blocks

In most cases, you won't be able to fit everything on one line that you want to achieve with an If...Then statement. In these cases, you can set up an If...Then code block, as the following shows.

```
If blnExitApp = True Then
  MsgBox("You have elected to close the application.")
  Quit
End If
```

As this example shows, you can embed more than one statement inside an If...Then block. In this example, if the value assigned to the blnExitApp variables is equal to True, then all of the statements in between the opening If...Then statement and the closing End If statement are executed. However, if the value assigned to blnExitApp is equal to False, then the code statements inside the If...Then block are skipped and program execution continues with the next programming statement following the If...Then block.

Tip Good programming practice is to use code blocks in place of single line If...Then statements. This way, if you have to come back later and insert additional code statements, the necessary structure will already be in place.

The If...Then...Else Block

You can expand the If...Then block to include an optional Else statement. When you do so, you provide an alternative course of action that should be taken if the tested condition turns out to be False instead of True. For example, suppose you create the application you see in Figure 6-1.

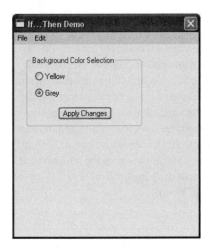

Figure 6-1. *Using conditional logic to modify a window's background color*

In this example, a GroupBox control has been added to the application's window and populated with two RadioButton controls, each of which is associated with a different color. A PushButton has also been added to the GroupBox control. By adding the following code statements to the PushButton control, you provide the user with the capability to change the window's background color.

```
If rbnYellow.Value = True Then
  Window1.HasbackColor = True
  Window1.BackColor = &cFFFF80
End If

If rbnGrey.Value = True Then
  Window1.HasbackColor = True
  Window1.BackColor = &cC0C0C0
End If
```

■Note A RadioButton control is used to present users with a choice between two options. By default, all RadioButton controls on a window function as a group, meaning only one RadioButton can be selected at a time. By grouping RadioButton controls together, using the GroupBox control as an example, you can create separate groupings of RadioButton controls, each of which is independent of other groups.

You can use the Properties window to specify a default RadioButton selection by enabling the Value property for one of the RadioButton controls in a grouping. Programmatically, you can change the currently selected RadioButton by setting its Value property to True. Similarly, you can check to see if a RadioButton control's Value property has been set, as the previous example shows.

As you can see, two If…Then blocks are set up. The first If…Then block checks to see if the Value property belonging to the first RadioButton control is set to True (for example, that it has been selected). If it was selected, then the next statement executes and sets the BackColor property of the window to Yellow.

The second If…Then block performs a second test, this time looking to see if the value of the second RadioButton control was selected. Figure 6-2 demonstrates how the selection of the RadioButton labeled Yellow changes the window's background color.

Figure 6-2. *Using If…Then blocks to process the value of RadioButton controls*

The problem with the previous example is this: if the user selected the first RadioButton control, REALbasic is still required to process the second If...Then block, even though it is not selected. Rather than creating multiple If...Then blocks, as was done in the previous example, you can set things up to be more efficient using the Else statement to set up an If...Then...Else block as the following shows.

```
If rbnYellow.Value = True Then
    Window1.BackColor = &cFFFF80
  Else
    Window1.BackColor = &cC0C0C0
End If
```

As you can see, this example is one line shorter than the previous example, yet it performs exactly the same thing, while simplifying the code so REALbasic only has to perform one conditional test.

The If...Then...ElseIf Blocks

REALbasic also provides you with the capability to set up If...Then...ElseIf blocks, which test for any number of possible conditions and execute the code statements associated with the first matching condition. For example, you could add an additional RadioButton control to the previous example, and then modify the code statements assigned to the PushButton control, as the following shows.

```
If rbnYellow.Value = True Then
    Window1.BackColor = &cFFFF80
  ElseIf rbnGrey.Value = True Then
    Window1.BackColor = &cC0C0C0
  ElseIf  rbnWhite.Value = True Then
    Window1.BackColor = &cFFFFFF
End If
```

In this example, three separate conditions are tested and, whichever one proves True, is executed, while the others are skipped.

Nesting If...Then Blocks

REALbasic also enables you to embed, or nest, If...Then blocks within one another. In doing so, you can create complex conditional tests that begin by testing for one condition, and then perform further testing when required, as the following example shows.

```
If blnGameOver = True Then

  If intNoOfPoints <= 1000 Then
    MsgBox("Continue your training my young padewan learner.")
  End If
```

```
If intNoOfPoints >= 1001 Then
  If intNoOfPoints <= 10000 Then
    MsgBox("Your Jedi skills are indeed most impressive!")
  End If
End If

If intNoOfPoints >= 10001 Then
  MsgBox("Congratulations Master Jedi, you are truly strong with the force.")
End If

End If
```

In this example, the value of blnGameOver is tested to see if it is equal to True (for example, if it is time to end the game). If it is time, a number of nested If…Then blocks are executed to determine the player's score.

■**Tip** You can create extremely complex testing logic by embedding If…Then statements and blocks. However, remember, nesting too deeply can make your program code difficult to maintain and understand. As an alternative to embedding If…Then statements, you can use logical operators to combine comparison operations. Logical operators are covered in the section "Logical Operators."

The Select…Case Block

At times, you might want to test a single condition against a number of possible values. While you can certainly perform this type of test using an If…Then…ElseIf block, REALbasic also provides you with the Select Case block, which is better suited to performing this type of test. While an *If…Then…ElseIf* block evaluates each ElseIf statement, a Select Case block stops executing once a matching Case statement is found, making it more efficient. The following outlines the syntax for the Select Case block.

```
Select Case expression
  Case value
    statements
  Case value
    statements
  Case Else
    statements
End Select
```

The Select…Case block begins with the Select Case statement and ends with the End Select statement. Individual Case statements are defined inside the Select Case block that identifies possible matching values. When a match occurs, the code statements in between the matching Case statement and the next Case statement are executed.

Note Select...Case statements can include an optional Case Else statement that executes only when none of the defined Case statements match up against the tested value. Note, the Select Case block accepts either Case Else or Else as the format of the optional Else clause.

As you can see, a Select Case block is easier to read when compared to nested If...Then blocks. In addition, Select Case blocks typically require less code statements to set up. The following example demonstrates how to set up a typical Select Case block.

```
Select Case strCustomerName
  Case "Walmart"
    MsgBox("Customer account number is 6765765765765.")
    Return
  Case "Target"
    MsgBox("Customer account number is 6769382576767.")
    Return
  Case "Roses"
    MsgBox("Customer account number is 1231435 456755.")
    Return
  Case "Sears"
    MsgBox("Customer account number is 98978562546573.")
    Return
  Case Else
    MsgBox("An account must be set up for this new customer.")
End Select
```

In this example, a message is displayed depending on whether the value assigned to the strCustomerName variables match any of the values specified in the Case statements. However, if no match is found, the Case Else statement executes.

Case statements are flexible. For example, you can set them up to check for a range of values using the To keyword, as the following shows.

```
Select Case intNoOfPoints
  Case 1 To 1000
    MsgBox("Continue your training my young padewan learner.")
    Return
  Case 1001 To 10000
    MsgBox("Your Jedi skills are indeed most impressive!")
    Return
  Case 10001 To 1000000
    MsgBox("Congratulations Master Jedi, you are truly strong with the force.")
    Return
End Select
```

You can also set up Case statements using different ranges or types of values, as the following shows.

```
Select Case intMonthOfBirth
Case 1, 4, 7, 10
  MsgBox("Department birthday celebrations occur on the 15th of the month.")
  Return
Case 2, 5, 8, 11
  MsgBox("Department birthday celebrations occur on the 21st of the month.")
  Return
Case 3, 6, 9, 12
  MsgBox("Department birthday celebrations occur on the 1st of the month.")
  Return
End Select
```

#If...#EndIf

One of REALbasic's primary selling features is its capability to compile applications that can run on different OS platforms. Each OS platform has certain, completely unique features. For example, only Windows OSs support the registry.

To develop applications that can execute on certain OSs, at times, you need to customize portions of your application to leverage OS-specific features. To provide you with a mechanism for handling these situations, REALbasic provides the #If...#EndIf block.

The #If...#EndIf block can be used to handle other situations, too, such as supporting the creation of applications that require features found in certain versions of REALbasic or that run differently in debug mode versus as a standalone application. REALbasic limits the #If...#EndIf block's functionality by only allowing it to work with a specific set of Boolean constants, which Table 6-1 shows.

Table 6-1. *REALbasic Boolean Constants*

Constant	Classification	Description
DebugBuild	Debug vs. Standalone	Evaluates to True when the application is run within the REALbasic IDE.
RBVersion	REALbasic Version	Returns a True or False value, indicating the version level being used to run a REALbasic application.
TargetHasGUI	Application Type	Returns a value of True if the application being run is a Desktop application (as opposed to a Console, Service, or Event Driven Console application).
TargetBigEndian	OS	Returns a value of True if the application being run uses the Big Endian byte order (e.g., Macintosh systems).

Continued

Table 6-1. *Continued*

Constant	Classification	Description
TargetLittleEndian	OS	Returns a value of True if the application being run uses the Little Endian byte order (e.g., PCs).
TargetCarbon	OS	Returns a value of True if the application being run executes Carbon/Mac OS X code (e.g., Mac Classic and Mac OS X).
TargetMachO	OS	Returns a value of True if the application is being run on a Macintosh computer running Mac OS X.
TargetMacOS	OS	Returns a value of True if the application is being run on a Macintosh computer running either Mac Classic or Mac OS X.
TargetMacOSClassic	OS	Returns a value of True if the application is being run on a Macintosh computer running Mac Classic.
TargetLinux	OS	Returns a value of True if the application is being run on a Linux computer.
TargetWin32	OS	Returns a value of True if the application is being run on a Windows computer.

To understand the #If...#EndIf statement, seeing it in action can help. The following statements demonstrate how to test for the OS being used to run the application.

```
#If TargetMachO
  MsgBox("This application is running on a computer running on Mac OS X.")
#ElseIf TargetWin32
  MsgBox("This application is running on a computer running on Windows.")
#ElseIf TargetLinux
  MsgBox("This application is running on a computer running on Linux.")
#EndIf
```

■**Note** As the previous example demonstrates, the Then keyword is optional when working with the #If...#EndIf statement.

For another example of how to use the #If...#EndIf code block, check out the RB Word Processor application in Chapter 9.

REALbasic Operators

As you have already seen in this book, REALbasic uses comparison operators in the formulation of program statements that involve conditional logic. REALbasic also uses mathematical operators when working with numbers. In addition to comparison and mathematical operators, REALbasic also supports the use of logical operators that facilitate the testing of more than one condition at a time.

Comparison Operators

For REALbasic to make any type of comparison, it must be told what type of comparison to make. In most of the examples you have seen up to this point, comparisons were made based on equality. In other words, the equals (=) operator was used to ask REALbasic to determine if two values were equal.

In addition to checking for equality, REALbasic provides you with a collection of other comparison operators that give you with the capability to check for a range of values. Table 6-2 provides a complete list of REALbasic's comparison operators.

Table 6-2. *REALbasic Comparison Operators*

Operator	Type	Example
=	Equals	If $X = 18$ Then
<>	Not Equals	If $X <> 18$
>	Greater Than	If $X > 18$
<	Less Than	If $X < 18$
>=	Greater Than or Equal To	If $X >= 21$
<=	Less Than or Equal To	If $X <= 21$

You have the chance to work with a number of these operators when you create the RB Number Guess game in the section "Creating a Computer Game."

■**Note** In addition to using REALbasic's comparison operators for the obvious task of comparing numeric data, you can also use them when you work with string values. String comparisons are case-insensitive, meaning "Bob" and "bob" are equal to one another. However, "Ann" is considered less than "Bob" because, alphabetically, "Ann" comes before "Bob."

Mathematical Operators

REALbasic's mathematical operators are based on the same set of operators we all use for common everyday math. Anyone familiar with a modern calculator should have no trouble recognizing each of the mathematical operators listed in Table 6-4 or understanding their function.

OPERATOR PREDEDENCE

One important concept you need to be aware of when working with mathematical operators is the order of precedence in which REALbasic performs mathematic operations. Table 6-3 lists the order in which REALbasic mathematic operator precedence occurs. Note, operators listed at the top of Table 6-3 are processed before those listed later in the table.

Table 6-3. *Order of Precedence for REALbasic Mathematic Operators*

Operator	Description
*, /, \	Multiplication and division occur first and are processed from left to right
Mod	Modulo is processed after all multiplication and division
+, -	Addition and subtraction are processed last, starting from left to right

To help better understand the order in which REALbasic processes mathematical operators, consider the following statement.

```
intTestValue = 10 /2 + 3 - 1 * 3
```

REALbasic solves this equation, as the following outlines.

1. Divide 10 by 2 to get 5.

2. Multiply 1 * 3 to get 3.

3. Add 5 + 3 - 3 to get 5.

If you want, you can use parentheses to control the order in which REALbasic solves an equation. For example, if the equation were rewritten as you see in the following:

```
intTestValue = 10 /2 + (3 - 1) * 3
```

REALbasic would solve it as shown here.

1. Subtract 1 from 3 to get 2.

2. Divide 10 by 2 to get 5.

3. Multiply 2 * 3 to get 6.

4. Add 5 + 6 to get 11.

Table 6-4. *REALbasic Mathematical Operators*

Operator	Type	Example
+	Add	$5 + 5 = 10$
-	Subtract	$10 - 5 = 5$
*	Multiply	$5 * 5 = 25$
\	Division (Integer)	$15 \setminus 2 = 7$
/	Division (Floating Point)	$15 / 2 = 7.5$
Mod	Modulo	$15 \, Mod \, 2 = 1$

An example of how to work with most of these mathematical operators was provided in RB Calculator application presented in Chapter 5.

Logical Operators

At times, you may want to combine comparison operations together to make a decision. For example, you might want to execute a given set of code statements only when both the values of X and Y are greater than to zero. You could set up this test as the following shows.

```
If X > 0 Then
  If Y > 0 Then
    MsgBox("Both X and Y are greater than zero.")
  End If
End If
```

Using the REALbasic And logical operator, however, you could rewrite these statements as in the following.

```
If X > 0 And Y > 0 Then
  MsgBox("Both X and Y are greater than zero.")
End If
```

As you can see, using the And operator saves you two lines of code and makes things easier to read and understand. Table 6-5 lists the logical operators supported by REALbasic and describes their function.

Table 6-5. *REALbasic Logical Operators*

Operator	Type	Example
And	Both comparisons are True	$X >= 0$ And $Y >= 5$
Or	Either comparison is True	$X = 0$ Or $Y = 0$
Not	Reverses the value of a Boolean value	Not $(X > Y)$

Creating a Computer Game

To finish this chapter, you learn how to create a REALbasic computer game called RB Number Guess. This game gives you the chance to apply the material you've just read and to reinforce your understanding of conditional logic even further.

Through the development of the RB Number Guess, you learn how to work with the Slider control, which the player uses on each turn to specify a new guess. This application also introduces you to the Random Class and shows you how to use it to generate a random number needed for game play. In addition, you get to work with various mathematical operators and define window properties.

While this chapter demonstrates how to create the RB Number Guess using the Windows version of REALbasic, you can easily adapt the game to work on Macintosh or Linux with only a few minor adjustments to the size and shape of the controls that make up the game's graphical user interface (GUI). Compiled examples of the application are available on the book's companion CD-ROM for Mac OS X, Windows, and Linux.

The objective of the game is for the user to guess a randomly generated number in as few guesses as possible. Rather than require the player to key in each guess, this game uses the REALbasic Slider control to collect user input, as Figure 6-3 shows.

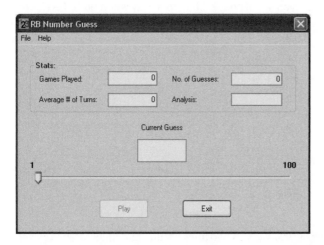

Figure 6-3. *The RB Number Guess game challenges the user to guess a number between 1 and 100, using the fewest possible number of guesses.*

The rest of the game's GUI is made up of the StaticText, EditField, and GroupBox controls you have already worked with in previous chapters. In addition, the game also has a small menu system, with menu items for terminating game play and displaying information about the game.

■**Note** When executed on Windows, the RB Number Guess game displays a number representing the current location of the Handle on the Slider control. This number dynamically changes as you move the Handle, allowing the player to specify, with precision, their next guess. This behavior is not replicated on Macintosh and Linux, though. Instead, players do not see this value until they have completed their turn and released the Handle. This application highlights an example of the many differences in how things work on Macintosh, Windows, and Linux. You may want to modify the game, so the Slider control is replaced with a EditField and PushButton control, allowing players to key in their guesses instead, when run on Macintosh or Linux. Making this modification gives you the opportunity to work with the #If...#EndIf statement and can help further enhance your appreciation of the types of obstacles that must be overcome when developing cross-platform applications.

Putting Together the Game's User Interface

The RB Number Guess game is primarily controlled through a Slider control and two PushButton controls. StaticText and EditField controls are used to display output. In addition, a GroupBox control is used to help organize the display of game statistics that are collected and displayed during and after game play.

The first step involved in creating the RB Number Guess game is to create a new REALbasic desktop application. Next, let's give the application its own icon by opening the Project Editor and setting the Icon property for App to 123.bmp. You can find a copy of this bitmap file along with the source code for this project on the book's companion CD.

■**Note** By setting the App item's Icon property, you change the icon associated with the application, giving it a more professional look. To do so, click the App item's Icon property. REALbasic responds by displaying the Edit Icon window. Right-click the Image area and select the Add menu item from the context menu that appears. REALbasic then displays an Open dialog, letting you specify the name and location of the desired graphic image. Once selected, click OK to close the Open dialog. The selected graphic now appears in the Edit Icon window. Click OK to close this window and return to the Project Editor.

Next, resize Window1, as specified in Table 6-6. Add a GroupBox control and populate it with four StaticText and four EditField controls. Then, add a Slider control and resize it, so it takes up most of the width of the window. Place two PushButton controls just beneath it and add two StaticText controls, one over each end of the Slider control. Finally, add a EditField Control and a StaticText control just over the top center location of the Slider control. When done, your new application's interface should look just like the example shown in Figure 6-3.

Once you add all the required controls, modify the property values for the window and its controls, as Table 6-6 specifies.

Table 6-6. *Property Modifications for the RB Number Guess Application*

Object	Property	Value
Window1	Title	RB Number Guess
	Width	471
	Height	292
EditField1	Name	edfGamesPlayed
	ReadOnly	True
	Text	0
EditField2	Name	edfAvgNoOfTurns
	ReadOnly	True
	Text	0
EditField3	Name	edfNoOfGuesses
	ReadOnly	True
	Text	0
EditField4	Name	edfAnalysis
	ReadOnly	True
EditField5	Name	edfDisplay
	TextFont	System
	Font.Size	24
	Font.Bold	True
	ReadOnly	True
StaticText1	Name	lblGamesPlayed
	Text	Games Played:
StaticText2	Name	lblAvgNoOfTurns
	Text	Average # of Turns:
StaticText3	Name	lblNumberOfGuesses
	Text	No. of Guesses
StaticText4	Name	lblAnalysis
	Text	Analysis:

Object	Property	Value
StaticText5	Name	lblCurrentGuess
	Text	Current Guess
StaticText6	Name	lblLowRange
	Bold	Checked
	Text	1
StaticText7	Name	lblHighRange
	Bold	Checked
	Text	100
GroupBox1	Name	grbStats
	Caption	Stats:
PushButton1	Name	btnPlay
	Caption	Play
	Enabled	False
PushButton2	Name	btnExit
	Caption	Exit
Slider1	Name	sdrControl
	Minimum	0
	Value	0
	Maximum	100

The next step in setting up the GUI for the RB Number Guess game is to create its menu system. To do so, double-click the MenuBar1 item found on the Project screen. This displays the menu in REALbasic's MenuBar Editor. By default, REALbasic automatically adds a File and Edit menu for your application. However, because the RB Number Guess game does not have a Edit menu, you should delete the View menu by selecting it and clicking Delete. Next, modify the menu system for MenuBar1, as Table 6-7 outlines.

Table 6-7. *Menus and Menu Items for the RB Number Guess Game*

Menu	Menu Item	Text Property
File	FileQuit	E&xit
Help	HelpAbout	&About

Because REALbasic automatically takes care of it for you, you needn't add the FileQuit menu item on the File menu. The user interface for the RB Number Guess game is now complete, as Figure 6-4 shows.

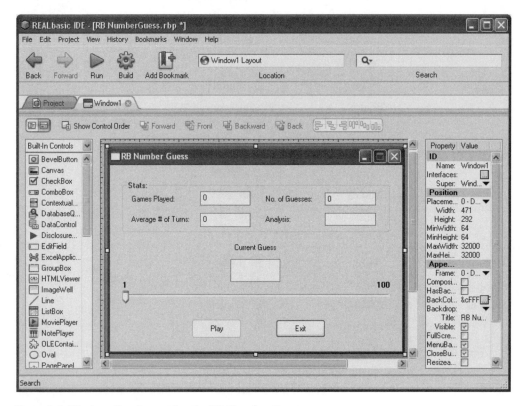

Figure 6-4. *The interface layout for the RB Number Guess game*

Defining Properties

The RB Number Guess game uses several variables to store and track information needed by the game. These variables are accessed by different parts of the application, so rather than declaring them as local variables, you must set them with a higher-level scope. To accomplish this, set up each of these variables as window properties with a public-level scope. Table 6-8 outlines these properties and their data type.

Table 6-8. *Custom Properties Added to the RB Number Guess Game*

Property	Data Type	Description
intNoGuessed	Integer	Keeps track of the number of guesses made
intSecretNumber	Integer	Stores the game's randomly generated secret number
intTotalNoOfTurns	Integer	Keeps track of the total number of turns taken

The following procedure outlines the steps involved in declaring each of these properties.

1. Double-click the application's window to switch over to the Code Editor.

2. Click the Add property button located on the Code Editor toolbar or click Project ➤ Add ➤ Property.

3. REALbasic responds by displaying a property declaration field at the top of the code pane. Enter intNoGuessed as Integer in the declaration field, as Figure 6-5 shows.

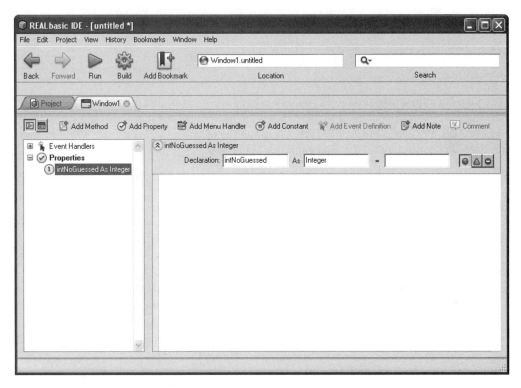

Figure 6-5. *Adding a new property to a window*

4. Repeat steps 2 through 4 to define the intSecretNumber and intTotalNoOfTurns properties.

Adding a Little Program Code

Once you finish adding the three properties, you are ready to begin writing the code statements needed to make the game work. Begin by switching back to the Window Layout view of the Windows Editor, and then double-click the window. REALbasic responds by opening the Code Editor and displaying the Open event belonging to the window. Enter the following code statements.

```
Dim r as New Random      'Instantiate a Random Object

intSecretNumber = r.InRange(1,100)      'Generate a random number
```

The first statement uses the New keyword to instantiate a Random object. The second statement uses the Random class's InRange method to randomly generate a number from 1 and 100, and to store it in the intSecretNumber property.

■**Note** The Random class is a built-in REALbasic class from which you can instantiate a new object based on that class. Classes and objects have not been covered yet, so for now, just enter these code statements as shown. You learn about classes and objects in Chapter 8.

Together, these two statements generate an initial secret number the player must guess to win the game. Next, switch back to the Window Layout view of the Windows Editor, and then double-click the Slider control. REALbasic responds by opening the ValueChanged Subroutine for the Slider control. Enter the following code statements.

```
intNoGuessed = intNoGuessed + 1      'Increment variable value by 1

edfNoOfGuesses.Text = CStr(intNoGuessed) 'Display the number of guesses

If sdrControl.Value = intSecretNumber Then  'Check to see if the player won

    edfAnalysis.Text = "You Win!"      'Update game status
    sdrControl.Enabled = False      'Disable access to the Slider control
    btnPlay.Enabled = True      'Enable access to the Play button

    'Display the total number of games played
    edfGamesPlayed.Text = CStr(Val(edfGamesPlayed.Text) + 1)

    'Calculate the total number of turns taken since the game was started
    intTotalNoOfTurns = intTotalNoOfTurns + intNoGuessed

    'Calculate the average number of turns per game (as an Integer value)
    edfAvgNoOfTurns.Text = CStr(intTotalNoOfTurns \ Val(edfGamesPlayed.Text))

End If
```

```
If sdrControl.Value < intSecretNumber Then   'See if the player's guess was low

    edfAnalysis.Text = "Too Low!"       'Update game status

End If

If sdrControl.Value > intSecretNumber Then 'See if the player's guess was high

    edfAnalysis.Text = "Too High!"      'Update game status

End If
'Do not update the display of the Slider control's value when it is zero
If sdrControl.Value <> 0 Then

    'Display the Slider control's value as the player moves the its handle
    edfDisplay.Text = Cstr(sdrControl.Value)

End If
```

■**Note** A *subroutine* is a collection of programming statements that can be called and executed as a unit. Subroutines are sometimes referred to as procedures.

This subroutine is called whenever the player moves and releases the Slider control's handle. It begins by incrementing the value of intNoGuessed by 1, and then displays its value in the appropriate EditField, after converting its value to a string data type. Three If...Then blocks are then set up, each of which tests for a different condition.

The first If...Then block executes when the player correctly guesses the game's secret number (for example, when sdrControl.Value is equal to intSecretNumber). When this occurs, a series of code statements are executed that update the information displayed in the GroupBox control. In addition, the Slider control is disabled to stop game play and the PushButton labeled Play is enabled, allowing the player to start a new game.

The second If...Then block executes when the value specified by the player is less than the game's secret number. Similarly, the third If...Then block executes when the value specified by the player is higher than the secret number. In both of these cases, a text string is displayed in the EditField control labeled Analysis to provide the player with a clue that guides her next guess.

■**Tip** Take note of the comments embedded throughout this subroutine. By embedding comments into your program code, you help to document it and make it easier to understand.

The way this game is played, the player is permitted to select a number between 1 and 100. However, the Slider control has been set up to allow input between 0 and 100. The reason is to provide the Slider control's handle a place to rest at the beginning of the game that does not represent a initial value (for example, to enable the user to start playing without have his first move preselected). Because of this set up, it is necessary to prevent the value of 0 from being displayed when the player moves the Slider control's handle all the way to the left. This is accomplished by adding a If…Then block to the Slider control's Mouse Move drag event, as the following shows.

```
'Do not update the display of the Slider control's value when it is zero
 If sdrControl.Value <> 0 Then

     'Display the Slider control's value as the player moves its handle
     edfDisplay.Text = Cstr(sdrControl.Value)

End If
```

As you can see, as long as the slider control's value is not equal to zero, it is displayed. The next set of code statements you need to add to the RB Number Guess games is associated with the PushButton control labeled Play (that is, btnPlay). This code, which the following shows, executes each time the player clicks the play button and, thus, belongs in the PushButton control's Action event.

```
'A new game is being started

Dim r as New Random      'Instantiate a Random Object

intSecretNumber = r.InRange(1,100)      'Generate a random number

sdrControl.Enabled = True    'Enable the Slider control to allow game play
sdrControl.Value = 0     'By default the Slider Control's value is set to zero

intNoGuessed = 0  'Reset the variable used to track the number of guesses made

edfNoOfGuesses.Text = CStr(intNoGuessed)  'Display the number of guesses made
edfDisplay.Text = CStr(sdrControl.Value)  'Display Slider Control's value

edfAnalysis.Text = ""    'Clear out the display of the previous game's status

btnPlay.Enabled = False    'Disable access to the Play button
```

The first two code statements instantiate a Random object and assign a randomly generated number (with a value between 1 and 100) to the `intSecretNumber` property. The next two statements enable the Slider control and set its initial value to zero. The property representing the number of guesses made is reset to zero, the rest of the EditField controls are updated and the PushButton control labeled `Play` is disabled, thus preventing the player from starting a new game until the current game ends.

Next, add the following code statement to the Action event belonging to the PushButton control labeled Exit.

```
Quit     'Terminate the application's execution
```

The last of the code to be added to this application supports the display of About information, which the player can access by clicking Help ➤ About. To add these statements, you must first add a menu handler to your application by clicking the Add Menu Handler button on the Code Editor. Once this is done, you can enter the two code statements shown in the following.

```
'Display About Message
MsgBox("RB Number Guess - By Jerry Ford - Copyright 2006")
```

Testing RB Number Guess

If you have not done so already, go ahead and save your application. Name it RB Number Guess or any other name you prefer. Now, take a little time to test the execution of the game to make sure it works as expected. Figure 6-6 demonstrates how the game looks when it's being played.

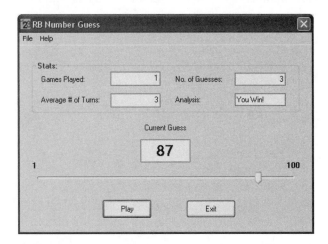

Figure 6-6. *Game stats are updated dynamically at the end of each move.*

Figure 6-7 shows the pop-up dialog window that appears if you click Help ➤ About.

Figure 6-7. *By adding an About menu item to your menu system, you provide a place for copyright or other useful application information.*

If you don't run across any errors when you test the RB Number Guess game, go ahead and compile standalone copies of the application. If you do run into errors when testing the application, they are most likely the result of typos you made when keying in program code statements. Go back and review your program code, and then fix any typos you find.

Summary

In this chapter, you learned the ins and outs of applying conditional logic to your REALbasic applications to alter the logical flow of program code. This included learning how to work with the many formats of the If...Then, as well as with the Select Case statements. You learned how to use #If...#EndIf to create conditional logic that executes based on the OS or version of REALbasic running it. You also learned how to work with REALbasic's mathematical, comparison, and logical operators. On top of all this, you had the chance to add custom window properties, and you learned how to generate random numbers and how to work with the Slider control.

CHAPTER 7

Iterative Processing

In Chapter 6, you learned how to set up conditional tests that control the logical flow of program code within your REALbasic applications. In this chapter, you learn how to set up loops to process large amounts of data or to repeatedly execute a set of statements over and over again. REALbasic provides support for a number of different types of loops and you learn how to work with each type. In addition, you also learn how to work with a number of new controls, such as the ListBox, ComboBox, PopupMenu, ProgressBar, and MoviePlayer controls.

Specifically, this chapter teaches you how to

- Set up and control different types of loops

- Programmatically break out of endless loops

- Terminate endless loops from within the REALbasic IDE

- Work with the ListBox, ProgressBar, PopupMenu, GroupBox, and MoviePlayer controls

Processing Data with Loops

Any time you need to process large amounts of data or to perform a series of code statements over and over again, you need set up a loop. A loop is just a series of statements, processed as a block, that execute repeatedly until a certain condition is met. For example, you could create a loop that collects user input until the user clicks a Finished button. You could also set up a loop to open a file and read every line in the file until the end of the file is reached. Or, you could set up a loop that iterates until a given variable is set to a certain value.

The number of cases where loops come in handy is endless. By enabling you to process the same code statements over and over again, loops help to streamline program code by letting you process any amount of data by reusing the same set of code statements.

Loops are ideal for driving any repetitive tasks and for processing the contents of arrays. You see examples of how to perform both of these types of tasks in this chapter. While, in most cases, you can use any one of the types of loops supported in REALbasic to perform a given task, each of these loops has certain qualities that differentiate them and make them better suited to particular types of tasks.

The following list identifies the different types of loops that REALbasic supports:

- **Do...Loop**. Creates a loop that iterates until terminated by an Exit statement.

- **For...Next**. Creates a loop that iterates a set number of times.

- **For...Each**. Creates a loop that iterates through every element stored in an array.

- **While...Wend**. Creates a loop that iterates as long as a specified Boolean condition remains True.

Each of these different types of loops is examined further in the following sections. In addition, this chapter also teaches you how to work with a number of new controls as you work your way through the following loop examples.

Do...Loop

The Do...Loop is the simplest type of loop supported by REALbasic. It supports a number of different variations. In its simplest form, the *Do...Loop* executes without checking for a predefined condition, using the following syntax.

```
Do
  Statements
Loop
```

Do is a keyword identifying the beginning of the loop. *Statements* is a placeholder representing code statements you embed inside the loop for repeated execution. *Loop* is a keyword that identifies the end of the loop. To get a good idea of how to work with this format or the Do...Loop, consider the following example.

```
Dim intCounter As Integer = 0

Do

  intCounter = intCounter + 1
  ListBox1.AddRow Str(intCounter)

  If intCounter = 10 Then
    Exit
  End If

Loop
```

This example begins by declaring a variable named intCounter with a data type of Integer and an initial value of zero. Next, a Do...Loop is set up that loads a list of numbers (1–10) into a ListBox control. The Do...Loop increments the value of counter by 1 each time the loop iterates. The ListBox control's AddRow method is used to add a number to the ListBox control. Note, the number added is stored in the intCounter variable. This variable has a data type of integer, so it must be converted to a string before it can be added to the ListBox control.

> **■Note** The ListBox control displays a list of String values from which the user can make a selection. You can add items to a ListBox from the REALbasic IDE by assigning data to its InitialValue property. REALbasic also lets you programmatically add items to a ListBox control using its AddRow method.

Because the Do…Loop does not specify a predefined condition that must be met for the loop to stop executing, it is up to the programmer to develop a means for stopping loop execution. In the previous example, this occurred when the value of intCounter was set equal to ten, at which time the Exit statement was executed. The Exit statement causes the immediate termination of a loop, allowing your application to continue processing, starting with the first code statement following the loop.

Figure 7-1 shows the output produced when this example is executed on a computer running Windows.

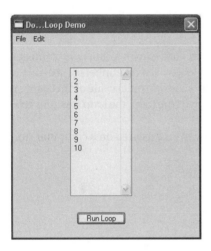

Figure 7-1. *Using a Do…Loop to populate a ListBox, as seen on Windows*

You should avoid using the Do…Loop and the Exit statement when creating loops within your REALbasic applications. Because the termination condition is not clearly identified at the beginning or the ending of the loop, the condition that will terminate loop execution is not readily evident. This is generally considered a poor programming practice because it forces you to read through all the code statements contained within the loop to identify how it is terminated.

A better way of setting up a Do…Loop is to include the optional Until keyword. This enables you to set up loops that execute until a specific condition becomes True or, to put it another way, the Do…Loop executes as long as a specified condition remains False. This form of the Do…Loop is perfect for situations where you know in advance what condition must be met for the loop to terminate its execution. For example, you might set up a Do…Loop to run until a variable was set equal to a certain value or until the user entered a certain command.

Using the Until keyword, you can set up two different forms of the Do...Loop. The following shows the syntax for the first form.

```
Do Until condition
  Statements
Loop
```

Condition is a Boolean expression that must evaluate to True for the loop to stop executing. Statements is a placeholder that represents the code statements you want executed when the loop executes. To see how this form of the Do...Loop works, consider the following example.

```
Dim intCounter As Integer = 1

Do Until intCounter  > 10

  ComboBox1.AddRow Str(intCounter)
  intCounter = intCounter + 1

Loop
```

This example begins by declaring a variable named intCounter with a data type of integer and an initial value of one. Next, a Do...Loop is set up that loads a list of numbers (1–10) into a ComboBox control, using the control's AddRow method. Because the initial value of intCounter is equal to one and is incremented by one on each iteration of the loop, the loop executes ten times before terminating its own execution.

Figure 7-2 shows the output produced when this example is executed on a computer running Linux.

Figure 7-2. *Using a Do...Loop to populate a ComboBox, as seen on Linux*

In this example, if the value assigned to `intCounter` had been set to 11 or greater at the start, the loop would have been skipped. This behavior occurs because the tested condition is checked at the beginning of the loop. The second way to use the Until keyword when setting up a Do…Loop is to move the Boolean expression to the end of the loop. The following shows the syntax for this form of the Do…Loop.

```
Do
  Statements
Loop Until condition
```

The result of moving the tested condition to the end of the loop is this: the Do…Loop executes once, no matter what the value of `intCounter` might be. Otherwise, this form of the Do…Loop works pretty much the same as the first form, as the following example shows.

```
Dim intCounter As Integer = 1

Do

  PopupMenu1.AddRow Str(intCounter)
  intCounter = intCounter + 1

Loop Until intCounter  > 10
```

In this example, the Do…Loop runs one time no matter what. However, because the initial value assigned to `intCounter` is one, it runs ten times, producing the same output as the previous example. Figure 7-3 shows the output produced when this example is executed on a computer running Mac OS X.

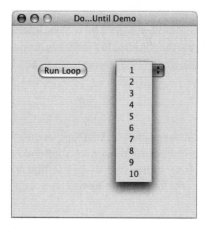

Figure 7-3. *Using a Do…Loop to populate a PopupMenu, as seen on Mac OS X*

The While…Wend Loop

The *While…Wend* loop provides the capability to execute one or more code statements, as long as an evaluated condition remains True. The following shows the syntax of the While…Wend loop.

```
While Condition
  Statements
Wend
```

Condition is a placeholder representing any valid Boolean expression, as the following example shows.

```
Dim intCounter As Integer = 1

While intCounter <=10

  EditField1.Text = EditField1. Text + Str(intCounter) + " " + EndOfLine
  intCounter = intCounter + 1

Wend
```

In this example, a While…Wend loop is used to populate an EditField control with ten numbers, each of which is displayed on a different line. The While…Wend loop tests a condition at the beginning of the loop. The While…Wend loop is similar to the Do…Until loop, but it lacks the Do…Until loop's flexibility. Specifically, the While…Wend loop does not provide the option of moving the conditional text to the end of the loop. You do not see this form of loop used often in REALbasic programs.

> ■**Note** The preceding example controlled when line breaks occurred in output by referencing an
> EndOfLine object. EndOfLine provides access to properties representing end-of-line markers on
> Macintosh, Windows, and Linux. You learn more about REALbasic classes later in Chapter 8.

Figure 7-4 shows the output that is produced when this example is executed on a computer running Windows. Note, if the value of intCounter is greater than ten to start with, then the While...Wend loop and all the statements contained within it are skipped.

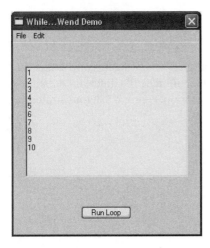

Figure 7-4. *Using a While...Wend loop to populate an EditField control, as seen on Windows*

The For...Next Loop

The For...Next loop is designed for situations in which you know exactly how many times a loop must execute. For...Next loops use a variable to keep track of loop execution to determine when the loop should cease execution. The value of the loop variable, or counter, can be increased or decreased, as appropriate during loop execution.

The following outlines the syntax of the For...Next loop.

```
For counter [As DataType] = start To | DownTo end [Step Value]
   Statements
Next [counter]
```

Counter is a local variable used to control loop execution. *DataType* is an optional parameter that provides you with the capability to declare the counter will be within the loop. If DataType is omitted, you must remember to declare the counter variable elsewhere within your code statements. *Start* sets the beginning value of the counter variable. *End* sets its ending value (for example, the value, which when reached, terminates the loop's execution). *Value* is an optional keyword. When used, it specifies the value to be used to increment or decrement the value of the counter variable as the loop processes. By default, the counter variable is automatically incremented by one on each iteration of a For...Next loop. However, by specifying the optional Step value you can change the incremental value. Finally, using the optional DownTo keyword, you can set up a For…Next loop to decrement, rather than increment, the counter variable.

If you define a For…Next loop's counter variable within the loop using the optional DataType keyword, the variable is local to that loop, meaning when the loop terminates, the variable ceases to exist. If your application must be able to read the value of the counter variable outside of the loop, then you need to define the variable outside the loop.

To see the For…Next loop in action, look at the following example.

```
For I As Integer = 1 to 100

  ProgressBar1.Value = ProgressBar1.Value + 1

Next
```

In this example, a For…Next loop is used to demonstrate how to visually control the display of data using a ProgressBar control. Specifically, the loop iterates 100 times, incrementing the ProgressBar control's Value property by one on each iteration. Figure 7-5 demonstrates the effect the For…Next loop has in this example.

Figure 7-5. *Using a For…Next loop to visually control a ProgressBar control, as seen on Linux*

■**Note** The ProgressBar control is commonly used to display a graphic representing the status of a process as it is being executed. By default, the ProgressBar control has an initial value of zero and a maximum value of 100. To indicate progress, all you have to do is to increment the ProgressBar control's Value property.

The For…Next loop is flexible. If you want, you can use the Step keyword to change the value used to increment the counter variable as the following shows.

```
For I As Integer = 1 to 100 Step 10

  ProgressBar1.Value = ProgressBar1.Value + 1

Next
```

As you can see, this example increases the value of the ProgressBar control's Value property by 10 (10 percent) on each iteration. If you need to, you can decrement the value of the counter variable, as you see in the following. For this example to work effectively, you must set the ProgressBar control's value property to 100.

```
For I As Integer = 100 DownTo 1

  ProgressBar1.Value = ProgressBar1.Value - 1

Next
```

■**Note** Because of the manner is which REALbasic compiles code statements, the For…Next, and For…Each loops are typically more efficient than the Do…Loop. Do…Until, and While…Wend loops in terms of resources consumed (memory and processor time) by your application.

The For…Each Loop

The For…Each loop is designed to automatically process each element stored in a single-dimension array. The syntax for the For…Each loop is outlined in the following:

```
For Each element [As DataType] In array
  statements
Next
```

Element is a variable used to represent an item stored in an array; *DataType* is optional. When used, it specifies the data type of the data stored in the array.

To better understand how the For…Each loop works, look at the example Figure 7-6 shows. In this example, an EditField has been set up to enable the user to enter a list of items for her Christmas wish list. Wishes are entered one at a time, by clicking the PushButton control labeled Add to List. Each item added is stored in array. Once the user finishes entering data, the list is displayed by a For…Each loop that executes when the PushButton control labeled Display List is clicked.

Figure 7-6. *Storing data in a array, as seen on Mac OS X*

In addition to creating the user interface, this example also requires you to declare a property with a public scope, as the following shows.

```
strWishListArray() As String
```

This property, named strWishListArray, defines an array with a data type of String. Note, the size of the array has not been specified. Once the required property is added, double-click the PushButton control labeled Add to List, and then add the following code statements.

```
If EditField1.Text <> "" Then

  strWishListArray.Append EditField1.Text
  EditField1.Text = ""
  EditField1.SetFocus

End If
```

These statements consist of an If…Then block, which takes the text entered by the user and adds it to the end of an array named strWishListArray. Note, the If…Then statement performs a check to make sure the user entered something into the EditField control before allowing a new element to be added to the array, using the Append function.

Next, add the following code statements to the PushButton control labeled Display List.

```
Dim strMessageText As String
Dim intCounter As Integer = 0

For Each I As String In strWishListArray

  intCounter = intCounter + 1
  strMessageText = strMessageText + Str(intCounter) + ". " + I + EndOfLine

Next

MsgBox "My Christmas wish list:" + EndOfLine + EndOfLine + strMessageText
```

The first two statements declare two variables. The first variable, named **strMessage** is used to display output extracted from the strWishListArray by the For...Each loop. The second variable, named intCounter, is used to format the display of output by numbering each item displayed.

Next, a For...Each loop is used to process each element in the strWishListArray array. Each time the loop iterates, the value assigned to intCounter is incremented by one. In addition, the value extracted from the array is appended to a display string. Once the For...Each loop has finished processing every element stored in the array, the resulting string is displayed using the MsgBox function.

Figure 7-7 shows the output generated when this application is run on Mac OS X.

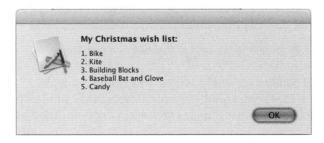

Figure 7-7. *Displaying the data stored in an array using a For...Each loop, as seen on Mac OS X*

Shortcuts for Creating Loops

REALbasic provides templates to assist you with the creation of loops in your program code. Specifically, it can assist you in setting up Do...Until and While...Wend loops. To see how this works, open a new REALbasic project, double-click Window1 and enter the following code statements.

```
Dim intCounter AS Integer = 0

intCounter = IntCounter + 1
If intCounter = 10 Then MsgBox "The number 10 has been reached!"
```

Next, select the last two of these statements and right-click to open the Code Editor's contextual menu. You see menu items for defining loops at the bottom of the menu. Click the Wrap in Do/Loop menu item. REALbasic responds by placing the selected code statements inside a Do...Until loop for you. However, because REALbasic does not know what condition you want the loop to test, it adds a placeholder of _condition_, as Figure 7-8 shows.

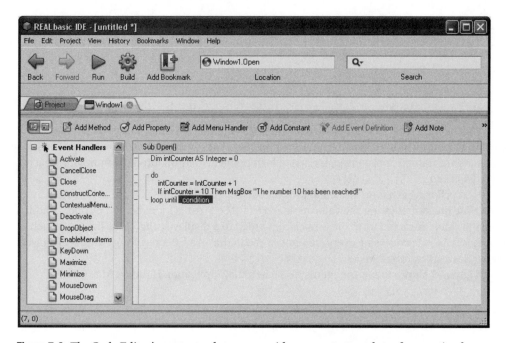

Figure 7-8. *The Code Editor's contextual menu provides access to templates for creating loops.*

Replacing *_condition_* with a valid Boolean expression is up to you. For this example, replace _condition_ with `intCounter > 15`. The end result of this example is a Do...Until loop that iterates 15 times, pausing on the tenth iteration to display a message in a pop-up dialog, as the following shows.

```
Dim intCounter As Integer = 0
do
  intCounter = IntCounter + 1
  If intCounter = 10 Then MsgBox "The number 10 has been reached!"
loop until intCounter > 15
```

■Note You can also use the Code Editor's contextual menu to access a template for setting up If...Then code blocks.

BREAKING OUT OF ENDLESS LOOPS

Every programmer accidentally creates an endless loop at some point when developing a new application. Endless loops often make themselves known by making your application nonresponsive, and by consuming large amounts of processor and memory resources. If, when testing a REALbasic application, you believe an endless loop may be running, you can usually stop it by switching over to the REALbasic IDE and clicking the Stop button located on the Run Screen. If this does not work, however, you can also try terminating your test application by pressing Ctrl+Alt+Del on Windows or Linux, or by clicking Control+Option+Escape on Macintosh.

Guarding Against Endless Loops

One of the dangers of working with loops is you may accidentally set them up in such a way that they never terminate, creating *endless* or *infinite loops*. In other words, the condition a loop tests to know when to stop is never satisfied. Endless loops, therefore, typically result from faulty logic. As the following example shows, accidentally setting up an endless loop is all too easy.

```
Dim intCounter As Integer = 1

Do Until intCounter  > 10

  ComboBox1.AddRow Str(intCounter)
  intCounter = intCounter - 1

Loop
```

This example was supposed to add a number to a row in a ComboBox control on each iteration of the Do…Until loop. The intention was to add ten numbers. However, because of a typo, faulty logic was introduced that prevents the loop from terminating. Specifically, instead of incrementing the value of intCounter by one on each iteration of the loop, the value of intCounter is decremented by one. As a result, no matter how many times the loop iterates, the value of intCounter will never become greater than ten. In fact, while the value of intCounter starts off as one, it gets smaller each time the loop is processed.

The point to take away from this example is to take extra care when coding loops in your applications. A loop is a powerful programming technique. However, its power can be turned against you when a loop is miscoded, as the previous example shows. In addition to being careful when you write your program code, it is equally important for you to test your applications thoroughly, to ensure every line of code is tested, even code for parts of the application that may not be often used.

Creating a REALbasic Movie Player

The final part of this chapter focuses on the development of another REALbasic application. This time, you learn how to create a desktop movie player. Using the RB Movie Player application, you can play any MPEG video on your computer.

■**Note** The primary component in the RB Movie Player application is the MoviePlayer control. The *MoviePlayer control* provides the capability to play movies within REALbasic applications. This control is designed to work with either Windows Media Player or Apple's QuickTime Player. On Windows, you have the choice of using either player. On the Macintosh, you must use the QuickTime Player. At press time, the control does not work with any players running on Linux. Therefore, the RB Movie Player application only runs on Windows and Macintosh.

As you create the RB Movie Player application, you learn how to work with MoviePlayer control. This control provides you with the capability to play MPEG movie files. You learn how to specify whether the control should display the Windows Media Player or the Apple QuickTime Player. You also learn how to programmatically stop and start movies.

This application also provides you with a sneak peak at how to work with folder items and shows you how to work with the standard Open dialog. This enables you to create applications that can browse folders and open any file.

This chapter explains the development of the RB Movie Player using the Windows version of REALbasic. However, you could just as easily use the Macintosh version of REALbasic to create this application. In fact, you could also use the Linux Professional version of REALbasic to create this application, as long as you compile your application to run on Windows or Macintosh.

Figure 7-9 provides a sneak peak at the RB Movie Player application. As you can see, it consists of just the MoviePlayer control, which provides an assortment of controls for playing movies, controlling speaker volume, and so on. In addition, the RB Movie Player application also has a menu system that provides control over a number of movie player functions.

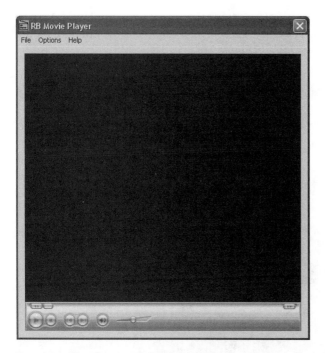

Figure 7-9. *The RB Movie Player application can be used to play any mpeg movie file.*

Assembling the Application's User Interface

The RB Movie Player consists of a menu system and a single MoviePlayer control. The first step
in creating the RB Movie Player application is to create a new REALbasic desktop application.
Once you create a new project, assign your application its own icon by opening the Project
Editor and assigning the Icon property for App to Movie.bmp. A copy of this icon is included on
the book's companion CD-ROM, along with the source code for this project.

Change the Width, Height, and Title properties for the application's window, as Table 7-1
specifies.

Table 7-1. *Property Modifications for the RB Movie Player Application*

Object	Property	Value
Window1	Title	RB Movie Player
	Width	466
	Height	455

Next, drag-and-drop an instance of the MoviePlayer control on to the window and resize it until it takes up most of the window's available space. When you finish, the interface for the RB Movie Player should look like the example in Figure 7-10.

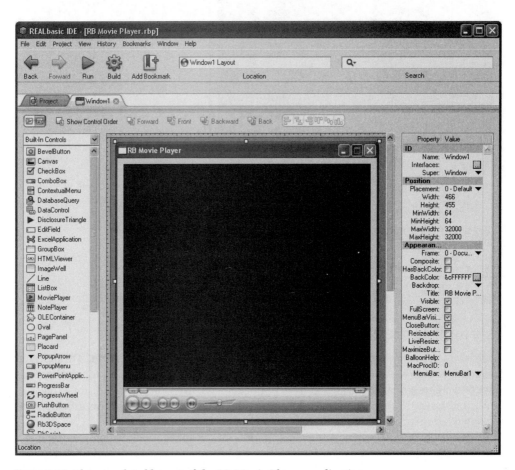

Figure 7-10. *The completed layout of the RB Movie Player application*

Once the application's user interface is set up, it's time to build the menu system. To do so, double-click the Menubar1 item located on the Projects screen. REALbasic responds by displaying the menu in the MenuBar Editor. By default, REALbasic adds both a File and Edit menu to your application. Because the RB Movie Player application does not need the Edit menu, you can remove it by selecting it and clicking Delete. Next, modify the menu system for MenuBar1 by adding and configuring the menu and menu items listed in Table 7-2.

Table 7-2. *Menus and Menu Items for the RB Movie Player Application*

Menu	Menu Item	Text Property
File	FileOpen	&Open Movie
	FilePlay	Pl&ay Movie
	FileStop	&Stop Movie
	FileQuit	E&xit
Options	OptionsMenu	&Options
	OptionsMediaPlayer	Media Player
	OptionsQuickTime	QuickTime
Help	HelpMenu	&Help
	HelpAbout	&About

Adding the Program Code

Once you finish configuring the application's user interface by adding the MoviePlayer control and setting up its menu system, you're ready to begin adding the code statements required to make the RB Movie Player application work. Start by switching back to the Windows Layout view of the Windows Editor, and then double-clicking the window. REALbasic responds by opening the Code Editor and displaying the Window1's Open event. Now, enter the following code statements.

```
'Load default configuration options for the RB Movie Player Application

MoviePlayer1.PlayerType = 1  'Set the default player is QuickTime

OptionsQuickTime.Checked = True  'Mark the QuickTime menu item as checked
```

The first statement is just a comment that documents the basic purpose of the statements that follow. The second statement sets the MoviePlayer control's PlayerType property equal to 1, making the QuickTime the default player. Table 7-3 lists the different player options available to REALbasic.

Table 7-3. *Players Supported by the MoviePlayer Control*

Player	Value	Description
Preferred player	0	On Windows, the preferred player is Media Player. On Macintosh, only the QuickTime player is supported.
Windows Media Player	2	Sets Media Player as the application's player.
Apple QuickTime	1	Sets QuickTime as the application's player.

The third previously shown statement sets the Checked property of the OptionsQuickTime menu item (the QuickTime menu item under the Options menu) equal to True, visually marking that menu item as the application's default option.

The rest of this application's code statements are associated with the various menu items that make up its menu system. For starters, click the Add Menu Handler button located on the Code Editor's toolbar and select the FileOpen menu item from the MenuItem Name drop-down list. Next, add the following code statements to the menu item's event handler.

```
'Prompt the user to select a movie

Dim MovieTypes as New FileType    'Declare a variable representing a FileType object

MovieTypes.Name= "Movie Files"    'Specify string identifying supported files
MovieTypes.Extensions=".mpg"      'Specify supported file types

'Declare variable representing a folder object
Dim f as FolderItem = GetOpenFolderItem(MovieTypes)

'Perform the following as long as the user did not click on the Cancel button
If f <> Nil then

  MoviePlayer1.Speaker=True  'Display the movie player's volume control
  MoviePlayer1.HasStep=True  ' Display forward and reverse arrows on slider
  MoviePlayer1.Movie=f.OpenAsMovie  ' Open the move selected by the user
  MoviePlayer1.Play   'Play the selected movie

  'Disable the Option menu's Media Player menu item
  OptionsMediaplayer.AutoEnable = False

  'Disable the Option menu's QuickTime menu item
  OptionsQuickTime.AutoEnable = False

End if
```

The first statement declares a variable named TextTypes based on the FileType class. The next two statements set the Name and Extensions properties of the FileType class. By specifying a specific file extension, you tell REALbasic to restrict the types of files the Open dialog window can display and open, which, for this application, is MPEG movies.

ACCESSING FILES USING A STANDARD OPEN DIALOG

The previous set of code statements established a reference to a MPEG file by declaring a variable with a data type of `FolderItem`. The `FolderItem` class can be used to represent a file or folder. Note, the `GetOpenFolderItem` function assigns an MPEG file to this variable. The `GetOpenFolderItem` does this by displaying a standard Open dialog, as 7-11 shows, and returning a reference to the file selected by the user. More information on how to work with files and folders is available in Chapter 9.

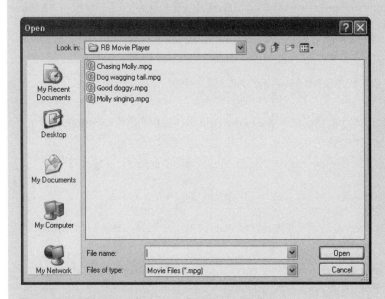

Figure 7-11. *The Open dialog, as shown in Windows*

Next, the `GetOpenFolderItem` function is used to display a standard Open dialog and retrieve a file, which is represented by a variable named `f`. The rest of the statements are embedded inside an If…Then loop, which allows them to execute only if the user selects an MPEG file. This way, if the user clicks the Open dialog's Cancel button, these statements will not execute. Assuming an MPEG file is selected, the next four statements set properties belonging to the MoviePlayer control. These statements enable the display of the control's volume control, as well as the forward and reverse arrows on the MoviePlayer control's slider. Then, the specified MPEG file is opened and played. The last two statements disable the Option menu's two menu items, preventing the user from changing the selected Movie Player (Media Player or QuickTime) once movie play has begun.

Next, add another menu handler and, this time, associate it with the FilePlay menu item. Then, add the following code statement.

```
MoviePlayer1.Play    'Play the selected movie
```

This statement plays (or replays) the currently selected movie file, using the MoviePlayer control's Play method. If a movie is already playing when the user clicks the FilePlay menu item, this code statement will not have any effect. The currently playing movie continues to run.

Now add another menu handler and assign the FileStop menu item to it. Then add the following code statement.

```
MoviePlayer1.Stop    'Stop movie playback
```

This statement executes the MoviePlayer control's Stop method to stop the playback of the currently playing movie. If no movie is being played, this statement has no effect. The next code statements to add to your application are for the Help menu's About menu item. Add another menu handler and assign it to the HelpAbout menu item. Then, add the statements listed in the following.

```
'Display information about the application and its author
MsgBox "RB Movie Player - By Jerry Ford - 2006"
```

Next, add another menu handler and assign the OptionsMediaPlayer menu item to it. Then, add the following code statements.

```
'Actions to take when the Option menu's Media Player menu item is selected

MoviePlayer1.PlayerType = 2   'Play the movie using the Media Player

OptionsMediaPlayer.Checked = True    'Mark the Media Player menu item as selected
OptionsQuickTime.Checked = False   'Unmark the QuickTime menu item
```

These statements assign the MoviePlayer control's PlayerType property a value of 2, which represents the Windows Media Player and marks the menu item as selected by setting its Checked property to True.

Finally, add one last menu handler and assign it to the OptionsQuickTime menu item. Then, add the following code statements, which specify QuickTime as the player to be used for movie playback.

```
'Actions to take when the Option menu's QuickTime menu item is selected

MoviePlayer1.PlayerType = 1   'Play movie using the QuickTime player

OptionsQuickTime.Checked = True   'Mark the QuickTime menu item as selected
OptionsMediaplayer.Checked = False   'Unmark the Media Player menu item
```

Testing RB Movie Player

If you have not done so yet, save your application and name it RB Movie Player. Before moving on, put the application through its paces to make sure it works as you expect. This should include playing a few video clips and testing each of the menu items you added to the application's menu system.

Note If you do not have any MPEG movie files on your computer, you can find plenty to download on the Internet. In addition, you can use any of the sample MPEG video files included, along with the source code for this application on the book's companion CD-ROM.

If you get any errors when you attempt to test your application, most likely you made one or more typos when keying in the application's code statements. If this is the case, double-check your typing for each statement that REALbasic flags as an error. Once you eliminate any errors, go ahead and compile your application.

Summary

In this chapter, you learned how to work with various forms of loops, including the Do...Loop, Do...Until, While...Wend, For...Next, and For...Each loops. These statements provide you with the capability to process large amounts of data and to execute code statements repeatedly with a minimum amount of program code. You also leaned how to work with the ListBox, ComboBox, PopupMenu, and ProgressBar controls, as well as how to work with a REALbasic function that provides access to a standard Open dialog that can be used when working with files and folders. And, last, you learned different ways to break out of endless loops.

CHAPTER 8

Object-Oriented Programming

In Chapter 7, you learned how to set up and execute loops to repeatedly execute sets of program statements over and over again. The focus of this chapter is object-oriented programming. Even though you have been creating object-oriented programs from the first chapter of this book, you now learn a little about what REALbasic does behind the scenes to help you develop object-oriented applications. This includes learning about REALbasic's built-in class hierarchy. You will also learn how to use classes as templates for creating your own custom subclasses. Finally, you also learn how to use modules to store program code that does not belong to any specific object.

In this chapter, you learn how to

- Customize REALbasic classes by adding your own properties, methods, and constants

- Use classes to instantiate objects

- Create modules and assign properties, methods, and constants to them

An Introduction to Object-Oriented Programming

Object-oriented programming (OOP) is a key feature of REALbasic. In OOP, data and code are stored together in objects. REALbasic provides programmers with access to a collection of pre-built program code and data in the form of classes. *Classes* provide templates for instantiating objects. *Instantiation* is the process of creating an object that inherits all the features of the class from which it is copied.

An object inherits the properties and methods belonging to a class. You can think of a class as being akin to a set of blueprints for a house. Using the same set of blueprints, a builder can build any number of houses, each of which can have the same set of features. Examples of classes from which objects can be instantiated include the PushButton, EditField, StaticText, and ProgressBar controls. Controls instantiated from these types of classes are referred to as *control objects*. REALbasic also provides access to other types of noncontrol classes, such as the Date class.

The PushButton, BevelButton, RadioButton, and CheckBox controls are all different subclasses of the RectControl class. The RectControl class is a subclass of the Control class and the Control class is a subclass of the Object class, which is the top-level class in the REALbasic class hierarchy. REALbasic class hierarchy is made up of hundreds of classes. You can view REALbasic's class hierarchy by right-clicking (Control-clicking on Macintosh) on any Windows

Editor to display the editor's contextual menu. Click Add, and then REALbasic displays a hierarchical listing of the subclasses located under the Object class, as you see in Figure 8-1.

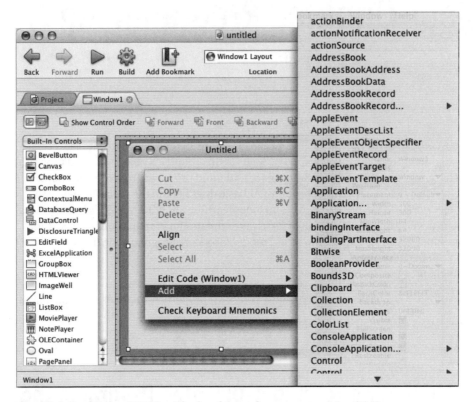

Figure 8-1. *Examining REALbasic's class hierarchy, as seen on Mac OS X*

■**Note** While you won't find any shortage of examples of how to work with different types of REALbasic classes in this book, the number of classes in the REALbasic class hierarchy are too numerous to cover. To learn more about a specific class, refer to REALbasic's Language Reference.

Advantages of Working with REALbasic Classes and Subclasses

Through the instantiation of objects from classes and subclasses, REALbasic significantly simplifies the coding process by masking the complexity of application development. For example, when you add a PushButton control to a window, you needn't concern yourself with telling REALbasic how to manage the control's behavior. The PushButton control's built-in properties and methods already provide all the code required to make the PushButton control work as you want it to. All you have to do is provide the program code you want executed when specific events occur, such as when a user clicks the PushButton.

Classes serve as templates from which objects can be instantiated. Classes promote code reuse by allowing code defined in one class to be used over and over again in objects instantiated from these classes. Classes provide REALbasic applications with a number of advantages, including:

- **Built-in source code**. Classes provide access to functionality provided by built-in methods, freeing you from having to reinvent the wheel by creating your own methods to develop similar functionality.

- **Reduced code maintenance**. The less code you must enter to make your applications work, the less code you have to update and debug.

- **Smaller applications**. Because subclasses inherit properties and methods belonging to parent classes, they can access parent properties and methods, and then reuse their code without you having to re-create them.

Instantiating Objects from Classes and Subclasses

To work with the methods and properties belonging to a particular class, you must first instantiate it. The steps you follow to instantiate a new object vary based on the type of objects you are working with. Objects based on REALbasic control classes, such as the PushButton and the EditField, are instantiated by placing a copy of them on a window. Other noncontrol classes are instantiated by first declaring a variable with a data type that matches the data type of the class, and then using the New keyword to instantiate a new object based on the specified class.

■**Note** You may be asking yourself right now what the difference is between a class and a subclass. A *subclass* is a class derived from another class. The parent class from which the subclass is derived is referred to as the *Super Class*. Subclasses automatically inherit all the properties, methods, constants, and events of their Super Class. For example, you might think of a car as being a subclass of a motor vehicle, inheriting properties such as color, wheels, and doors, as well as methods, such as stop and go. However, a subclass does not inherit any properties, methods, or constants that are assigned a scope of protected. A subclass is itself a class and can be used as the Super Class for other subclasses. For example, using the automobile analogy, you could think of a car, which is a subclass of a motor car, also as being the Super Class of a Ford Taurus.

Working with Control Classes

Because every application you have worked on in this book has depended on the use of controls in the development of its graphical user interface (GUI), you have been instantiating new objects from day one. In addition, you have been customizing these objects by modifying their properties and adding code statements to their methods.

Control classes provide an unlimited supply of interface controls that you use when building your application's GUI. Each time you add a control to a window, you are adding a new object that inherits all the properties and methods of the class that defines the control.

REALbasic provides you with the capability to create new control subclasses based on existing control classes. In this way, you can take any control class and modify it to suit your specific needs. When you create your own control subclass, REALbasic adds it to your application's Project menu.

■Tip If you choose, you can export any control subclass you define to your desktop. Doing so enables you to import the Control subclass into other REALbasic applications. The easiest way to export a subclass is to right-click it in the Project Editor, select the Export option from the context menu that appears, and then specify the location where you want to store the subclass. REALbasic saves the subclass as a file with a file extension of .rbo, as Figure 8-2 shows.

StatesListBox.
rbo

Figure 8-2. *REALbasic assigns a unique icon to exported control subclasses, as seen on Windows.*

To import a copy of a control subclass into another REALbasic application, all you have to do is drag-and-drop the icon representing the exported control subclass into the Project Editor of another REALbasic application.

To get a better understanding of how to create your own custom control subclasses, consider the following example. For this example, let's assume you spend a lot of time developing custom mailing-list applications for small businesses. One of the features common to each mailing list program is the need to specify the state where customers reside.

One way to accomplish this is to add an instance of a ListBox control to a window, and then to supply code statements that populate the ListBox with a list of all 50 states. You could then copy-and-paste this control from the REALbasic project into other REALbasic projects, as needed. A more convenient way of dealing with this situation, however, would be to create a customized subclass based on the ListBox class, add the required code statements, and then export it, so the control subclass can later be imported into any REALbasic application that needs this functionality.

The following procedure outlines the steps involved in creating and exporting this new class, named StatesListBox.

1. From within the REALbasic Project Editor, click the Add Class button located on the Project Editor toolbar or click Project ➤ Add ➤ Class.

2. Rename the class to StatesListBox by modifying its Name property in the Properties pane.

3. Set the class's Super Class to ListBox by expanding the Super property and clicking Control ➤ RectControl ➤ ListBox, as you see in Figure 8-3.

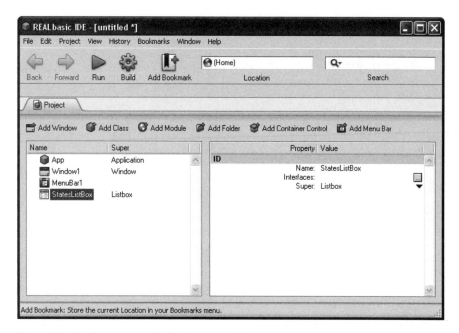

Figure 8-3. *Configuring a subclass's Super Class as seen on Windows*

4. Double-click the new class to open the Code Editor.

5. Expand the Event Handlers node in the Browser pane, select the Open event, and add the following code statements.

```
'Load values representing all 50 states

AddRow "ALABAMA - AL"
AddRow "ALASKA - AK"
AddRow "ARIZONA - AZ"
AddRow "ARKANSAS - AR"
AddRow "CALIFORNIA - CA"
AddRow "COLORADO - CO"
AddRow "CONNECTICUT - CT"
AddRow "DELAWARE - DE"
AddRow "FLORIDA - FL"
AddRow "GEORGIA - GA"
AddRow "HAWAII - HI"
AddRow "IDAHO - ID"
AddRow "ILLINOIS - IL"
AddRow "INDIANA - IN"
AddRow "IOWA - IA"
AddRow "KANSAS - KS"
AddRow "KENTUCKY - KY"
AddRow "LOUISIANA - LA"
AddRow "MAINE - ME"
```

```
AddRow "MARYLAND - MD"
AddRow "MASSACHUSETTS - MA"
AddRow "MICHIGAN - MI"
AddRow "MINNESOTA - MN"
AddRow "MISSISSIPPI - MS"
AddRow "MISSOURI - MO"
AddRow "MONTANA - MT"
AddRow "NEBRASKA - NE"
AddRow "NEVADA - NV"
AddRow "NEW HAMPSHIRE - NH"
AddRow "NEW JERSEY - NJ"
AddRow "NEW MEXICO - NM"
AddRow "NEW YORK - NY"
AddRow "NORTH CAROLINA - NC"
AddRow "NORTH DAKOTA - ND"
AddRow "OHIO - OH"
AddRow "OKLAHOMA - OK"
AddRow "OREGON - OR"
AddRow "PALAU - PW"
AddRow "PENNSYLVANIA - PA"
AddRow "RHODE ISLAND - RI"
AddRow "SOUTH CAROLINA - SC"
AddRow "SOUTH DAKOTA - SD"
AddRow "TENNESSEE - TN"
AddRow "TEXAS - TX"
AddRow "UTAH - UT"
AddRow "VERMONT - VT"
AddRow "VIRGINIA - VA"
AddRow "WASHINGTON - WA"
AddRow "WEST VIRGINIA - WV"
AddRow "WISCONSIN - WI"
AddRow "WYOMING - WY"
```

6. Open the Project sheet, right-click the StatesListBox class, and select Export from the displayed context menu.

7. The Save As dialog appears. Specify the location where you want to save the Class file, and then click OK.

Once you finish the development of a new control subclass, you can add it to any window. To do so, open a REALbasic project and switch to the appropriate Windows Editor. Next, drag-and-drop an instance of the StatesListBox on to the Project Editor. You can then use the control class just as any other control class provided by REALbasic. To add an instance of it to a window, use the drop-down list located at the top of the Controls pane to select the Project Controls option. This displays a list of all the controls located on the project's Property Sheet, as Figure 8-4 shows.

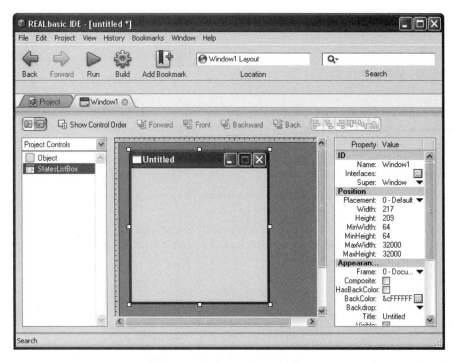

Figure 8-4. *You can instantiate any control subclass located on the Project Editor by dragging-and-dropping it on to a window, as seen on Windows.*

Once visible, you can add this control to the window, just as if it were a built-in REALbasic control. When you test your application, you see this control is automatically populated with entries representing each state.

Working with Noncontrol Classes

To work with control classes, you simply have to add them to windows. However, REALbasic supports a whole range of noncontrol classes, which you can also add to your applications. In fact, you have already done so on a number of occasions. For example, back in Chapter 3, you worked with the Date class when you developed the RB Clock application. Likewise, in Chapter 7, you learned how to work with the EndOfLine class when formatting string output.

To work with classes other than those associated with controls, you need to program-matically instantiate objects based on those classes. The first step in doing this is to define a variable that represents the new object. When you declare the variable, you must also assign it a data type that matches the class from which the object will be instantiated. For example, to work with the Date object, you must define a variable with a data type of Date, as the following shows.

```
Dim dteMyAnniversary
```

Declaring a variable in this manner does not instantiate an object. It merely establishes a reference, which you can then use to instantiate the object using the New keyword, as you see in the following.

```
dteMyAnniversary = New Date
```

■Tip REALbasic also enables you to declare and instantiate an object in a single statement, as the following shows.

```
Dim dteMyAnniversary As New Date
```

Once you instantiate an object, you can access any of the properties and methods belonging to its parent class. For example, in the case of the Date class, you could set its Year property to 1991, as the following shows.

```
dteMyAnniversary.Year = 1991
```

You can work with some classes within REALbasic without having to formally instantiate them using the New keyword. For example, the EndOfLine class's Windows property, which you used in Chapter 7 to control string formatting within data displayed using the MsgBox function, was accessed by simply setting up an expression, as the following shows.

```
MsgBox "Greetings!" + EndOfLine + EndOfLine + "Welcome to my application."
```

The MsgBox function used in the previous example provides you with the capability to display a text message in a pop-up window without having to add a new window to your application, and then configure its interface. While certainly convenient, REALbasic provides a more flexible, object-oriented alternative to the MsgBox function in the form of the MessageDialog class.

The *MessageDialog class* provides you with detailed control over the pop-up window displayed, which you do not get with the MsgBox function. For example, using the MessageDialog class, you can specify what combination of buttons are displayed, what icon is displayed, and which buttons are set up as the default Cancel and Action buttons. You can also specify a high-level explanatory message, as well as a second, more detailed, message string. In addition, on Windows and Linux, you can also specify a string to be displayed in the pop-up window's title bar.

The MessageDialog class is another example of a noncontrol class. To use it, you must instantiate, as the following shows.

```
Dim popup as New MessageDialog
Dim result as New MessageDialogButton
```

This first statement declares a variable named popup and uses it to instantiate a MessageDialog object. The second statement declares a variable named result and uses it to instantiate a MessageDialogButton object.

The MessageDialogButton class represents a button in a MessageDialog pop-up window, which has three possible values, as shown in the following list. Use the MessageDialogButton class and an If…ElseIf…Then block or a Select…Case block to determine which of these buttons the user may have clicked.

- **ActionButton**. A button set up to perform the default action.

- **CancelButton**. A button set up to perform an action if the user clicks Cancel

- **AlternateActionButton**. A button set up to perform an alternative action.

Once instantiated, you can configure any of the MessageDialog class's properties, which you see in the following list:

- **ActionButton**. A button set up to perform the default action.

- **AlternateActionButton**. An optional button set up to perform an alternative action.

- **CancelButton**. An optional button that executes an action if the user clicks Cancel.

- **Explanation**. A text string representing the primary message to be displayed in the pop-up dialog window. On Macintosh, this text string is displayed in a smaller font below the Message property.

- **Icon**. A graphic icon displayed in the pop-up dialog window. You can specify an icon type either as an Integer value or by its REALbasic supplied constant value. Table 8-1 lists the supported range of values for this property.

- **Message**. A text string representing summary text. On Macintosh, this text string is displayed in a larger font just above the Explanation property.

- **Title**. A text string displayed in the titlebar of Windows and Linux pop-up dialog windows.

Table 8-1. *Icons Available for Display by the MessageDialog Class*

Value	Constant	Icon*
-1	GraphicNone	No graphic is display
0	GraphicNote	A Note graphic is displayed
1	GraphicCaution	A Caution graphic is displayed
2	GraphicStop	A Stop graphic is displayed
3	GraphicQuestion	A Question graphic is displayed

* Note: The appearance of these icons varies between operating systems (OSs), especially on the Macintosh, where the Note, Stop, and Question icons are all displayed as application icons.

The MessageDialog class also provides you with access to two methods, which the following shows:

- **ShowModal**. Displays the pop-up dialog windows and returns a value representing the button clicked by the user.

- **ShowModalWithin**. Displays the pop-up dialog as a sheet window (on Macintosh) and returns a value representing the button clicked by the user.

The best way to learn how the MessageDialog class works is to use it. The following example demonstrates how to use the MessageDialog to display a text message, and then determine which button the user clicks.

```
Dim popup As New MessageDialog  'Instantiate a MessageDialog object
Dim result As MessageDialogButton  'Instantiate a MessageDialogButton object

'Set various properties belonging to the MessageDialog class
popup.icon = MessageDialog.GraphicNote  'Display an informational icon
popup.ActionButton.Caption = "Yes"  'Set text shown on the action button
popup.CancelButton.Caption = "No"   'Set text shown on the cancel button
popup.CancelButton.Visible = True    'Display the cancel button
popup.Message = "Application Shutdown" 'Display short message
popup.Explanation = "Are you sure that you want to quit?" 'Display message

'Display the popup windows and capture the button clicked by the user
result = popup.ShowModal

Select Case result  'Figure out which button the user clicked
  Case popup.ActionButton
    'Insert statements here
  Case popup.CancelButton
    'Insert statements here
End select
```

Comments were embedded in this example to explain line-by-line how things work.

Event-Driven Programming

In object-oriented applications, programs typically execute code in response to actions taken by the user. For example, if the user clicks an Open menu item, an application may display an Open file dialog. If the user clicks a PushButton control labeled Exit, the application might terminate its execution. Applications of this nature are referred to as event-driven applications.

Working with Event Handlers

Event-driven programming provides you with the capability to associate program code with events belonging to specific objects. Code associated with a specific event is stored in an *event handler*. When an application runs and events occur, REALbasic automatically tracks all activity and determines when events occur. If an event occurs for which you provided program code, the code statements located in that object's event handler are executed.

REALbasic controls provide the building blocks for developing application interfaces. Each control is designed to respond to a specific collection of actions. For example, the *PushButton control* responds to a number of different actions, such as click and double-click.

If you are new to object-oriented programming, then you may be surprised at the number of different events your REALbasic applications are capable of responding to. REALbasic provides a large collection for controls. Each control has its own particular set of events it is capable of responding to. As Figure 8-5 shows, you can use the Browser windows, located on the left-hand side of the Code Editor, to explore the range of events supported by controls you add to windows.

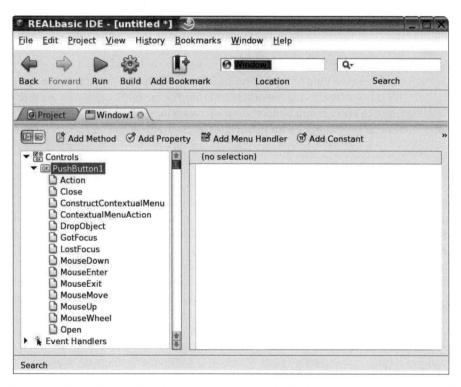

Figure 8-5. *Browsing the list of events supported by the PushButton control, as seen on Linux*

REALbasic organizes controls and their event handlers in a hierarchical fashion in the browser page. To view the event handlers associated with a particular control you added to a window, expand the control's entry in the Browser pane. A list of controls you added to the windows is displayed. Expand any control to see event handlers it supports.

To enter program code you want executed in response to a particular action, select the event hander associated with the affected control and enter the code statements in the right-hand side of the Code Editor.

■**Tip**   Once you add program code to an event handler, REALbasic uses bold text to highlight the event handler and the control in the Code Editor's browser. This makes it easy to identify which controls and event handlers have code associated with them.

Working with Menu Handlers

While REALbasic automatically provides access to event handlers for any control you add to a REALbasic application, it does not do the same for menu handlers. A *menu handler* is similar to an event handler, but it only executes in response to selections made by the user to menu items you add to your REALbasic applications.

To add program code to respond to menu events, you must first add a menu handler to your application. This is done by clicking the Add Menu Handler button located on the Code Editor toolbar. You need to add a menu handler for each menu item you add to your application. More information on how to work with menu handlers is available in Chapter 4.

Working with Modules

As you write more and more REALbasic applications, you may come across situations in which you need to add properties, methods, and constants to your application that are not associated with a particular object. In these situations, where do you define these nonobject-related properties, methods, and constants? The answer is modules.

A *module* is a container for storing nonobject-related resources. Modules are not classes. They do not have a Super Class and you can't use them as a template for creating subclasses. Modules are not instantiated using the New keyword. Module functionality is limited. Modules can only contain properties, methods, and constants.

To help further explain modules and their usefulness, consider a situation in which you are creating a scientific application. This application might need to perform a number of different calculations based on specific formulas. Access to these methods might be required from various parts of the applications. Yet, the calculations themselves might not be associated with a particular object. One way to implement this is to develop methods designed to perform the calculations the application needs to perform. For these methods to execute, they might also need access to a collection of scientific data, such as the value of pi. This data could be stored in constants. In addition, you might want to store data produced by these methods using properties. In this scenario, modules provide a means for storing all the properties, methods, and constants required to perform the scientific calculations.

Adding Modules to REALbasic Applications

Modules are added to REALbasic applications from the Project screen. You can add a new module by clicking the Add Module button on the Project Editor toolbar or by clicking Project ➤ Add ➤ Module, as Figure 8-6 shows. By default, REALbasic names the first module added to application Module1. Using the Properties pane, however, you can rename the module by changing the value assigned to its Name property to something that better describes the module's purpose.

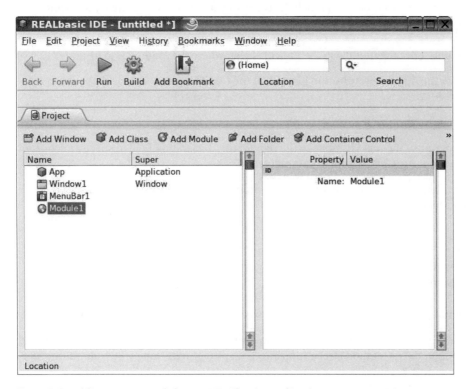

Figure 8-6. *Adding a new module to a REALbasic application, as seen on Linux*

Scoping Modules Resources

Each property, method, and constant you add to a module has a scope that defines which parts of the applications are able to access them. Three different levels of scope are supported, as you see in the following.

- **Global**. Makes the property, method, and constant available to all parts of the application using the name assigned (for example, "dot" notation is not required).

- **Public**. Makes the property, method, and constant available to all parts of the application using "dot" notation (for example, Module1.*ResourceName*).

- **Protected**. Limits access to the property, method, and constant available to code within the module using the name assigned (for example, "dot" notation is not required).

Adding a Property to a Module

You add a property to a module in much the same way that you add a property to a window. The following procedure identifies the steps required to perform this task.

1. Double-click the module in the Project screen where the ~~method~~ *property* is to be added.

2. Click the Add Property button located on the Code Editor toolbar or click Project ➤ Add ➤ Property.

3. Enter the name of the property into the field provided and specify its data type.

4. Click one of the three buttons to the right of the Declaration field to specify a scope for the property (Global, Public, or Protected).

5. Optionally, document the property by adding a comment in the space provided below the Declaration area.

Adding a Method to a Module

You add methods to modules using the same basic procedure used to add methods to windows, as the following procedure outlines.

1. Double-click the module in the Project screen where the method is to be added.

2. Click the Add Method button located on the Code Editor toolbar or click Project ➤ Add ➤ Method. The Method Declaration area is displayed at the top of the code editing area, as Figure 8-7 shows.

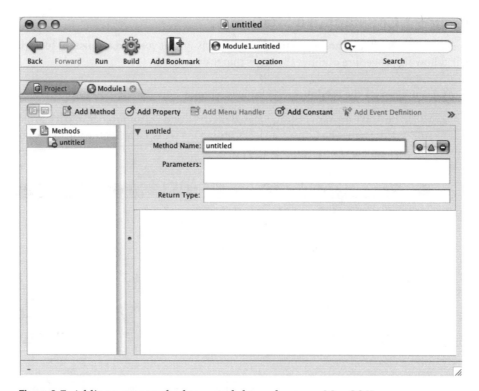

Figure 8-7. *Adding a new method to a module, as shown on Mac OS X*

3. Enter the name of the method in the Method Name field.

4. Enter any required parameters and their data types in the Parameters field.

5. By default, REALbasic defines the method as Subroutine. If necessary, convert the method to a Function by specifying the data type of a value that will be returned by the method.

6. Click one of the three buttons to the right of the Method Name field to specify a scope for the method (Global, Public, or Protected).

Adding a Constant to a Module

You add a constant to a module in much the same way that you add a constant to a window.
The following procedure outlines the steps that are involved.

1. Double-click the module in the Project screen where the ~~method~~ *constant* is to be added.

2. Click the Add Constant button located on the Code Editor toolbar or click Project ➤
   Add ➤ Constant. The Constant Declaration area is displayed at the top of the code editing area, as you see in Figure 8-8.

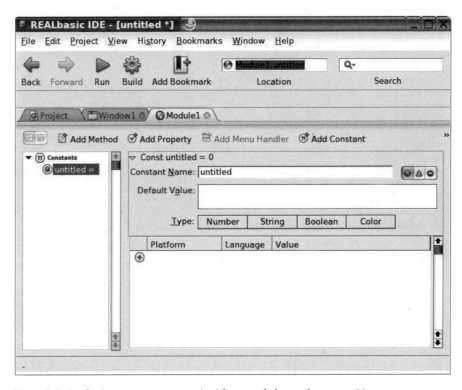

Figure 8-8. *Declaring a new constant inside a module, as shown on Linux*

3. Enter the name of the constant in the Constant Name field.

4. Enter the value to be assigned to the constant in the Default Value field.

5. Specify the data type for the constant by clicking one of the buttons representing the
   Number, String, Boolean, or Color data types.

6. Click one of the three buttons to the right of the Constant Name field to specify a scope
   for the property (Global, Publish, or Protected).

Working with Windows

A key part of any desktop application is the development of its GUI, the foundation of which is windows. Windows store controls and provide an organizational tool for managing properties, methods, and constants. An understanding of how to apply OOP to windows, therefore, is essential to any REALbasic programmer.

·Up to this point in the book, all the applications you worked with have consisted of a single window. REALbasic automatically opened these windows each time you ran your applications. Often, though, applications are made up of collections of different windows. You can add additional windows to your application from the Project screen by clicking the Add Window button located on the Project toolbar or by clicking Project ➤ Add ➤ Window. REALbasic responds by adding a new window to your application, as Figure 8-9 shows. You can then change the window's name or its type by modifying its Name and Frame properties in the Properties pane.

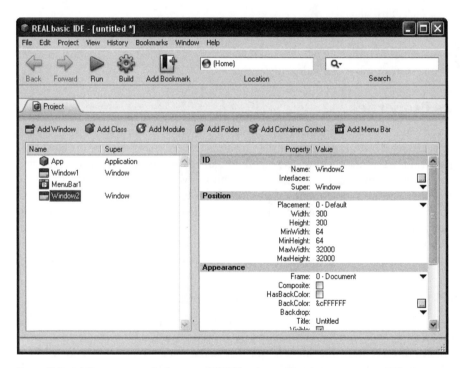

Figure 8-9. *Adding a new window to a REALbasic application, as seen on Windows*

Any time you develop an application that consists of more than one window, you need to know how to open these windows. One way to do this is by making a reference to a property of the window you want opened. For example, if you develop an application that has a second window, which you renamed SupportWindow, you could display it by adding the following code statement to a menu item or PushButton control located on the application's primary window.

```
SupportWindow.Title = "Additional Support"
```

In this example, SupportWindow is opened and the specified text string is displayed in its title bar. If you don't need to make any changes to the window you want to open, you can take a more direct approach to opening it, as you see in the following.

```
SupportWindow.Show
```

Here, the window class's Show method was used to open the window. If you create an application that lets the user open multiple copies of the same window at the same time, as is the case if you create a word processor application that supports the simultaneous opening of multiple document files, you need to take a slightly different approach when you open new windows. Specifically, you need to declare a variable representing each instance of the window the user opens, and then use the New work to instantiate each new instance, just as you do with other types of objects. For example, the following statements open two copies of the same window.

```
Dim w1 As New SupportWindow
Dim w2 As New SupportWindow
```

By using variables to represent windows in this manner, your REALbasic applications can track and manage any number of window instances.

Windows Properties

To REALbasic, a window is simply another type of object. However, because windows provide the foundation of most desktop applications, they are an especially important type of object. You can customize windows by adding properties, methods, and constants to them. These properties, methods, and constants can then be used by the controls you add to these windows.

Properties define information about objects. REALbasic classes provide a number of predefined properties, which are inherited by objects instantiated from these classes. In addition, REALbasic lets you add custom properties to windows to store information specific to a particular object. You learned how to add properties to REALbasic applications as part of the development of the RB Number Guess game in Chapter 6.

Windows Constants

Constants define information that does not change during program execution. REALbasic provides access to a number of predefined constants. In addition, you can add your own constants to application windows to store information specific to a particular object. See Chapter 5 for information on how to add constants to REALbasic windows.

Associating New Methods with Windows

Methods are collections of programming statements. Whether you realize it or not, you have been working with methods from your first REALbasic application. REALbasic makes things easy for you by automatically creating most of the methods you need to work with as you write your applications. In many cases, all you have to do is find the right method and add your program code to it. For example, if you create a new REALbasic application and double-click Window1, REALbasic responds by opening the Code Editor and displaying a place for you to add code statements that will execute when the window opens. If you look at the top of the edit area, you see the following statement:

```
Sub Open()
```

Figure 8-10 shows an example of what you see when you do this on Linux. This statement identifies the beginning of a new method. In this case, the method is a subroutine named Open that does not receive any input when called.

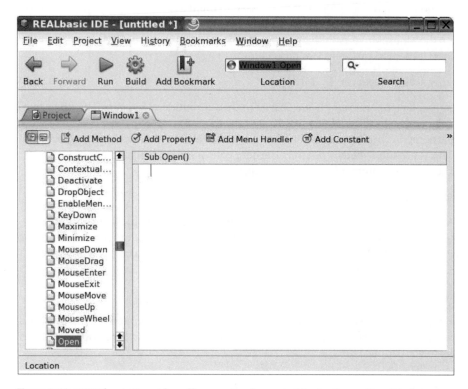

Figure 8-10. *REALbasic Event handlers are implemented in the form of methods, as seen on Linux.*

■**Note** Visual Basic programmers making the switch to REALbasic will appreciate that REALbasic not only automatically builds method statements, but it also removes them from the code-editing area. This makes focusing on the job to be done easier because the opening and closing subroutine and function statements aren't mixed in.

REALbasic methods consist of two parts. The first part is the *parameter line,* where the method name is defined, as well as any parameters that may be passed to the method for processing as input. The second part is the program code you add to make the method do something. REALbasic supports two different types of methods: subroutines and functions.

A *subroutine* is a method that does not return any data when it runs, whereas a *function* is designed to return data.

Methods are a key component of any REALbasic application. All event handles and menu handlers are methods. In addition, you can add additional functionality to your REALbasic applications by adding your own custom subroutines and functions.

Parameter Input

Subroutines and functions can process input passed to them as parameters. To process these parameters, they must be defined in the method's opening statements. For example, if you were to open the MouseMove event handler for Window1, you would see REALbasic automatically sets up this method to accept two parameters.

```
Sub MouseMove(X As Integer, Y As Integer)
```

Both parameters in this example are passed to the subroutine as integers. The first value passed is assigned to a local variable named *X* and the second variable passed is assigned to a local variable named *Y*. Unlike subroutines, functions can return a result to the statements that call them. This is accomplished by defining the data type of the value the function returns at the end of the opening statement, as the following shows.

```
Function MouseWheel(X As Integer, Y As Integer, Delta As Integer) As Boolean
```

Here, REALbasic has set up the MouseWheel event handler for Window1 to accept two Integers as input. This method is also designed to return a Boolean value of True or False to the procedure that calls it. In this example, the programmer must include a code statement that passes back the Boolean value, as the you see in the following.

```
Return True
```

Each of the two methods you just looked at are automatically generated for you by REALbasic. However, you can also add your own custom methods to windows to provide additional functionality to your applications.

Adding Methods to Windows

The following procedure outlines the steps involved in adding a new method to a window.

1. Open the Code Editor for one of the windows in your application.

2. Click the Add Method button or click Project ➤ Add ➤ Method.

3. The Method Declaration area is displayed at the top of the Code Editor.

4. Enter the name to be assigned to the method in the Method Name field.

5. If the method is going to receive input, defining a parameter for each input, separated by commas in the Parameters field. You must also specify the data type for each parameter.

6. If the method will return a value, then you must enter its data type in the Return type field.

7. Click one of the three buttons to the right of the Method Name field to specify a scope of the method (Public, Protected, or Private).

8. Enter the program code statements that will make up the method in the code area.

Note If you are creating a function, REALbasic automatically changes the method to a function as soon as you enter a data type in the Return type field.

The best way to learn to work with custom methods is to look at some examples. Figure 8-11 shows a subroutine named DisplayMsg, created to display any string passed to it as an argument in a pop-up dialog window.

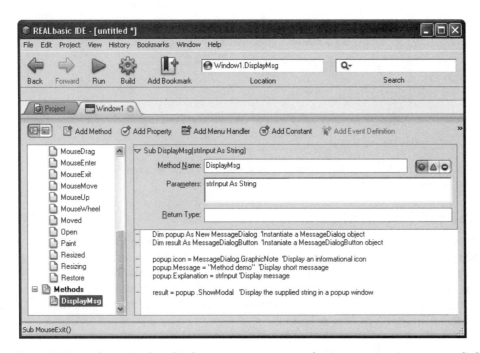

Figure 8-11. *A subroutine that displays any message passed to it as a string in a pop-up dialog, as seen on Windows*

Note Comments are embedded alongside each statement to provide an explanation of what each statement does.

Figure 8-12 shows a function named GetRandomNumber, which was created to return a randomly generated number between 1 and 100.

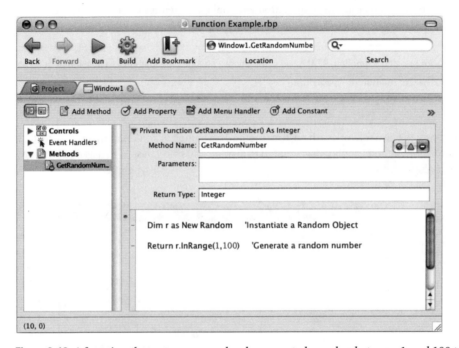

Figure 8-12. *A function that returns a randomly generated number between 1 and 100 to any calling statement, as seen on Mac OS X*

Setting a Default Values for a Parameter

If you need to, you can also provide REALbasic with default values for some or all of your method's parameters. To do so, all you must do is add an assignment statement to the end of each declaration in the Parameters field located in the method declaration area.

Figure 8-13 shows a function with a parameter that includes a default value.

As the following shows, this function might be called, in which case the default value assigned to the function's parameter is used.

```
strSecretNumber = GetRandomNumber
```

On the other hand, this function could be called as you see in the following.

```
strSecretNumber = GetRandomNumber(10)
```

When called this way the function replaces the default value assigned to its parameter with the value passed to it. In this case, it's the number 10.

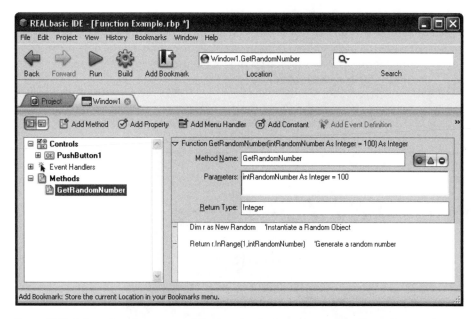

Figure 8-13. *A function that uses a default value in the event no argument is passed, as seen on Windows*

■**Note** You can also specify a parameter as being optional by preceding its declaration with the Optional keyword. When this method is called and a value is not passed for an optional parameter, REALbasic substitutes the default value for the parameter's data type (0 for numbers and "" for strings).

Building the RB Picture Viewer

This chapter concludes by demonstrating how to create another REALbasic desktop application. This application, called the *RB Picture Viewer,* provides the user with a program that can display any of the following graphic file types: .jpeg, .jpg, .gif, .bmp, .pct, and .png.

The development of the RB Picture Viewer demonstrates how to work with the ImageWell control as a tool for displaying graphics. In developing this application, you get the chance to add a constant and a method to the application's main window. You also add a second window to the application and use the Window class's Show method to control its display. Last, you also get the opportunity to put the MessageDialog class to work to develop the display of the application's About menu.

This chapter demonstrates the development of the RB Picture Viewer using the Linux version of REALbasic. However, you can just as easily create this application using the Macintosh or Windows version of REALbasic. All the steps involved are the same. Figure 8-14 provides a look at the RB Picture Viewer when it first starts. The RB Picture Viewer is made up of a single control and is controlled by its menu system.

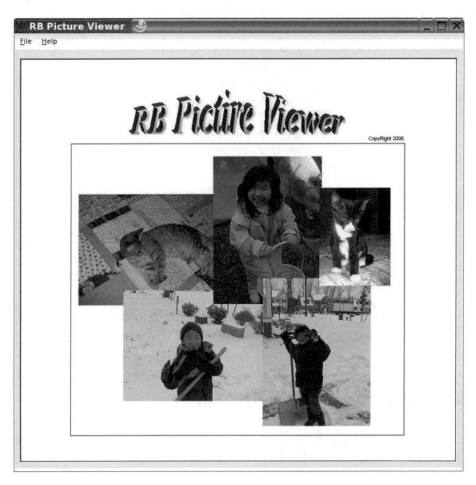

Figure 8-14. *RB Picture Viewer can be used to view an assortment of graphics, as seen on Linux.*

Putting Together the Application's User Interface

The RB Picture Viewer application is made up of a menu system and a single ImageWell control. The first step in creating the application is to create a new REALbasic desktop application. Begin by assigning your application its own icon. You do this by opening the Project Editor and assigning the Icon property for App to Camera.bmp. You can find a copy of this bitmap file on this book's companion CD-ROM.

Next, change the properties for the application's main window (Window1), as specified in Table 8-2.

Table 8-2. *Property Modifications for the RB Picture Viewer Application*

Object	Property	Value
Window1	Title	#cTitlebarMsg
	Width	873
	Height	826
	Resizable	Checked
	MaximizeButton	Checked

Note, the size of the window will be larger than that of the area available in the Window Editor, so you need to scroll up and down to access the entire window. Also, note the specification of #cTitlebarMsg as the Title property's value. The # character tells REALbasic the value being assigned is a constant. You add this constant to the application a little later. Now, add a ImageWell control to Window1 and resize it until it takes up most of the window's available space, and then modify the properties belonging to the ImageWell control, as listed in Table 8-3.

Table 8-3. *Property Modifications for the Imagewell Contol*

Object	Property	Value
ImageWell	Name	ImgDisplay
	LockLeft	Checked
	LockTop	Checked
	LockRight	Checked
	LockBottom	Checked
	Image	RBPictureViewer.bmp*

* You will find a copy of the RBPictureViewer Bitmap file on the book's companion CD-ROM.

Now that Window1 has been set up, let's get to work on its menu system. Start by double-clicking Menubar1 item located on the Projects screen. REALbasic displays a default set of menus and menu items in the MenuBar Editor. The application does not use the Edit menu, so delete Edit menu by selecting it and pressing Delete. Now, modify the menu system by adding and configuring the menu and menu items listed in Table 8-4.

Table 8-4. *Menus and Menu items for the RB Picture Viewer Application*

Menu	Menu Name	Menu Item	Text Property
File	FileOpen		&Open
		FileQuit	E&xit
Help	HelpMenu		&Help
		HelpAbout	&About
		HelpOnlineSupport	O&nline Support

The RB Picture Viewer application provides access to an Online Support web page. This is accomplished by adding a second window to the application, and then adding an HTMLViewer control to display the specified web page.

Begin by opening the Project screen, and then clicking the Add Window button located on the Project Editor toolbar. Select the new window and make the property modifications listed in Table 8-5.

Table 8-5. *Property Modifications for the URLSite Window*

Object	Property	Value
Window2	Name	URLSite
	Title	Online Support Page
	MaximizeButton	Checked

Now add an HTMLViewer control to the URLSite window and resize it, so it takes up most of the available display area. Then, select the HTMLViewer control and make the following property modifications to the window, as Table 8-6 shows.

Table 8-6. *Property Modifications for the URLSite Window*

Object	Property	Value
HTMLViewer	Name	hvrDisplay
	LockLeft	Checked
	LockTop	Checked
	LockRight	Checked
	LockBottom	Checked

Adding Custom Constants and Methods

The RB Picture Viewer application's main window is Window1. This is where most of the application's programming logic is stored. Before the coding process begins, though, you need to add a constant and a method to Window1. The constant is used to store a text string containing the name of the application. This constant is used to display the application's name in the title bar of its main window and in the Help menu's About window. The method is used to store code statements responsible for opening and selecting graphics.

To add the constant, open the Code Editor for Window1. Next, click the Add Constant button located on the Code Editor's tool bar. A constant declaration area is displayed at the top of the code editor. Enter cTitlebarMsg in the Constant Name field and assign a value of RB Picture Viewer in the Default Value field, as Figure 8-15 shows.

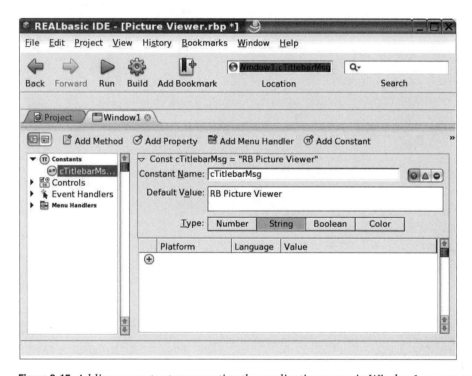

Figure 8-15. *Adding a constant representing the application name in Window1, as seen on Linux*

To add a new method, click the Add Method button located on the Code Editor's tool bar. A method declaration area is displayed at the top of the Code Editor. Enter OpenImage in the Method Name field and assign a value of Picture in the Return Type field, as you see in Figure 8-16.

Figure 8-16. *Defining a new method in the RB Picture Viewer application, as seen on Linux*

Adding a Little Program Code

Once you finish configuring the application's user interface and its menu system, and you add the required constant and method to Window1, it's time to start adding the program code. Start by adding the following code statements to the new OpenImage method you just added to Window1.

```
'Declare variable to represent the FileType object
Dim ImageTypes As New FileType
'Declare a variable representing a Picture object
Dim pctImage As Picture

ImageTypes.Name= "Image Files"  'Specify string identifying supported files

'Specify supported file types
ImageTypes.Extensions=".jpeg; .jpg; .gif; .bmp; .pct; .png"

'Declare variable representing a folder object
Dim f as FolderItem = GetOpenFolderItem(ImageTypes)
```

```
If f <> Nil then   'Perform only if the user did not click on the Cancel
  pctImage = f.OpenAsPicture    'Set variable equal to the select image
  Return pctImage      'Return value representing the selected image
End if
```

■Note Comments embedded alongside each statement provide a detailed explanation of what each statement does.

Next, let's add the code for each of the menu items on MenuBar1. Start by clicking the Add Menu Handler button located on the Code Editor's tool bar, and then select the FileOpen menu item from the MenuItem Name drop-down list. Add the following code statements to the menu item's event handler.

```
'Call the OpenImage Function to retrieve a picture to be displayed
ImgDisplay.Image = OpenImage()
```

Click the Add Menu Handler button again. This time, select the HelpAbout menu item from the MenuItem Name drop-down list. Add the following code statements to the menu item's event handler.

```
Dim mdgAbout as New MessageDialog    'Instantiate a MessageDialog object
Dim mdbResult as MessageDialogButton    'Declare a variable to store result

mdgAbout.Title = cTitlebarMsg     'Display a message in the titlebar
mdgAbout.icon=MessageDialog.GraphicNote    'Display a note icon
mdgAbout.ActionButton.Caption="OK"  'Specify text for the ActionButton

mdgAbout.Message="RB Movie Player"
mdgAbout.Explanation="By Jerry Ford - 2006"

mdbResult  = mdgAbout.ShowModal     'Display the popup dialog
```

Now, click the Add Menu Handler button again. This time, select the HelpOnlineSupport menu item from the MenuItem Name drop-down list. Add the following code statements to the menu item's event handler.

```
URLSite.Show  'Display the URLSite window
```

You are finished adding the program code required for Windows1. Before you begin testing your new application, though, you need to perform one final step. Specifically, you need to open the Code Editor for the URLSite window and add the following code statement to the HTMLViewer control's (hvrDisplay) Open Event handler.

```
hvrDisplay.LoadURL "http://www.apress.com"
```

> ■**Note** The hvrDisplay.LoadURL "http://www.apress.com" statement used to display the application's Online Support pages points to the website of this book's publisher. In real life, you'd want to substitute your own website for this URL.

Testing RB Picture Viewer

If you have not done so yet, go ahead and save your application, and name it RB Picture Viewer. Then, test it to make sure it does not have any errors. If it does have errors, then you probably made a typo or two, which you'll need to track down and correct. If you do not have any image files handy, you can find a small collection of graphics files included along with the source code for this application on the book's companion CD-ROM. Figure 8-17 shows how the RB Picture Viewer looks when viewing one of these sample graphics images.

Figure 8-17. *Viewing a picture using the RB Picture Viewer application, as seen on Linux*

Summary

In this chapter, you learned concepts critical to object-oriented programming. This included learning about REALbasic's class hierarchy and how to work with various REALbasic classes. You learned how to customize REALbasic's built-in classes by adding your own properties, methods, and constants. You learned how to create, customize, export, and import your own control classes. Finally, you learned how to work with modules as a means of making resources available globally to your REALbasic applications.

PART 3

■■■

Advanced Topics

CHAPTER 9

■ ■ ■

Processing Text Files

In Chapter 8, you learned about object-oriented programming and how to work with a number of REALbasic classes. In this chapter, you learn how to use REALbasic to build applications that can open, create, and save text files. This includes learning how to work with a number of new functions and classes. You learn how to interact with files and folders, and how to work with styled text that contains different font types, font sizes, and various styles, such as boldface, italics, and underlined. You also learn how to print text documents. Finally, you put all this new information to work through the development of your own word processing application.

Specifically, you learn how to

- Define different file types within your REALbasic applications

- Work with files and folders

- Work with standard dialog windows

- Read to and write from text files

- Work with styled text

Working with Plain and Styled Text Documents

Nearly any application you might work with today reads and writes to text files in one way or another. A *text file* is a document made up of plain-text characters with no special formatting. On Windows, text documents can be created using Notepad. On Macintosh, you can use the SimpleText application. Different implementations of Linux include an assortment of different text editors, including the VI editor.

Today, most people are used to working with styled text. For example, word processors like Microsoft Word enable you to create formatted documents that include bold, italic, and underlined text. *Styled text* also includes text files that can mix and match font types and font sizes. Using REALbasic, you can create and modify both plain text and styled text files.

Defining File Types

To work with files, REALbasic needs to know a little something about their content. You provide REALbasic with this information by telling it about the file type of the files you want to work within your applications. A *file type* provides information about the content of a file and the manner in which information is stored within it.

On Mac OS X, Windows, and Linux, the file type is identified by the three-character file extension added to the end of filenames. For example, a file with the name SampleReport.doc is a Microsoft Word file, whereas files with extensions of .gif or .jpg are different kinds of graphic files.

■**Note** Mac Classic file types are identified by four-character File Type and Creator codes.

Specifying File Types in Your REALbasic Applications

Telling REALbasic about the different file types you plan on supporting in your applications is easy. REALbasic does this in the form of File Type Sets. A *File Type Set* is a REALbasic item you add to the list of files managed in the Project Editor, and then use to define each file type your application will support.

To add a File Type Set, open the Project Editor screen and click Project ➤ Add ➤ File Type Set. This adds a File Type Set Editor to a REALbasic project, as you see in Figure 9-1.

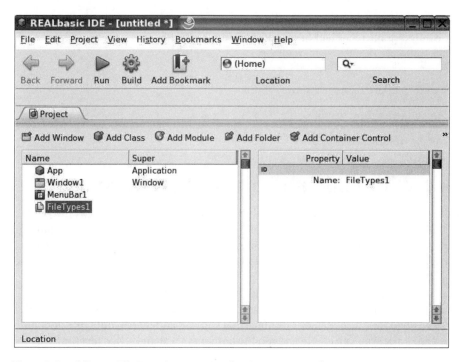

Figure 9-1. *Adding a File Type Set to a REALbasic project, as shown on Linux*

The File Type Set Editor lets you define information about the different types of files your application will support. This information includes the following:

- **Display Name**. The name displayed in a standard dialog window, indicating the file types the application works with.

- **Object Name**. The name of the file type as known to the application. Note, an object name cannot include blank spaces.

- **MacType**. A four-character code that identifies a file type on Mac Classic.

- **MacCreator**. A four-character code used on Mac Classic to identify the file type.

- **Extensions**. A three-character filename extension that identifies the file type on Windows, Linux, and Mac OS X.

- **Icon**. An optional graphic icon that can be used to associate files generated by the application with the application.

To define a new file type, all you have to do is open the File Type Set Editor, click the Add File Types button, and then add an entry for each of the previously discussed fields.

Working with File Types

Once defined, you can begin working with specified file types. For example, the following statement shows how to display the Open file dialog window and configure it to display JPEG files.

```
TargetFile = GetOpenFolderItem(FileTypes1.JPEG)
```

In this example, the Open dialog window is restricted to opening only JPEG files. You can configure the Open dialog window to open multiple files by separating each file type using semicolons, as you see in the following:

```
TargetFile = GetOpenFolderItem(FileTypes1.JPEG;FileTypes1.GIF)
```

If you want, you can configure the Open dialog window so it can open any file types you have defined, as the following shows.

```
TargetFile = GetOpenFolderItem(FileTypes1.All)
```

Accessing Files and Folders

The next step after defining the types of files you'll work with in your application is to set up references to specific files and folders. To REALbasic, files, folders, and the disk drives (or volumes) they reside on are all considered *FolderItems*. REALbasic provides you with a number of ways of establishing references to FolderItems. For example, you can use the Open dialog window or you can specify the pathname to a specific file or folder.

Once you set up a FolderItem reference, you can manipulate it in a number of ways using properties and methods that belong to the FolderItem class. For example, you can use FolderItem properties to get a file or folder's name, and FolderItem methods to copy, move, or delete files and folders.

Specifying File or Folder Location

One way to establish a reference to a file or folder is to specify the path to the file. For example, to access a file that resides in the same folder as REALbasic, you could establish a file reference as shown in the following:

```
Dim TargetFile As FolderItem
TargetFile = GetFolderItem("Config.txt")
```

As you can see, if no path information is provided, REALbasic assumes the specified file resides in the same folder as REALbasic or the completed application. You can now reference the specified file within your program code as TargetFile. Similarly, to access the folder where REALbasic resides, specify "" in place of a filename, as you see in the following:

```
Dim TargetFolder As FolderItem
TargetFolder = GetFolderItem("")
```

To access a file or folder in a different location, you must tell REALbasic in what disk drive the file or folder resides and provide the path to the file or folder. One way to do this is to begin by referencing the disk drive where the file or folder resides, and then use the FolderItem class's Child method.

To reference a specific disk drive, use the Volume function. Each disk drive to which a computer is connected is automatically assigned a volume number, starting with Volume(0), which represents the boot drive (for example, the disk drive where the operating system (OS) files have been installed).

The Child method provides REALbasic with the relative location of a file or folder. For example, the following statements point REALbasic to a file named Config.txt, which is located in a folder named Configuration on the computer's boot drive.

```
Dim TargetFile As FolderItem
TargetFile = Volume(0).Child("Configuration").Child("Config.txt")
```

Another helpful property you may want to use is the Parent property, which can be used to specify a reference to a folder relative to a file or folder it contains. For example, the following statement establishes a reference to the parent folder of the REALbasic folder.

```
Dim TargetFile As FolderItem
TargetFile = GetFolderItem("").Parent
```

Note Once you establish a file or folder reference, you can use any of the FolderItem class's properties to get information about the specified file or folder. For example, the following code statements establish a reference to the REALbasic folder, and then display a pop-up dialog window that shows how many files are stored in that folder using the FolderItem class's Count property.

```
Dim TargetFile As FolderItem
TargetFile = GetFolderItem("")
MsgBox("There are " + Str(TargetFile.Count) + _
   " files in REALbasic's folder")
```

Accessing Special Folders

Macintosh, Windows, and Linux all have certain *special folders* used by specific parts of the OS. For example, both Macintosh and Windows make use of special folders that represents the user's Desktop. Likewise, Linux OSs also have certain folders that have special importance. Examples include each users' /home folder and the /etc, /bin, and /lib folders.

REALbasic helps to make accessing special folders easier by providing a SpecialFolder object that gives you access to properties representing various special folders on Macintosh, Windows, and Linux. For example, the following code statements show how to set up a reference to the Desktop special folder on Macintosh, Windows, and Linux.

```
Dim TargetFolder As FolderItem
TargetFolder = SpecialFolder.Desktop
```

The major advantage of accessing special folders in this manner is you don't have to know or specify the actual location of these folders. REALbasic takes care of determining this for you.

Using Open File and Folder Dialog Windows

In situations where you want to give the user the capability to specify which file an application should open, REALbasic provides you with access to a standard Open dialog window. You can call on the Open dialog window in two ways. The first way is to use the GetOpenFolderItem function, which you saw in Chapter 8, when you created the RB Picture Viewer. As a quick review, look at the following example.

Note Both the GetOpenFolderItem and the OpenDialog class return a value of Nil if the user clicks Cancel instead of selecting a file.

```
Dim TargetFile As FolderItem
TargetFile = GetOpenFolderItem("text")
If TargetFile <> Nil Then
  'Add code to open and process the selected file
End If
```

In this example, the GetOpenFolderItem displays the Open dialog window, waits for the user to select a text file, and then returns a reference to the selected file. The other option open to you is the OpenDialog class. Using this class, you can create a highly customized Open dialog window by setting any of the following properties:

- **Left**. Together, with the Top property, specifies the location where the upper left-hand corner of the Open dialog window is displayed.

- **Top**. Together, with the Left property, specifies the location where the upper left-hand corner of the Open dialog window is displayed.

- **InitialDirectory**. Specifies the default directory opened by the Open dialog window.

- **Filter**. Specifies the types of files that can be opened.

- **ActionButtonCaptain**. Specifies the text displayed on the Action button.

- **CancelButtonCaption**. Specifies the text displayed on the Cancel button.

- **Title**. Specifies the text string displayed in the Open dialog window's title bar.

- **PromptText**. Displays a text message.

The following example demonstrates how to work with the OpenDialog class.

```
Dim dlg as OpenDialog    'Declare variable represening the OpenDialog
Dim TargetFile as FolderItem 'Declare variable to represet a FolderItem
dlg = New OpenDialog    'Instantiate a OpenDialog object

dlg.InitialDirectory = Volume(0).Child("Diary") 'Set default directory
dlg.Title = "Select A Diary Entry"    'Specify a titlebar message
dlg.Filter = "FileTypes1/TEXT"    'Specify accessable file types
'Customise text displayed on the Action button
dlg.ActionButtonCaption = "Open File"

TargetFile = dlg.ShowModal()    'Display the Open dialog window

If TargetFile <> Nil   Then    'Make sure the user selected a file
  'Open and process the selected file
End If
```

Figure 9-2 demonstrates how the customized Open dialog window looks when this example is run.

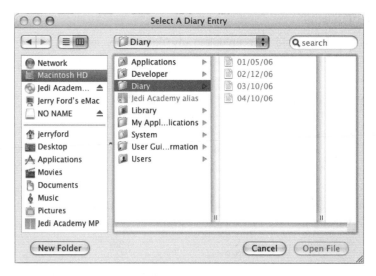

Figure 9-2. *A customized Open dialog window, as seen on Mac OS X*

■Tip You cannot use the standard Open dialog window to select a folder. Instead, REALbasic provides you with access to the SelectFolder function and the SelectFolderDialog class. Instead of returning a reference to a selected file, the SelectFolder function and SelectFolderDialog class return a reference to the selected folder, unless the user clicks the Cancel button, in which case a value of Nil is returned. The SelectFolderDialog class supports the same set of properties as the SelectFileDialog class.

Verifying Path and File or Folder Existence

Things have a tendency to move around a lot on computers, especially on computers shared by two or more people. As a result, files and folders may not always be where you expect them. To guard against this possibility and to prevent errors from occurring, it is important for you to add checks to your program code that ensure a specified path is valid and a specified file or folder exists.

If either of these two conditions is true, REALbasic returns a value of Nil in place of the file or folder reference. You should always check for these.

```
Dim TargetFile As FolderItem
TargetFile = Volume(0).Child("Configuration").Child("Config.txt")
If TargetFile <> Nil Then   'Ensure that the specified path is valid
  If TargetFile.Exists = True  Then 'Ensure that the specified file exists
    'Insert code here to process file
  End If
End If
```

Deleting Files and Folders

Using the FolderItem class's Delete method, you can delete any file or folder, as the following shows.

```
Dim TargetFile As FolderItem
If TargetFile <> Nil Then  'Ensure that the specified path is valid
  If TargetFile.Exists = True  Then 'Ensure that the specified file exists
    TargetFile = Volume(0).Child("Configuration").Child("Config.txt")
    TargetFile.Delete
  End If
End If
```

Be careful when deleting files and folders using the FolderItem class's Delete method. Resources deleted this way are deleted and not sent to the Trash Bin.

Tip Instead of deleting a file, you have the option of moving it into the special trash folder, where it can later be deleted or restored. To accomplish this, use the FolderItem class's MoveFileTo method in conjunction with the Trash special folder, as shown in the following:

```
TargetFile = Volume(0).Child("Configuration").Child("Config.txt")
TargetFile.MoveFileTo(SpecialFolder.Trash)
```

Process Text Files

Once your application has created or opened a text file, you'll want to do something with it. This means reading its contents, writing something to it, or, perhaps, just printing it, which is discussed in the section "Printing Files."

Reading from Text Files

As you might expect, REALbasic provides a number of different ways of reading from text files. For example, you can read a file all at once or you can read and process it line by line. One way to read a text file is to use the TextInputStream's ReadLine method, as you see in the following example.

```
Dim InputFile As FolderItem   'Declare a variable representing the FolderItem object
'Declare a variable representing the TextInputStream object
Dim SourceStream As TextInputStream

'Display the Open dialog window
InputFile = GetOpenFolderItem("FileTypes1/PlainText")
```

```
If InputFile <> Nil Then   'Make sure the user did not click on Cancel

  'Retrieve a reference to the TextInputStream
  SourceStream = InputFile.OpenAsTextFile

  While Not SourceStream.EOF  'Loop until end-of-file is reached
    'Write a line from the source file to the EditField
    EditField2.Text = EditField2.Text + SourceStream.ReadLine + EndOfLine
  Wend

  SourceStream.Close   'Close the file once it has been read

End If
```

As you can see, a FolderItem reference is established using the GetOpenFolderItem function. Then, a check is made to make sure the user did not click the Open dialog window's Cancel button. Next, a reference to the TextInputStream is set up, using the FolderItems class's OpenAsTextFile method. TextInputStream is responsible for copying text from the file to the application. This is accomplished using a While…Wend loop that repeatedly executes the ReadLine method, pulling in a line of text at a time. The While…Wend loop iterates until the file's end-of-file marker is reached. Also, note, this example ends by executing the TextInputStream object's Close method. This is a critical step that ensures the file is properly closed and made available to other applications.

Or, you can read a file in a single step, instead of processing it line by line, as the following shows. To do so, you use the TextInputStream class's ReadAll method.

```
Dim InputFile As FolderItem  'Declare a Folderitem variable

'Declare variable representing a TextInputStream
Dim SourceStream As TextInputStream

InputFile = GetOpenFolderItem("text/plain")  'Display the Open dialog

If InputFile <> Nil Then   'Make sure user did not click on Cancel

  'Retrieve a reference to the TextInputStream
  SourceStream = InputFile.OpenAsTextFile

  'Write the contents of the file into the EdifField
  EditField1.Text = SourceStream.ReadAll

  SourceStream.Close   'Close the file once it has been read

End If
```

Writing to Text Files

The FolderItem class also provides you with methods for writing text to files. For example, using the AppendToTextFile method, you can add text to the end of any file. If you want to work with a new text file, you can use the CreateTextFile method instead. Both of these methods return a TextOutputStream object. This object provides access to methods you can use to write to the file. The following example shows how to write to a new text file using the CreateTextFile method.

```
'Declare a variable representing the FolderItem object
Dim OutputFile As FolderItem

'Declare a varialbe representing the TextOutputStream object
Dim OutputStream As TextOutputStream

'Display the Save dialog window
OutputFile = GetSaveFolderItem("FileTypes1/PlainText", "untitled.txt")

'Make sure the user did not click on the Cancel button
If OutputFile <> Nil Then

  OutputStream = OutputFile.CreateTextFile   'Create a new text file

  'Write the contents of the EditField to the specified file
  OutputStream.WriteLine EditField1.Text

  OutputStream.Close   'Close the file once it has been read

End If
```

As you can see, this example uses the TextOutputStream object's WriteLine method to write the contents of single line EditFields to a text file. The TextOutputStream object's Close method is then executed as the final step of working with the file.

Working with Styled Text

REALbasic EditField controls provide you with the capability to handle both plain and styled text. *Styled text* is text that has been formatted in some manner. Using the EditField control, you can add word processing-like capabilities to any REALbasic application. All that's required is to enable the EditField control's Styled property.

Examples of styled text include text that has been underlined or text that has been made italic or bold. Styled text also includes text that consists of different fonts and font sizes. The EditField control provides a set of methods you can use to toggle off and on different font styles. For example, the following statement would toggle the display of text between bold and nonbold.

```
EditField1.ToggleSelectionBold
```

Likewise, the following two statements could be used to toggle between italic and underline font styles.

```
EditField1.ToggleSelectionItalic
EditField1.ToggleSelectionUnderline
```

In similar fashion, you can use the EditField control's SelTextSize and SelTextFont properties to change the font size and font type of any selected text. For specific examples of how to work with EditField properties related to styled text, check out the RB Word Processor application in the section "Creating a REALbasic Word Processor."

Reading Styled Text

The preceding examples showed how to read and write plain text files. However, if your application contains Styled text, you'll need to use different methods to ensure the styled text is properly handled. For example, to read a file containing styled text, you need to use the FolderItem class's OpenStyledEditField method to read it, as shown in the following.

```
'Declare variable representing the FolderItem object
Dim SourceFile as FolderItem

SourceFile = GetOpenFolderItem("Text")    'Display the Open dialog

If SourceFile <> Nil Then    'Make sure user did not click on Cancel

  'Read and copy the contents of the file into the EditField
   SourceFile.OpenStyledEditfield EditField1

End If
```

In this example, the contents of the text file selected by the user are read into an EditField control, preserving any styled text. Note, for this example to work, the EditField control's Multiline and Styled properties must be enabled.

Writing Styled Text to Files

To write a file containing styled text to a file, you need to use the SaveStyledEditField method, as the following shows.

```
'Declare a variable representing the FolderItem object
Dim SourceFile as FolderItem

'Display the Save dialog window
SourceFile = GetSaveFolderItem("plain/text","Untitled.rtf")
```

```
If SourceFile <> Nil Then  'Make sure the user did not click on Cancel

  'Write the contents of the EditField to the specified text file
  SourceFile .SaveStyledEditField EditField1

End If
```

This example takes any styled text located in an EditField1 and writes it to a file, while preserving its format.

Saving Files

Once your application is done making changes to a text file, you'll want to save it. To do so, you can use either the GetSaveFolderItem function or the SaveAsDialog class to display the standard Save As dialog window, which the user can then use to specify the name and location where the file should be saved.

To use the GetSaveFolderItem function, you need to specify the file type and a default name for the file. The file type should match the information stored in the application's File Set Type. For example, the following code statements demonstrate how to display the standard Save As dialog window to enable the user to specify the name and location where the file should be stored.

```
Dim TargetFile As FolderItem
TargetFile = GetSaveFolderItem("text", "Untitled")
If TargetFile <> Nil Then
  'Insert code here to save file
End If
```

Note, in this example, a default filename of Untitled was specified.

The SaveAsDialog class supports all the properties supported by the OpenDialog and SelectFolderDialog classes. In addition, the SaveAsDialog class also supports the SuggestedFileName property, which you can use to provide the user with a suggested default name for the file being saved. See the following example.

```
Dim dlg as SaveAsDialog  'Declare variable representing the SaveAsDialog
Dim TargetFile as FolderItem 'Declare variable to represent a FolderItem
dlg = New SaveAsDialog   'Instantiate a SaveAsDialog object

dlg.InitialDirectory = Volume(0).Child("Diary") 'Set default directory
dlg.SuggestedFileName = "Untitled"   'Specify a default filename
dlg.Title = "Save Diary File"   'Specify a titlebar message

'Customise text displayed on the Action and Cancel buttons
dlg.ActionButtonCaption = "Save File"
dlg.CancelButtonCaption = "Don't Save"
```

```
TargetFile = dlg.ShowModal()'Display the Open dialog window

If TargetFile <> Nil then    'Make sure the user selected a file
  'Enter statement to save file
End If
```

Printing Files

In addition to opening, writing to, reading from, and saving files, REALbasic lets you print them. REALbasic also provides you with the capability to display a Page Setup dialog window to enable the user to specify printing preferences. REALbasic also lets you display a Print dialog, and to print both styled and nonstyled text. And, REALbasic provides you with the capability to print directly to the printer, without using the Print dialog at all.

Working with the Page Setup Dialog Window

You might want to use the Page Setup dialog window in any application you let the user create and print documents. In the section "Creating a REALbasic Word Processor," you see it used in a word processor application.

To display and work with the Page Setup dialog window, shown in Figure 9-3, you need to define and instantiate a PrinterSetup object, which provides access to settings from the Page Setup dialog. You also want define a variable to store print settings provided by the Page Setup dialog. You can then display the dialog and assign its settings, as seen the following example.

Figure 9-3. *Collecting user print settings using the Page Setup dialog window, as seen on Windows*

```
Dim prs as PrinterSetup    'Declare a PrinterSetup variable

'Define a variable to hold Page Setup settings
Dim strPrintSettings As String

prs = New PrinterSetup    'Instantiate the Printer Setup object

If prs.PageSetupDialog then 'Display the Page Setup dialog window
   strPrintSettings = prs.SetupString   'Assign Page Setup settings
End if

MsgBox strPrintSettings   'Display print settings
```

In this example, all the settings managed by the Page Setup dialog window are assigned to a variable named strPrintSettings. The contents of this variable are then displayed in a pop-up window, as you see in Figure 9-4. However, if the user clicks on Cancel, a Nil value is returned in place of print settings.

Figure 9-4. *Examining the settings stored in the Page Setup dialog window, as seen on Windows*

■**Note** The Linux version of REALbasic does not support the Page Setup dialog window. If you attempt to use it, REALbasic returns a value of False and the dialog window is not displayed.

Using the Print Dialog Window

To present the user with a Print dialog, you can use the OpenPrinterDialog function. If the user clicks the dialog's OK button, REALbasic returns a graphic's object whose methods can then be used to print the file. Otherwise, a Nil value is returned. The following example demonstrates how to work with the OpenPrinterDialog function.

```
Dim gphFile As Graphics    'Declare a Graphics object

gphFile = OpenPrinterDialog()    'Display the Print dialog window

If gphFile<> Nil Then   'Submit print job if user didn't click on Cancel

  'Print text with a 1-inch margin on the left and top side of the page
  gphFile.DrawString _
    "Once upon a time there was a little boy named William.", 100, 100

  gphFile.NextPage    'print the current page and create a new page

  'Print text with a 1-inch margin on the left and top side of the page
  gphFile.DrawString "The End!", 100, 100

End
```

REALbasic uses the Graphics object to handle printing, which is why the preceding example began by declaring a Graphics object named gphFile. Next, the OpenPrinterDialog function was used to display the Print dialog windows, as Figure 9-5 shows.

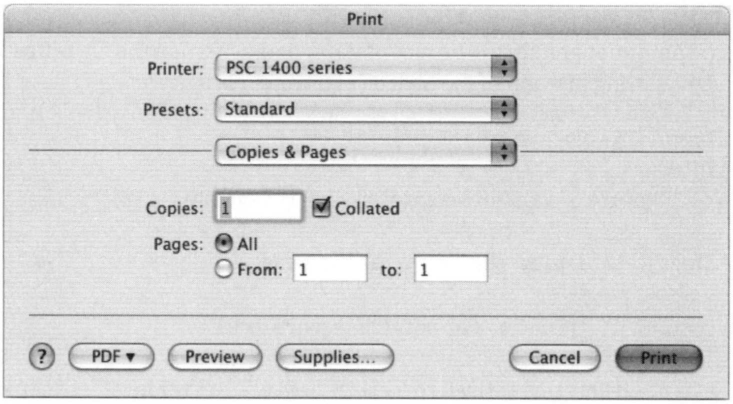

Figure 9-5. *Displaying the Print dialog window on Mac OS X*

If the user clicks Cancel, a value of Nil is returned and nothing happens. Otherwise, the Graphic class's DrawString method is used to draw text. The text is drawn at a location specified by *X* and *Y* coordinates. These coordinates represent pixel locations starting from the upper left-hand corner of the printed page. Next, the Graphic class's NextPage method is used. This method prints the current page and creates a new one. A second page is then drawn and printed in similar fashion.

Bypassing the Print Dialog Window

If you prefer, you can skip the display of the Print dialog window and use the OpenPrinter function to handle file printing. Except for pausing to display a Print dialog window, this function works identically to the OpenPrinterDialog function, as the following example shows.

```
Dim gphFile As Graphics    'Declare a Graphics object

gphFile = OpenPrinter()    'Retrieve a Graphics object required to print

'Print text with a 1-inch margin (72 pixels equals an inch)
'on the left and top side of the page
gphFile.DrawString _
   "Once upon a time there was a little boy named William.", 72, 72

gphFile.NextPage    'Print the current page and create a new page

'Print text with a 1-inch margin (72 pixels equals an inch)
'on the left and top side of the page
gphFile.DrawString "The End!", 72, 72
```

Printing Styled Text

If a file contains styled text, you want to retain the format of the styled text when the file prints. To do so, you can use the DrawString method of the StyledTextPrinter class.

```
'Declare a variable representing the StyledText printer class
Dim stp As StyledTextPrinter
Dim gphFile As Graphics    'Declare a variable representing the Graphic class

gphFile = OpenPrinterDialog()    'Display the Print dialog window

If gphFile <> Nil then    'Print if the user did not click on Cancel

  'Use the EditField's StyledTextPrinter method to return a StyledTextPrinter object
  'using the specified Graphics object and width (in pixels)
  stp = EditField1.StyledTextPrinter(gphFile, 72 * 7.5) 'Pixels times inches

  'Specify start coordinated of the upper left-hand corner of the print page and the
  'height of the printed image
  stp.DrawBlock 100, 100, 72 * 10   '72 pixels by 10 inches

End If
```

Notice, in this example, the DrawBlock method was used in place of the DrawString method, which is a requirement for printing styled text.

Creating a REALbasic Word Processor

This chapter wraps up by showing you how to create a REALbasic word processor application. This application, called the RB Word Processor, gives you a chance to work with most of the information you learned in this chapter.

This chapter demonstrates how to develop the RB Word Processor using the Windows version of REALbasic. However, as with the other sample applications you worked on in this book, you can also create the application using either the Macintosh or Linux version of REALbasic. All the steps are the same. Figure 9-6 provides a look at the RB Word Processor in action. As you can see, it consists of a menu system, an EditField control, and a number of PushButton and BevelButton controls.

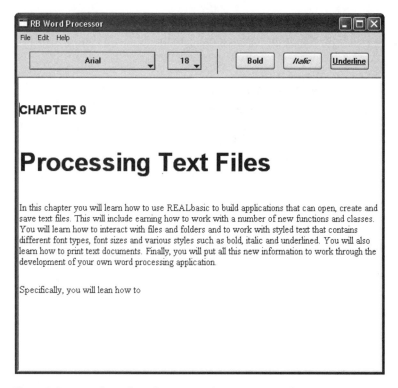

Figure 9-6. *A sneak peak at the RB Word processor application*

Putting Together the User Interface

The first step in creating the RB Word Processor application is to create a new desktop application. Next, modify the properties specified in Table 9-1.

Table 9-1. *Property Modifications for the RB Word Processor Application*

Object	Property	Value
Window1	Name	EditorWindow
	Title	RB Word Processor
	Width	587
	Height	536
	Resizable	Checked
	MaximizeButton	Checked

Now, add an EditField control to the window and resize it until it takes up most of the window's available space. Next, modify the properties belonging to the EditField control, as you see in Table 9-2.

Table 9-2. *Property Modifications for the EditField Control*

Object	Property	Value
EditField1	Name	edfTextArea
	Left	0
	Top	50
	Width	587
	Height	486
	LockLeft	Checked
	LockTop	Checked
	LockRight	Checked
	LockBottom	Checked
	MultiLine	Checked
	Styled	Checked

Now, it's time to add controls that will be used to format text. First, drag-and-drop a BevelButton control to the upper left-hand area of the window, just above the EditField control. The *BevelButton control* is similar to the PushButton control, except it can be configured to act like a drop-down list, which is how it is used in this application. Specifically, this control is used to display a list of fonts. Modify its properties as shown in Table 9-3.

Table 9-3. *Property Modifications for the First BevelButton Control*

Object	Property	Value
BevelButton1	Name	bbFontType
	Caption	
	Hasmenu	1 – Normal menu
	Bold	Checked
	TextSize	0

Add another BevelButton control just to the right of the first one. This control is used to display a list of font sizes. Modify its properties, as you see in Table 9-4.

Table 9-4. *Property Modifications for the Second BevelButton Control*

Object	Property	Value
BevelButton2	Name	bbFontSize
	Caption	
	Hasmenu	1 – Normal menu
	Bold	Checked
	TextSize	0

Now, select the Line control, and then draw a vertical line about a quarter inch to the right of the second BevelButton control. This line is used to visually organize and separate the two BevelButton controls from the other controls you are about to add.

Next, add three PushButton controls to the right of the Line control, and then modify their properties, as you can see in Table 9-5.

Table 9-5. *Property Modifications for the Three PushButton Controls*

Object	Property	Value
PushButton1	Name	pbBold
	Caption	Bold
	Bold	Checked
PushButton2	Name	pbItalics
	Caption	Italic
	Bold	Checked
	Italic	Checked

Continued

Table 9-5. *Continued*

Object	Property	Value
PushButton3	Name	pbUnderline
	Caption	Underline
	Bold	Checked
	Underline	Checked

Now that the window and its controls are set up, it's time to put together the application's menu system. Double-click the Menubar1 item located on the Projects screen. REALbasic displays a default set of menus and menu items. Modify the menu system by adding and configuring the menu and menu items you see in Table 9-6.

Table 9-6. *Menus and Menu Items for the RB Word Processor Application*

Menu	Menu Name	Menu Item	Text Property	Key	MenuModifier
File	FileMenu		&File		
		FileNew	&New	N	Checked
		FileOpen	&Open	O	Checked
		FileSave	&Save	S	Checked
		FilePrint	&Print	P	Checked
Help	HelpMenu		&Help		
		HelpAbout	&About		

The menu items for the File menu should be added in the order listed in Table 9-6. In addition, you should also add three Line Separator bars. Place the first Line Separator bar after the Open menu item, add the second one just after the Save menu item, and put the last one just after the Print menu item. Once this is done, the application's interface is complete.

Defining Supported File Types

To work properly, you must tell REALbasic what types of files the RB Word Processor should work with. To do this, you need to add a File Type Set by opening the Project Editor and clicking Project ➤ Add ➤ File Type Set. Next, open the File Type Set Editor by double-clicking the File Type Set you just created and click the Add File Types button.

The RB Word Processor application should handle both text and rtf files, so you need to add two separate entries to the File Type Set. For the first entry, enter a Display Name of rtf, an Object Name of rtf, a MacType of TEXT, a MacCreator of MSWD, and an .rtf Extension. For the second entry, enter a Display Name of text, an Object Name of text, a MacType of Text, a MacCreator of ????, and a .txt Extension.

Adding Custom Constants and Properties

This application makes use of the MessageDialog class to display pop-up windows. To standardize the display of the text displayed in the title bar of these pop-up windows, a constant name cTitlebarMsg is added to the application's window. To do so, open the EditorWindow screen and click the Add Constant button. Name the constant cTitlebarMsg and assign it a default value of RB Word Processor. Then, click the String button to specify its data type.

You also need to add a pair of custom properties to the application. To add the first property, click the Add Property button, declare a new property with a name of NewChanges, and assign it a date type of Boolean as follows:

```
NewChanges As Boolean
```

The application toggles the value assigned to this property to identify when a text document has an unsaved change. Next, click the Add Property button again and type the following statement into the declaration field:

```
PageSetup As String
```

This property is used to store Page Setup settings specified by the user when printing text files. Now that you've added the application's custom constants and properties, all that remains is to add the program code required to tie everything together.

Adding Code That Supports the Menu System

Like most desktop applications, the RB Word Processor makes a lot of its functionality available to the user via its menu system. Because this application involves a fairly sizeable amount of code, the code for each menu item is covered separately in the sections that follow.

Coding the New Menu Item

The first menu item located in the File menu is the New menu item. When selected, a new window should be opened, enabling the user to begin working on a new document while keeping any other windows open. The user should be able to open a new text document at any time, even when the application does not have any visible windows displayed.

Menu systems on Windows and Linux are attached directly to the top of Windows. However, on the Macintosh, menu systems are displayed at the top of the viewing area. On Macintosh, it is possible for no windows to be visible and yet to have the application's menu system displayed. To support the application on Macintosh, you need to make the New menu item available at all times, even when no windows are open. Therefore, adding the menu handler for the New menu item to the window will not suffice. Instead, you need to add the menu handler to the App class object. Any code added to the App class object is made available to the entire application, not only to a particular window.

To add the menu handler for the New menu item, select the App screen and click the Add Menu Handler button. Enter FileMenu in the MenuItem Name field, and then add the following code statements.

```
'Declare a variable representing a new window
Dim TextWindow as EditorWindow
TextWindow = New EditorWindow  'Instantiate and display the new window
```

The first statement declares a variable named TextWindow based on the EditorWindow. The next line instantiates and displays the new window, enabling the user to work with more than one text document at a time.

Coding the Open Menu Item

The following shows the code for the FileOpen menu handler. This code, like the rest of the code in this application, is associated with the application's window and not with the App class object. It uses the GetOpenFolderItem function to display a standard Open dialog window and enables the user to select a text file. On Windows, the Open dialog displays RTF files. On Macintosh and Linux, TEXT files are displayed in the dialog.

```
Dim SourceFile As FolderItem   'Declare a variable representing the FolderItem
Dim TextWindow as EditorWindow   'Declare a variable representing a Window

'Display different file types based on the operating systems in use
#If TargetWin32 = True
   SourceFile = GetOpenFolderItem("rtf")  'On Windows use RTF
#Else
   SourceFile = GetOpenFolderItem("text") 'On Macintosh/Linux use Text
#Endif

If SourceFile <> Nil then 'Make sure the user did not click on cancel

   TextWindow = New EditorWindow   'Instantiate a new window

   'Open new window and display contents of the file (as styled text)
   SourceFile.OpenStyledEditField TextWindow.edfTextArea

   'Set the titlebar text equal to name of the file
   TextWindow.Title = SourceFile.Name

End If
```

If the user selects a file, the OpenStyledEditField method is used to open it, so any styled text in the file is retained.

Coding the Save Menu Item

The following shows the code for the FileSave menu handler. It uses the GetSaveFolderItem function to display a standard Save As dialog window and the SaveStyledEditField function to save the text document using the user supplied filename.

```
Dim TargetFile As FolderItem   'Declare a FolderItem variable
```

```
'Display different file types based on the operating systems in use
#If TargetWin32 = True
  TargetFile  = GetSaveFolderItem("rtf", "Untitled")  'Windows uses RTF
#Else
  'Macintosh and Linux uses TEXT
  TargetFile  = GetSaveFolderItem("text", "Untitled")
#Endif

If TargetFile  <> Nil Then  'Make sure the user did not click on cancel

  'Save contents of EditField in the specified file (as styled text)
  TargetFile.SaveStyledEditField edfTextArea

  'Set the titlebar text equal to the name of the opened file
  Title = TargetFile.Name

  'Disable the FileSave menu item
  FileSave.Enabled = True

  'Since changes have been saved set NewChanges property to False
  NewChanges = False

End If
```

Note, the method ends by displaying the FileSave menu item and changing the value of NewChanges property to False, indicating no unsaved changes exist. For the Save menu to work properly, it needs to be enabled at the appropriate time. This is accomplished by opening the TextChange event handler belonging to the edfTextArea control and adding the following statements.

```
'Update this property to show that the user has made a change
NewChanges = True
```

This event handler executes any time the user makes a change in edfTextArea. To finish things up for the Save menu item, you also need to add the following code statements to the edfTextArea control's EnableMenuItems event handler.

```
'If this property is equal to True then enable the Save menu item
If NewChanges = True Then
  FileSave.Enabled = True
End If
```

This menu handler executes any time the user accesses the application's menu system. Its job is to enable the Save menu item when the value of NewChanges is set equal to True.

Coding the Print Menu Item

The next step is to add the code for the FilePrint menu handler. Begin by keying in the following code statements.

```
Dim PrintSettings As PrinterSetup    'Declare a PrinterSetup variable
Dim StpObject As StyledTextPrinter 'Declare StyledTextPrinter variable
Dim GObject As Graphics    'Declare a Graphics object variable

'Set default width and height settings
Dim PrintWidth As Integer =  504  '504 pixels equals 7.5 inches
Dim PrintHeight As Integer = 648  '648 pixels equals 9 inches
```

As you can see, a PrinterSetup object is declared, followed by a StyledTextPrinter and a Graphics object. The StyledTextPrinter object is used to allow the application to print styled text and the Graphics object's DrawBlock method is used to print the text document. A pair of variables is then declared. These variables are used to define the width and height of printed pages.

Next, append the following code statements to the FilePrint menu handler. Because Linux does not provide support for the Print Setup dialog, a #If...#EndIf block is set up to allow the embedded code statements to execute only on Windows and Macintosh.

```
#If TargetLinux = False Then  'Linux does not have a Print Setup dialog

  PrintSettings = New PrinterSetup 'Instantiate the PrinterSetup object

  'Load any settings previously specified by the user
  If PageSetup <> "" Then
    PrintSettings.SetupString = PageSetup  'Assign saved print settings
  End if

  'Display the Page Setup dialog and collect setting updates
  If PrintSettings.PageSetupDialog Then
    PageSetup = PrintSettings.SetupString  'Save print settings
  End if

  If PageSetup <> "" Then   'If specified use Page Setup settings
    PrintSettings.SetupString = PageSetup  'Assign the settings
    PrintWidth = PrintSettings.Width  'Retrieve the width setting
    PrintHeight = PrintSettings.Height   'Retrieve the height setting
    'Display the Print dialog using the above settings
    GObject = OpenPrinterDialog(PrintSettings)
  Else  'Use hardcoded value for page height and width
    GObject = OpenPrinterDialog() ' Display default Print dialog
  End If

#Else
  GObject = OpenPrinterDialog()  'Display the Print dialog on Linux
#Endif
```

As you can see, a PrinterSetup object is instantiated. Then, any previously specified print settings set by the user are assigned to the SetupString property belonging to the PrintSettings PrinterSetup object. A Page Setup dialog is then displayed, enabling the user to change print settings. If the user made any changes to the page Setup settings, they are retrieved and passed to the OpenPrinterDialog function. If the user did not make any change to the Page Setup settings, the OpenPrinterDialog is called without being passed any settings.

The last statement embedded in the #If…#EndIf block only executes if the application is run on a Linux system, in which case all the preceding statements are skipped and the OpenPrinterDialog functions is executed. Note, each time the OpenPrinterDialog function is called, a value is assigned to GObject. Now, to finish the FilePrint menu handler, append the following code statements to the statements you just keyed in.

```
If GObject <> Nil Then 'Make sure the user did not press Cancel button

  'Pass the graphics object to the EditField's StyledTextPrinter method
  'Pad the PrintWidth value by a half inch to accomidate styled text
  StpObject = edfTextArea.StyledTextPrinter(GObject, PrintWidth - 36)
  Do Until StpObject.EOF   'Loop until every page has been printed
    'Set the location of the upper left-hander corner
    StpObject.DrawBlock 36, 36, PrintHeight
    If Not StpObject.EOF Then  'if not at end of page keep going
      GObject.NextPage   'Set up a new page
    End If
  Loop

End If
```

These code statements check to make sure the user did not click the Print Dialog's Cancel button and are responsible for printing document text a page at a time, using the Graphic class's DrawBlock method.

Coding the Exit (Quit) Menu Item

The following shows the code for the FileQuit menu handler. It uses the MessageDialog class to display a pop-up dialog window in case the user tries to close down the application without saving any unsaved changes in a text file.

```
If NewChanges = True Then   'Display popup if there are unsaved changes

  'Declare and instantiate a MessageDialog object
  Dim mdgAbout as New MessageDialog
  Dim mdbResult as MessageDialogButton 'Declare variable to hold result

  'Update the display of text in the titlebar
  mdgAbout.Title = "Warning: You have unsaved changes!"
  mdgAbout.icon = MessageDialog.GraphicCaution    'Display caution icon
  mdgAbout.ActionButton.Caption = "Quit Anyway"  'Set ActionButton text
  mdgAbout.CancelButton.Visible = True   'Display of the Cancel button
  mdgAbout.Message = "You have unsaved changes."  'Display a summary
```

```
    'Display primary warning message
    mdgAbout.Explanation = _
      "Please confirm that you still want to close this application."

    mdbResult  = mdgAbout.ShowModal      'Display the popup dialog

    If mdbResult = mdgAbout.CancelButton Then 'The user clicked on Cancel
      Return True    'Prevent the window from closing
    End If
  End If
End If
```

Note the Return True statement in the last If...Then statement. This statement executes when the user elects to click the pop-up dialog window's Cancel button. By returning a value of True, this statement stops the application from closing. This enables the user to save any unsaved text files before exiting the RB Word Processor application.

Coding the Help Menu's About Menu Item

The following shows the code for the HelpAbout menu handler. It uses the MessageDialog class to display a pop-up dialog window that gives the user a little information about the application and its author.

```
'Declare and instantiate a MessageDialog object
Dim mdgAbout as New MessageDialog
Dim mdbResult as MessageDialogButton 'Declare a variable to hold result

mdgAbout.Title = cTitlebarMsg     'Display a message in the titlebar
mdgAbout.icon=MessageDialog.GraphicNote     'Display a note icon
mdgAbout.ActionButton.Caption="OK"     'Specify ActionButton text

mdgAbout.Message="RB Word Processor"
mdgAbout.Explanation="By Jerry Ford - 2006"

mdbResult  = mdgAbout.ShowModal      'Display the popup dialog
```

Adding Code That Supports the Window and Its Controls

To wrap up your work on the RB Word Processor application, you need to add the code statements required to make the application's controls function. This includes BevelButton controls, the three PushButton controls, and the addition of a little code to the EditField control's SelChange event handler.

Coding the bbFontType Control

Let's begin by selecting the bbFontType control's Action event handler and adding the following code statements. The first code statement is responsible for displaying whichever font the user might select in the BevelButton control's Caption.

```
'Set the BevelButton's caption equal to the value selected by the user
bbFontType.Caption = bbFontType.List(bbFontType.MenuValue)

'Set the font type of the selected text equal to the font type
'specified in the BevelButton control's Caption
edfTextArea.SelTextFont = bbFontType.Caption
```

Earlier, when you added the application's EditField control, you left its TextFont and Text-Size properties equal to System and 0. The result of this is the default font and font size of each OS is used as the application's default font and font size. By selecting a different font type from the BevelButton control's drop-down list, the user can change the font type applied by the word processor. The last statement's job is to update the font type applied to any currently selected text.

For the user to be able to select a font type, a list of available fonts must first be loaded into the BevelButton control. You can accomplish this by adding the following code statements to the bbFontType control's Open event handler.

```
'Declare variable to be used as a counter in a For...Next loop
Dim intCounter As Integer

'Loop through each font and add to list in the BevelButton control
'FontCount is a function that returns the number of fonts installed
For intCounter = 1 to FontCount - 1
  'Font is a function that retrieves the names of fonts
  bbFontType.AddRow Font(intCounter)
Next

'Set value displayed on BevelButton equal to currently selected font
bbFontType.Caption = edfTextArea.SelTextFont
```

Note, the last code statement sets the BevelButton control's Caption based on the EditField control's default font type (which is set by the OS).

To finish your work on the first BevelButton control, you must add the following code statements to the EditField control's SelChange event handler.

```
'Update the caption of the BevelButton that represents font type each
'time the user repositions the cursor
If edfTextArea.SelTextFont <> bbFontType.Caption Then
  bbFontType.Caption = edfTextArea.SelTextFont
End If
```

The SelChange event occurs whenever the user repositions the cursor in the EditField control. These statements check to see if the currently selected font type matches the font type displayed in the bbFontType control's Caption and changes the value assigned to the Caption property if no match occurs.

Coding the bbFontSize Control

Next, you need to set up the BevelButton control (bbFontSize) with the capability to display different font sizes. Do so by opening the control's Action event handler and entering the following code statements.

```
'Set the BevelButton's caption equal to the value selected by the user
bbFontSize.Caption = bbFontSize.List(bbFontSize.MenuValue)

'Set the text size of the selected area in the EditField equal to the
'font size specified in the BevelButton control's Caption
edfTextArea.SelTextSize = Val(bbFontSize.Caption)
```

For the user to be able to pick a font size, you need to populate the second BevelButton control (bbFontSize) with a list of font sizes. To do so, add the following code statements to the control's Open event handler.

```
'Populate this menu with a list of typical font size values
bbFontSize.AddRow "8"
bbFontSize.AddRow "9"
bbFontSize.AddRow "10"
bbFontSize.AddRow "11"
bbFontSize.AddRow "12"
bbFontSize.AddRow "14"
bbFontSize.AddRow "16"
bbFontSize.AddRow "18"
bbFontSize.AddRow "20"
bbFontSize.AddRow "22"
bbFontSize.AddRow "24"
bbFontSize.AddRow "26"
bbFontSize.AddRow "28"
bbFontSize.AddRow "36"
bbFontSize.AddRow "48"
bbFontSize.AddRow "72"

'Set the BevelButton's Caption display the default font size
bbFontSize.Caption = Str(edfTextArea.SelTextSize)
```

Note, the last statement updated the control's Caption, based on the EditField control's currently selected font size.

Like the BevelButton control that manages the display of the font type, the *bbFontSize control* is responsible for keeping the user abreast of the size of the currently selected font size when the user repositions the cursor to a different location in the EditField control. To accomplish this, add the following code statements to the edfTextArea control's SelChange event handler.

```
'Update the caption of the BevelButton representing font size each time
'the user repositions the cursor
If Str(edfTextArea.SelTextSize) <> bbFontSize.Caption Then

  'If more than one font size is selected display a empty string in the
  'BevelButton representing font size. Otherwise display the font size
  If edfTextArea.SelTextSize <= 0 Then
    bbFontSize.Caption = ""
  Else
    bbFontSize.Caption = Str(edfTextArea.SelTextSize)
  End If

End If
```

In the event the user selects text made up of different size fonts, REALbasic sets the value of SelTextSize equal to zero. Rather than showing this value to the user, the last If…Then…Else code block substitutes an empty string.

Coding the bbBold Control

Now, let's move on to the bbBold PushButton control and add the following code statements to its Action event.

```
'Use the EditField's ToggleSelectionBold method to apply or remove
' bold text formatting
edfTextArea.ToggleSelectionBold
```

When executed, the net effect of this code is to toggle any selected text off from nonbold to bold and vice versa.

Coding the bbItalics Control

Next, add the following code statements to the bbItalics control's Action event handler.

```
'Use the EditField's ToggleSelectionBold method to apply or remove
' italic text formatting
edfTextArea.ToggleSelectionItalic
```

Coding the bbUnderline Control

Finally, add the following code statements to the bbUnderline control's Action event handler.

```
'Use the EditField's ToggleSelectionBold method to apply or remove
' underline text formatting
edfTextArea.ToggleSelectionUnderline
```

Testing RB Word Processor

That's it! Go ahead and save and test the RB Word Processor application. Given the size and complexity of this application, you're probably going to have a few typos to deal with. If you don't have the time to create this application from scratch, but you still want to see how it works, you can find its source code on this book's companion CD-ROM. Once you get the application to compile successfully, save it, and then put it through its paces by testing and validating the operation of all its features and functionality.

Summary

In this chapter, you learned how to work with text files and folders, including special folders. You learned how to define the file types your applications will be able to work with. You learned how to create, open, format, save, and print text files. You also learned how to work with an assortment of new functions and classes that provide access to standard windows, such as the Open and Save As dialogs.

CHAPTER 10

■ ■ ■

Working with Databases

In Chapter 9, you learned how to programmatically create and work with text files. REALbasic also provides robust support for databases. REALbasic's own database, the REAL SQL database, is built right into REALbasic Standard and Professional. REALbasic can also be set up to work with a number of popular third-party databases. Using REALbasic to create a front-end database interface, you can build applications that can send and retrieve any amount of data to and from back-end databases. This chapter demonstrates how to set up and programmatically interact with REAL SQL Databases.

Specifically, you learn how to

- Create new REAL SQL databases from both program code and the REALbasic IDE

- Define database schemas

- Add, modify, and delete database records

- Create database front ends

REALbasic's Database Support

A *database* is a repository for storing and retrieving data. Databases can be used to store small collections of data, such as information about a personal collection of books, music, or videos. Databases can also be used to efficiently store enormous amounts of data. For example, your local utility company, cable company, and telephone company all store information about you stored in a database somewhere. Using this information, they keep track of where you live, how much you spend, when your next payment is due, and whether you owe them any money.

REALbasic's built-in database, the REAL SQL database, is not only perfect for developing small database applications, it is also capable of handling massive amounts of data. However, it is a file-based database, as opposed to a server database, which means only one person at a time can access and work with a REAL SQL database.

The REAL SQL database is included in both the Standard and Professional Editions of REALbasic. Other third-party databases (such as MySQL and SQL Server) are only supported by the Professional Edition of REALbasic. While the REAL SQL database isn't sufficient for large industrial-sized databases, you might also use it as a temporary database when you develop database front-end applications. Once completed, you can modify the application to use the database of your choice.

■Note A front-end *database application* is simply a graphical user interface (GUI) that provides the user with access to the data stored in a database. The job of the front-end application is to submit requests to the back-end "database" and retrieve any returned data. In database terminology, the back-end database application is also referred to as a *data source*.

Database Plug-Ins

To work with a third-party database, you need to add a plug-in for that database to REALbasic's plug-ins folder. A *plug-in* is a file that provides REALbasic with everything it needs to work with a particular database. You can find a collection of plug-ins for a number of popular databases located in the download area at `www.realbasic.com`.

■Tip If you want to work with a database for which no plug-in is available at REALbasic's website, visit that database vendor's website to see if they provide a plug-in of their own for REALbasic. In addition, REAL Software provides a plug-in software developer's kit (SDK), which you or a third party can use to create a plug-in for virtually any database. You can download this SDK from the download area at `www.realbasic.com`.

Structured Query Language

The job of the front-end database application is to package database requests and submit them to the back-end database, which might be a REAL SQL database or one of the many supported third-party databases. To accomplish this task, REALbasic front-end applications use Structured Query Language (SQL) statements to request data from the database. For third-party database back-ends, the job of the associated plug-in is to translate front-end application commands into a format the database understands and to pass it along.

■Tip A complete overview of SQL is beyond the scope of this book. Instead, this book endeavors to present you with the basic steps required to perform common database tasks. REALbasic's built-in database, the REAL SQL database, is based on the SQLite database, which provides support for a subset of SQL. For specifics on the supported SQL commands, check out `www.sqlite.org`. If you are working with a different database, you need to refer to the vendor's website for that database to see what documentation is available regarding the database's SQL support.

Creating and Opening REAL SQL Databases

REALbasic provides you with everything you need to create new databases using commands available within the REALbasic IDE. This includes creating new REAL SQL databases or any third-party database for which plug-ins have been added to REALbasic's plug-ins folder. In addition, using the REALbasic REALSQLDatabase class, you can programmatically create new REAL SQL databases.

Creating a New REAL SQL Database from the IDE

To create a new REAL SQL database from the REALbasic IDE, open the Project screen and click Project ➤ Add ➤ Database ➤ New REAL SQL database. (Note, if you installed any third-party database plug-ins, you should also see entries for those databases listed.) REALbasic responds by displaying a standard Save or Save As dialog, enabling you to specify the name and location of the database you want to create.

Once added to your REALbasic application, the new database is displayed as a file item in the Projects screen, as shown in Figure 10-1.

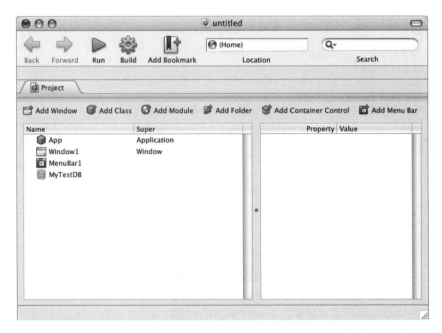

Figure 10-1. *Adding a new REAL SQL database to your application, as shown on Mac OS X*

Creating a Database in Code

Programmatically, you can create a REAL SQL database using the REALSQLDatabase class's DatabaseFile property. Once created, you can perform other commands, as the following example shows.

```
Dim TestDB As REALSQLdatabase
Dim TargetFile As FolderItem
Dim blnResult As Boolean

TestDB = New REALSQLdatabase
TargetFile = GetFolderItem("MyTestDB")

TestDB.DatabaseFile = TargetFile
blnResult = TestDB.CreateDatabaseFile

If blnResult = True Then
  'Add code statements here to perform database tasks
  TestDB.Close
  MsgBox "Database created"
Else
  MsgBox "Database Error: " + TestDB.ErrorMessage
End If
```

This example begins by declaring variables that represent the REALSQLDatabase and FolderItem objects. In addition, a Boolean variable named blnResult is declared. A REALSQLDatabase object is then instantiated as TestDB. Next, the GetFolderItem method of the FolderItem class is used to create a new file named MyTestDB in the same folder where REALbasic resides. The next two code statements use the REALSQLDatabase class's DatabaseFile property to associate the new database with the just-created file and the CreateDatabaseFile method to set up the database file. Finally, an If...Then...Else block is set up that checks to ensure the database was successfully created. Embedded within the If...Then...Else block are statements that close the database connection or display error text, when appropriate.

Connecting to an Existing Database from the IDE

If you already have a database you want your REALbasic application to work with, you can connect to it by clicking Project ➤ Add ➤ Database ➤ Select REAL SQL Database. REALbasic responds by displaying a standard Open dialog, enabling you to specify the name and location of the database. Once added, a new item representing the database is displayed in the Projects screen.

Connecting to an Existing Database in Code

You can also programmatically connect to a REAL SQL database using the REALSQLDatabase class's Connect method. Once connected, you can perform other commands, as the following example shows.

```
Dim TestDB As REALSQLdatabase
Dim TargetFile As FolderItem
Dim blnResult As Boolean

TestDB = New REALSQLdatabase
TargetFile = GetFolderItem("MyTestDB")

TestDB.DatabaseFile = TargetFile
blnResult = TestDB.Connect()

If blnResult  = True Then
  'Add code statements here to perform database tasks
  TestDB.Close
  MsgBox "Database connection established"

Else
  MsgBox "Database Error: " + TestDB.ErrorMessage
End If
```

In this example, the FolderItem class's GetFolderItem method is used to retrieve a reference to the specified database. Next, the REALSQLDatabase class's Database property is used to tell REALbasic the specified file is a database. The REALSQLDatabase class's Connect method is then used to establish a connection to the database.

Defining Database Schema

Once you create a new REAL SQL database, you need to specify its schema. If you have connected to an existing database instead of creating a new one, you can view and modify that database's schema. *Schema* is a fancy word for referring to a database's structure, which is made up of one or more tables. Each database table consists of one or more columns and each column is used to store data.

You can view a database's schema from the REALbasic IDE by opening the Project Editor screen and double-clicking the database. Doing so opens the window, as you see in Figure 10-2.

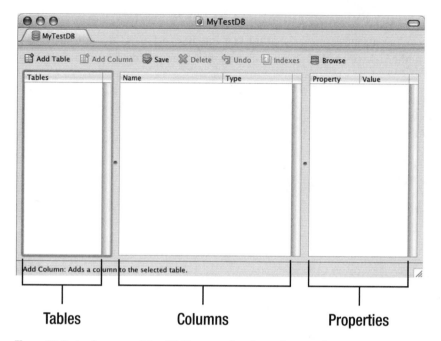

Figure 10-2. *As shown on Mac OS X, a new database does not have any tables defined.*

As Figure 10-2 shows, REALbasic lays out a database schema in three panes. The first pane contains a listing on any defined tables. The second pane displays a list of any columns added to the selected table. The third pane display the properties associated with the selected table or column. Above the three panes is a toolbar. Here, you see buttons that let you add new tables and columns, as well as save any changes or delete a selected table or column.

Adding Tables, Columns, and Indexes from the IDE

Every database must contain at least one table to be useful (although you can create empty databases if you want.) You can add and define a new table using the following procedure.

1. Double-click a database to open it.

2. Click the Add Table button. REALbasic responds by adding a new table with a name of *Untitled*.

3. Select the new table and change its name to something more descriptive by modifying its Name property.

4. Click the Add Column button to add a column to the table.

5. Select the new column and change its name to something more descriptive by modifying its Name property.

6. In the Properties pane, select the appropriate data type for the column by clicking the Type property. This displays a pop-up window showing all the data types supported by the database.

7. Add and configure as many columns as necessary.

8. Click the Save button.

9. Add as many additional tables as required by repeating Steps 2–8.

Figure 10-3 demonstrates how a small customer database created using the previous procedures might look.

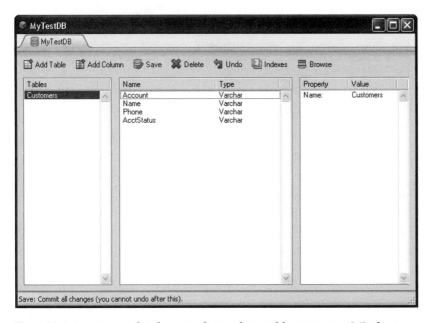

Figure 10-3. *A customer database made up of one table, as seen on Windows*

■**Note** Any property not supported by a particular type of database is grayed out in the Properties pane. A *Primary key* is a column used to link two or more tables together. For example, in a billing application that consists of a table containing customer addresses and a second table containing custom account balances, a customer-ID column might be marked as a primary key in both tables. Primary keys allow database queries to tie both tables together and pull out all data related to a particular customer. A *Mandatory key* marks a column as required (that is, one that cannot be set equal to null).

Once you finish laying out the schema for the database, you may want to add an index. An *index* is a column that will be searched often or used when sorting data. Indexing speeds data retrieval. Consider indexing columns that will be searched on or sorted often. Avoid indexing every column, which makes things run slower by forcing the database to make too many index updates when adding and removing data to and from the database. Do not index columns that will rarely be searched or that contain only a small subset of values.

To add an index to a database, its schema already needs to be defined. You can then define one or more database indexes using the following procedure.

1. Double-click a database to open it.

2. Select the table for which the index is being added and click the Indexes button. REALbasic responds by opening an Indexes sheet, as Figure 10-4 shows.

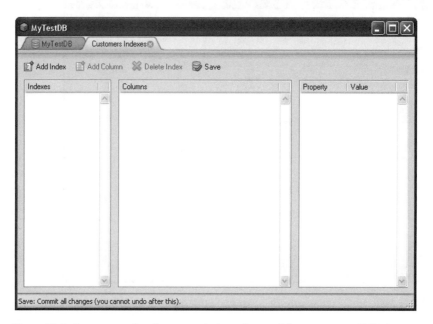

Figure 10-4. *A customer database consisting of two tables, as seen on Windows*

3. Click the Add Index button. REALbasic responds by adding a new index with a name of Untitled, as Figure 10-5 shows.

Figure 10-5. *Adding an index to a REAL SQL database table, as seen on Windows*

4. Select the new index and change its name to something more descriptive by modifying its Name property.

5. Click the Add Column button. The Select Column window appears and displays a listing of columns from the database.

6. Select the name of the column to be indexed.

7. If desired, create additional indexes by repeating steps 2–6.

8. Click Save.

Adding Tables, Columns, Indexes, and Records in Code

If you prefer, you can also programmatically add tables, columns, and indexes to a REAL SQL database. To do so, you need to programmatically create a new database or connect to an existing database, as previously shown. Regardless of whether to build or connect to a database, you need to add code to your database set-up application that defines its schema, creates indexes, and adds data.

If you are creating a new database, as you saw earlier, you need to define the database schema and any required indexes to it. You can do so by adding the following code statements after the execution of the statement containing the `CreateDatabaseFile` method.

```
TestDB.SQLExecute("Create Table Customers(Account Integer(" _
  + "Name varchar, Phone Integer, AcctStatus varchar)")
```

```
TestDB.SQLExecute ("Create Index AccountIndex On Customers (Account)")
```

The first statement uses the `REALSQLDatabase` class's `SQLExecute` method to create and add a new table to the database. In this example, the table is named Customers. Four columns are added to the table. The first column is named Account and is assigned a data type of Integer. The second column is named `Name` and is set up with a data type of `Varchar`. The third column is named `Phone`. It is used to store phone numbers. Note, for this example, the assumption is that phone numbers will consist only of numeric characters and will not begin with 0. The last column is named `AcctStatus` and it has a data type of `Varchar`.

The second statement uses the `SQLExecute` method to create and add an index to the database. The name of the index is `AccountIndex`. It is assigned to the `Customers` table (the only table currently in the database) and sets the `Account` column as the index.

If your application is connecting to an existing REAL SQL database, then you can skip the previous steps, assuming the database schema and index(s) are already defined.

Once a database is created and its schema defined, or an existing database is opened, you can populate it with data. To do so, you can use properties belonging to the `DatabaseRecord` class. This means adding the following declaration statement to the beginning of the database application.

```
Dim DBRecord As DatabaseRecord
```

This statement declares a variable based on the `DatabaseRecord` class. Using properties belonging to this class, you can then add data to the database, as the following shows.

```
DBRecord = New DatabaseRecord
```

```
DBRecord.IntegerColumn("Account") = 12345
DBRecord.Column("Name") = "Jerry Lee Ford, Jr."
DBRecord.IntegerColumn("Phone") = 9999999
DBRecord.Column("AcctStatus") = "Overdue"
```

```
TestDB.InsertRecord("Customers", DBRecord)
TestDB.Commit
```

```
DBRecord = New DatabaseRecord
```

```
DBRecord.IntegerColumn("Account") = 23456
DBRecord.Column("Name") = "Donal W. Lazyfeather"
DBRecord.IntegerColumn("Phone") = 5555555
DBRecord.Column("AcctStatus") = "Overdue"

TestDB.InsertRecord("Customers", DBRecord)
TestDB.Commit
```

The first four statements add data to the database using the `DatabaseRecord` class's `IntegerColumn` and `Column` methods. Each of these methods takes an argument that must match up against a table's column. Once data is assigned to each column, it is inserted into the database as a record using the `Database` class's `InsertRecord` method, which takes as arguments the name of the table and the name of the `DatabaseRecord` object. Once the record is inserted, the `Database` class's `Commit` method is used to save the change (addition) to the database. As you can see, a second record is then added to the database using the same set of methods.

■**Note** As you have just seen, you can create a new database and define its schema and indexes either from the REALbasic IDE or via code. You can also populate a new database with records via code. However, while you can modify existing database records, as the next section shows, you cannot add records to a database directly from the REALbasic IDE as you can via code. You can develop a GUI database front-end that supports database data entry, however, as you see in the section "The RB Book Database."

Querying Database Data

The REALbasic Database Editor provides you with the capability to view, search, sort, and update data already stored in a database. Doing so requires you to submit a SQL statement to retrieve and modify database records. The Database Editor provides you with two ways of submitting SQL statements. For those with little SQL background, you can fill out a GUI window that translates selections into SQL statements. For those with an understanding of SQL, an advanced option enables you to submit your own SQL statements.

Letting REALbasic Generate Your SQL Statements

To view existing database data, create a new REALbasic project and connect to a database. Double-click the database on the Project Editor screen to open the database using the Database Editor. From here, you can select and view the tables and columns that make up the database's schema. To view the data currently stored in the database, click the Browse button located in the Database Editor's toolbar. REALbasic responds by adding a new screen to the Database Editor, as Figure 10-6 shows.

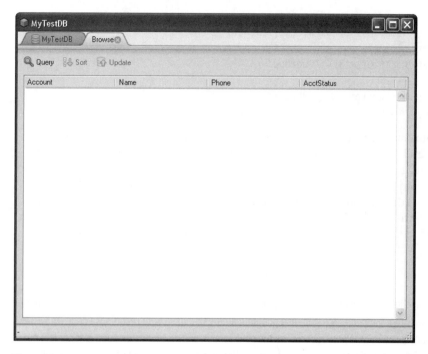

Figure 10-6. *You must submit a query to view data stored in the database, as seen on Windows.*

To view database data, you must submit a query. To do so, click the Query button. This displays the Select from window, as Figure 10-7 shows.

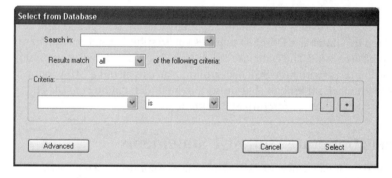

Figure 10-7. *REALbasic can automatically create SQL statements for you, based on criteria you supply, as seen on Windows.*

To submit a simply query, all you have to do is fill in the fields shown on the Select from window. To do so, select a table in the database from the Search in drop-down list. You then select a column from the table by selecting it from the first drop-down list in the Criteria section. Next, you must specify the type of operation you want to perform. Your choices are as follows:

- Is

- Is not

- Starts with

- Ends with

- Contains

- Greater than

- Less than

Then, you must key in a value in the third field in the Criteria section. REALbasic takes this information, generates a SQL statement for you, and submits it when you click the Select button. For example, using the database created in the previous example, you can view a list of all customers with overdue accounts by filling out the Select from window, as Figure 10-8 shows.

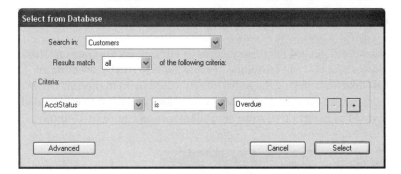

Figure 10-8. *Providing REALbasic with the information needed to build a simple database query, as seen on Windows*

After clicking the Select button, the results you see in Figure 10-9 are displayed in the Database Editor's Browse screen.

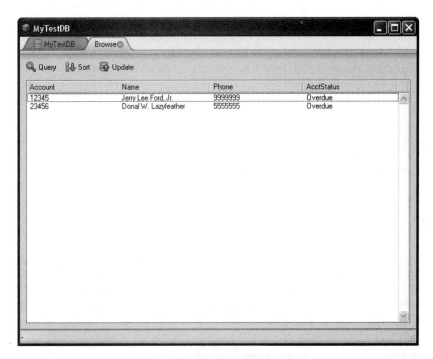

Figure 10-9. *Viewing the results of a simple database query, as seen on Windows*

From here, you can sort the displayed database records by clicking the Sort button. This opens the Sort Data window where you can select one or more fields to sort by selecting an entry from the Column List field and clicking the Move button to add them to the Sort Order field. All records are sorted based on the first specified column. If a second column were added to the Sort Order field, it would be used to perform a secondary sort, as Figure 10-10 shows.

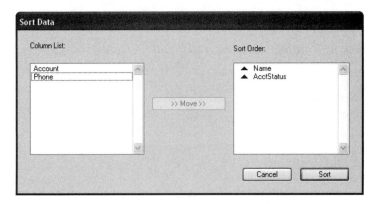

Figure 10-10. *Sorting the results of a database query, as seen on Windows*

Note the presence of the arrows, just to the left of the column name in the Sort Order field. They specify whether you want to sort a column based on ascending or descending order. You can toggle between ascending and descending sorts by clicking these arrows. The results of the sort operation are displayed in the Browse screen, as Figure 10-11 shows.

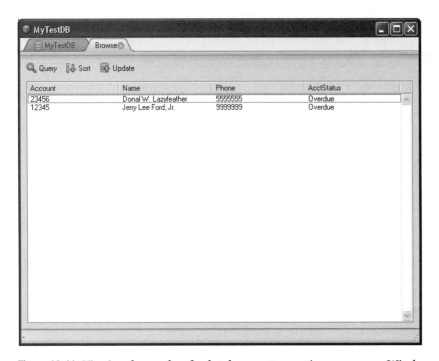

Figure 10-11. *Viewing the results of a database sort operation, as seen on Windows*

If necessary, you can create more complex queries by clicking the plus (+) button to the right of the third entry field in the criteria section to add another row. REALbasic lets you enter as many rows as you want. You then need to tell REALbasic how to match up data in the database against the different criteria you specified. This is done by selecting a value of either All or Any from the Results match drop-down list. Selecting All tells REALbasic to display only those records that match each of the stated criteria. Selecting Any tells REALbasic to display any record that matches at least one of the specified criteria.

Advanced SQL Query Statements

If you know enough about SQL to generate your own statements, you can do so by clicking the Advanced button in the lower-left hand corner of the Select from window. The Select from window changes and displays a single multiline EditField control into which you can type any SQL statement supported by the target database.

A number of good reasons exist for submitting your SQL queries using the advanced option. For starters, you can define a query using the simple version of the Select from windows, and then click the Advanced button to see the resulting statement REALbasic generates based on your specified criteria. You can use this approach as a self-learning technique for SQL. For example, Figure 10-12 shows the SQL statement generated based on selection criteria of overdue accounts.

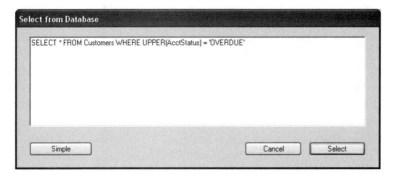

Figure 10-12. *Viewing the query that REALbasic generates on your behalf, as seen on Windows*

Another reason for generating your own SQL statements is because the simple version of the Select from window only lets you generate a small set of SQL statements. To generate a more complex query, you must use the Advanced option. For example, by default, the simple version of the Select from window does not provide you with the capability to select which columns you want returned as part of the query. Instead, all columns are returned. By replacing the * character following the opening SELECT keyword with a comma-delimited list of column names, you can restrict the columns that are returned.

Changing Column Data

REALbasic's Database Editor is not intended to be used as a data entry editor for databases, but you can use it to modify data stored in table columns. You cannot, however, use it to add or remove database records. To modify column data, you must generate a query, and then click the Update button when reviewing the query results. This opens the Update Database records window, as you see in Figure 10-13.

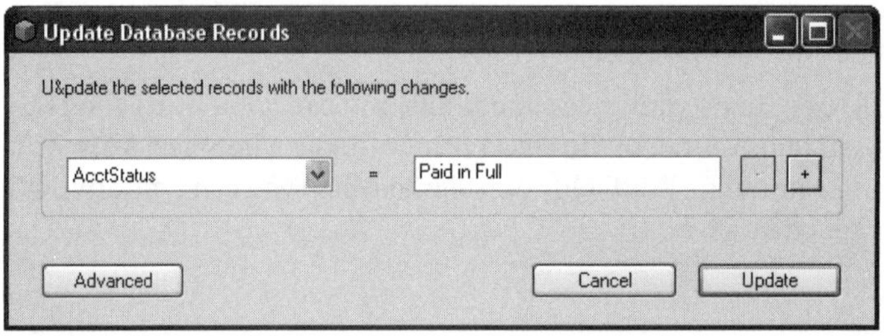

Figure 10-13. *Modifying database data associated with specifc columns, as seen on Windows*

In the example in Figure 10-13, all data stored in the selected table's `AcctStatus` column would be changed to `Paid in Full`. If you are comfortable generating your own SQL statements, an advanced version of the Update Database records window is also available.

■**Note** You can add new records to a database by keying in an Insert statement using the Advanced option.

Developing Database Front-Ends

As you already learned, REALbasic provides everything you need to build effective database front-end applications, regardless of whether the back-end database is a REAL SQL database or a third-party database. REALbasic provides two database-specific controls designed to facilitate the creation of front-end database applications: the DatabaseQuery and the DataControl controls.

The DatabaseQuery Control

The DatabaseQuery control, like other REALbasic controls, can be found in REALbasic's list of built-in controls. You add the *DatabaseQuery control* to an application like any other control, although, while you can see and interact with the control within the REALbasic IDE, it is invisible to the end user.

The DatabaseQuery control has only two properties: the `Database` property is used to associate the control with a specific database and the `SQLQuery` property contains a SQL statement automatically executed when the control is loaded. The purpose of this statement is to retrieve records from the database. The DatabaseQuery control has one method named `RunQuery`, which you can programmatically execute from within program code.

Using the DatabaseQuery control and a REALbasic programming technique, known as object binding, you can create a simple user interface to display database records. For example, using the REAL SQL database from previous examples, and a ListBox control and object binding, you can set up a simple user interface that provides a table level view of all the data stored in a particular database table.

■**Note** *Object binding* is the process of linking a control to a resource, such as a DatabaseQuery control to a ListBox control, to perform an action without program code.

To set this up, all you have to do is create a new project, add the MyTestDB to it, and then add a DatabaseQuery and a ListBox control to the window. Set the DatabaseQuery control's Database property equal to the name of the database. This links the control to the database. Then, set the SQLQuery property equal to `Select * From Customers`. This SQL statement tells REALbasic to retrieve all the records from the Customers table. Next, select the ListBox control and set its ColumnCount property equal to 4 the number of columns in the database). This

Bindings were deprecated in RB2007 r5

enables the ListBox control to display all the columns in the database. All that remains is for you to link the DatabaseQuery control to the ListBox control using object binding. To do so, select the Database Query control, press Control, and then select the ListBox control (on Macintosh, press the Command key). Then, click Project ➤ Add ➤ Binding. REALbasic responds by displaying the Visual Bindings window with the following four options:

- Bind ListBox1 with list data from DatabaseQuery1

- Bind DatabaseQuery1 with string data from ListBox1

- DatabaseQuery1 when ListBox1 gains focus

- DatabaseQuery1 when ListBox1 loses focus

Select the `Bind ListBox1 with list data from DatabaseQuery1` option and click OK. REALbasic responds by displaying a black line that visually links the two controls, as you see in Figure 10-14.

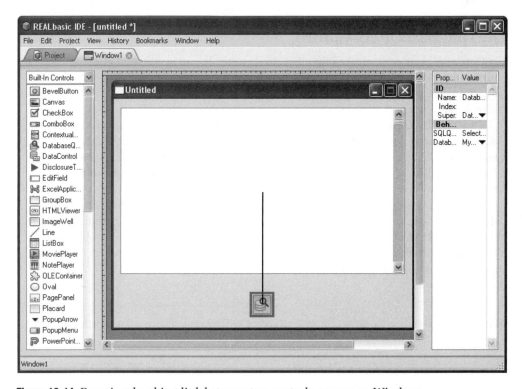

Figure 10-14. *Examining the object link between two controls, as seen on Windows*

Now, run the new application and you see the ListBox control display all the records stored in the Customers table, as you see in Figure 10-15.

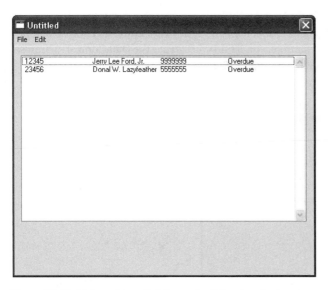

Figure 10-15. *Using object linking to build a simple database table-viewing application, as seen on Windows*

The DataControl

Using REALbasic's DataControl control, you can create a user interface for viewing, changing, and adding database records. To work with it, drag-and-drop an instance of the control on to a window. As you can see in Figure 10-16, the control has buttons for displaying the first, previous, next, and last records in a database.

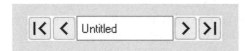

Figure 10-16. *Using object linking to build a simple database table-viewing application, as seen on Windows*

To set up the control, you need to assign its Database property to the name of a database you added to the application. You also need to set its TableName property to the name of one of the tables in the database. Last, you need to assign a valid SQL query to the SQLQuery property, just as you did earlier with the DatabaseQuery control.

For the DataControl control to be useful, you need to associate it with other controls on the window, such as EditField, RadioButton, CheckBox, and PushButton controls. For example, assuming you just set the properties for the DataControl control, you could display data stored in the Name column of the Customer table in the MyTestDB database by adding an EditField to the window, and then set its DataSource property to DataControl and its DataField property to

Name. Setting the DataSource property links the EditField control to the DataControl, which, in turn, is linked to the database. Setting the DataField property links the EditField control to a specific database column. If you run this example, you'll find you can use the DataControl to browse through all the names stored in the database. Figure 10-17 demonstrates how this example would look when run on Windows.

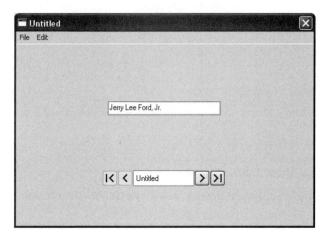

Figure 10-17. *Using the DataControl control to browse information stored in a database*

The RB Book Database

This chapter wraps up by showing you how to programmatically create a database that stores information about a user's personal library, including book titles, author names, publishers, and ISBN numbers. In addition, a category column is defined, which can be used to group related books into subjects, such as programming, networking, biography, historical, and so on.

In following along with this exercise, you learn how to create and execute a new type of REALbasic program, known as a *console application*, which is a program that does not have a GUI. Although you can run console applications directly from the desktop, typically, they are executed from the command line, allowing the applications to display text output and to interact with the user when appropriate, using a text-based interface.

When run, the console application creates a new REAL SQL database called PersonalBookDB. In addition, the console application populates the application with three sample records. Once created, you can use this database as a back-end for other REALbasic applications. As an example, you learn how to create a small front-end utility that lets you add as many new records as you want—one at a time—to the database. Of course, you can also view and edit database records using the REALbasic Database Editor, as you saw earlier.

Note Only the Professional version of REALbasic provides full support for console applications. However, the Standard version of REALbasic enables you to create demo applications. A *demo application* is simply an application that stops running after five minutes. The console application you develop here only runs for a moment as it creates the database. Therefore, the five-minute demo execution limitation imposed on REALbasic's Standard version has no impact on the execution of the console application developed in this chapter.

In demonstrating how to create these two database applications, this chapter uses the Linux version of REALbasic, but you can just as easily create these applications using either the Macintosh or Windows versions of REALbasic. All the steps are the same.

Creating the PersonalBookDB Database

Let's begin by creating the console application to be used to generate the PersonalBookDB. The first step is to create a new REALbasic project by clicking File ➤ New Project. When prompted to select the type of application you want to create, select Console Application. Because console applications do not have a GUI, REALbasic responds by opening the Project Editor. As you can see, console applications consist of a single App item. Double-click it and REALbasic responds by opening the Code Editor. Next, expand the Event Handlers entry in the browser area, as Figure 10-18 shows.

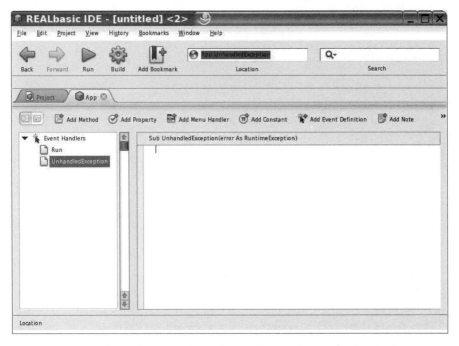

Figure 10-18. *Console applications do not have a GUI and consist only of code statements, as seen on Linux.*

As you can see in Figure 10-18, console applications have only two event handlers, one of which is the Run Event Handler. This event handler is executed whenever the console application is executed. The following lists the program code for the console application.

```
'Declare a database representing a REAL SQL Database
Dim BookDB As REALSQLdatabase
Dim TargetFile As FolderItem  'Declare a FolderItem
Dim DBRecord As DatabaseRecord  'Declare a DatabaseRecord variable
Dim blnResult As Boolean  'Declare Boolean variable

BookDB = New REALSQLdatabase  'Instantiate a REALSQLdatabase object

'Create a file to store the new database
TargetFile = GetFolderItem("PersonalBookDB")

BookDB.DatabaseFile = TargetFile  'Associate database with the file

BlnResult = BookDB.CreateDatabaseFile  'Create the database

If BookDB.Connect() Then  'Proceed if the connection is successful

  'Use the SQLExecute method to add a table in the new database
    BookDB.SQLExecute("Create Table BookCollection(Title varchar," _
    + "Author varchar, ISBN varchar," _
    + "Publisher varchar, Category varchar, Location varchar)")

  'Create a index for the table
  BookDB.SQLExecute _
    ("Create Index TitleIndex On BookCollection (Title)")

  DBRecord = New DatabaseRecord  'Instantiate a new record

  'Assign elements to table columns
  DBRecord.Column("Title") = "Beginning REALbasic"
  DBRecord.Column("Author") = "Jerry Lee Ford, Jr."
  DBRecord.Column("ISBN") = "159059634X"
  DBRecord.Column("Publisher")="Apress"
  DBRecord.Column("Category") = "Programming"
  DBRecord.Column("Location") = "Shelf 4"

  'Use the InsertRecord method to add the record to the table
  BookDB.InsertRecord("BookCollection", DBRecord)

  DBRecord = New DatabaseRecord  'Instantiate a new record
```

```
'Assign elements to table columns
DBRecord.Column("Title") = "Beginning SuSe Linux"
DBRecord.Column("Author") = "Keir Thomas"
DBRecord.Column("ISBN") = "1590594584"
DBRecord.Column("Publisher") ="Apress"
DBRecord.Column("Category") = "Operating Systems"
DBRecord.Column("Location") = "Shelf 7"

'Use the InsertRecord method to add the record to the table
BookDB.InsertRecord("BookCollection", DBRecord)

DBRecord = New DatabaseRecord   'Instantiate a new record

'Assign elements to table columns
DBRecord.Column("Title") = "Beginning Ct"
DBRecord.Column("Author") = "Ivor Horton"
DBRecord.Column("ISBN") = "1590592530"
DBRecord.Column("Publisher") ="Apress"
DBRecord.Column("Category") = "Programming"
DBRecord.Column("Location") = "Shelf 1"

'Use the InsertRecord method to add the record to the table
BookDB.InsertRecord("BookCollection", DBRecord)

BookDB.Commit  'Complete the database transaction
BookDB.Close   'Terminate the database connection

'Display an message informational message
StdOut.WriteLine "DataBase creation and population: Completed!"

Else  'Proceed if an error occurred connectingto the database

'Display the error message that occurred
StdOut.WriteLine "DataBase Error: " + BookDB.ErrorMessage

End If
```

As you can see, the code statements listed here are well-documented with embedded comments that outline exactly what is going on, every step of the way. Once you add these statements, go ahead and save the application, and then assign it the name of DBCreator. When you are ready, go ahead and run it. You can do so in either of two ways. First, you can run it like any other application by opening it from the desktop. Or, you can open and execute the application from the command prompt. When executed this way, you see a text message generated at the end of the application's execution that either tells you the database was successfully created or displays an error message.

■**Note** On Linux, you can get to a command prompt by opening a Terminal window. On Windows, you can get to the command prompt by clicking Start ➤ Accessories ➤ Command Prompt. On Mac OS X, you can get to the command prompt by opening the Applications folder, followed by the Utilities folder, where you find the Terminal utility.

Once you successfully run the application, create a new REALbasic desktop application and add the database it. Next, double-click the database to open the Database Editor and select the BookCollection table. You should see the columns Figure 10-19 shows.

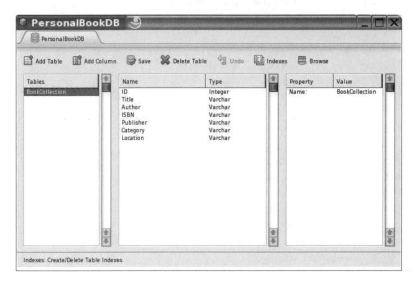

Figure 10-19. *Examining the schema for the PersonalBookDB database, as seen on Linux*

Next, click the Query button and submit a query to make sure all three initial records were added to the database. To do so, click the Advanced button, type `Select * From BookCollection`, and then click Select. If everything looks in order, you are ready to continue and create the desktop application that will let you add new book entries into the database. Go ahead and keep this new project open because you use it in the next section to create a front-end database application.

Creating a Utility to Add New Books

To create a front-end database desktop application that enables you to add additional books to the PersonalBookDB, take the new project you just created and added the database to, and save it as DBAdd. Begin by selecting the Title property for Window1 to RB Book Add. Next, add six StaticText and six EditField controls in two columns. Then, add a PushButton control to the window, and align it and the rest of the controls, as Figure 10-20 shows.

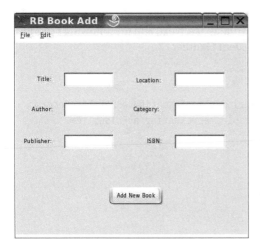

Figure 10-20. *Building a front-end user interface for the PersonalBookDB database, as seen on Linux*

Next, modify the properties belonging to the controls you just added to the windows, as Table 10-1 specifies.

Table 10-1. *Modifying Properties Belonging to Controls on the DBAdd Application*

Object	Property	Value
StaticText1	Text	Title:
StaticText2	Text	Author:
StaticText3	Text	Publisher:
StaticText4	Text	Location:
StaticText5	Text	Category:
StaticText6	Text	ISBN:
PushButton1	Name	pbtAdd
	Caption	Add New Book
EditField1	Name	edfTitle
EditField2	Name	edfAuthor
EditField3	Name	edfPublisher
EditField4	Name	edfLocation
EditField5	Name	edfCategory
EditField6	Name	edfISBN

As you can see from the name assigned to the StaticText and EdifField controls, they are individually associated with specific columns in the database. Next, add the following program code to the pbnAdd PushButton control's Action Event Handler.

```
Dim dbFile As FolderItem
Dim BookDB As REALSQLdatabase
Dim DBRecord As DatabaseRecord  'Declare a variable representing a DatabaseRecord
Dim TargetFile As FolderItem  'Declare a variable representing a FolderItem

If edfTitle.Text <> "" Then

  BookDB = New REALSQLdatabase

  TargetFile = GetFolderItem("PersonalBookDB")
  BookDB.DatabaseFile = TargetFile

  If BookDB.Connect() then

    DBRecord = New DatabaseRecord  'Instantiate a new record

    'Assign elements to table columns
    DBRecord.Column("Title") = edfTitle.Text
    DBRecord.Column("Author") = edfAuthor.Text
    DBRecord.Column("Publisher") = edfPublisher.Text
    DBRecord.Column("Location") = edfLocation.Text
    DBRecord.Column("Category") = edfCategory.Text
    DBRecord.Column("ISBN") = edfISBN.Text

    'Use the InsertRecord method to add the record to the table
    BookDB.InsertRecord("BookCollection", DBRecord)
    BookDB.Commit  'Complete the database transaction

    BookDB.Close  'Terminate the database connection

    MsgBox "Book added to database"

    'Clear out the EditField controls to allow for a new entry
    edfTitle.Text = ""
    edfAuthor.Text = ""
    edfPublisher.Text = ""
    edfLocation.Text = ""
    edfCategory.Text = ""
    edfISBN.Text = ""
```

```
Else

  'Display the error message that occurred
  MSgBox "DataBase Error: " + BookDB.ErrorMessage

End If

Else

  MsgBox "Error: Empty database records cannot be processed."

End If
```

This code executes each time the pbnAdd PushButton control is clicked. The job of the pbnAdd PushButton is to collect data keyed in by the user and to load it into the database as a new record. Note, to prevent blank records from being added to the PersonalBookDB, a check is made to ensure the user has entered something into the EditField control representing the Title column in the database's BookCollection table.

Once you finish adding the required program code, save the DBAdd application and compile it. Add a few new book entries to the database. Then, close the application and return to the REALbasic IDE. Open the Project Editor and double-click the PersonalBookDB item. Check to make sure the new records you just added were properly added to the database.

Summary

In this chapter, you learned a little about the basics of database program development. This included learning how to open and create REAL SQL databases, using both the REALbasic GUI and program code. You also learned how to specify database schema, and how to add and modify database records. You learned how to work with both the Database Query and DataControl controls, as well as how to work programmatically with a number of REALbasic database-related classes.

CHAPTER 11

■ ■ ■

Working with Graphics and Audio

In earlier chapters, you gained some experience working with graphics in your REALbasic applications: you learned how to use the ImageWell control to display different types of graphic files. In this chapter, you learn much more about REALbasic's built-in support for graphics. Specifically, you learn how to use Canvas control, as well as properties and methods belonging to the Graphics class, to create new graphic images of your own. You also learn how to work with a number of different REALbasic methods, classes, and controls that support audio file playback.

Specifically, you learn how to

- Play audio files

- Use the Macintosh and Windows speech synthesizer to pronounce text strings

- Play musical notes on computers running Macintosh and Windows

- Create and manipulate graphics

Adding Sound Effects to REALbasic Applications

Up to this point in the book, all the sample applications you created and worked on, except one, have had one thing in common: they have been mute. The lone exception was the RB Movie Player application, where you learned how to use the MoviePlayer control to facilitate the playing of movie files on Macintosh and Windows, using QuickTime and the Windows Media Player.

REALbasic provides you with the capability to liven your desktop applications using a number of different audio options, including

- Using the Beep method to play the computer's default beep sound

- Using the Sound class to play audio files

- Using the Speak method to pronounce text strings using the operating system's built-in speech synthesizer

- Using the NotePlayer control to play musical notes using a variety of simulated instruments

---

■**Note** The Sound class, the Speak method, and the NotePlayer control only work on Macintosh and Windows.

Getting the User's Attention

You can get the user's attention when your application runs in a number of different ways. For example, you can change the display of information in various controls displayed on the application's user interface. You can also display messages in pop-up windows.

Another simple, yet effective, way to get the user's attention is to make some noise, or more specifically, to play the computer's default beep sound. For example, you might develop an application that performs a particularly lengthy and time-consuming calculation. An effective way to let the user know when the calculation is complete and the results are available is to play a beep sound.

All you must do to make a little noise is to execute REALbasic's built-in Beep method, which plays the computer's default beep sound. To execute this method, call the Beep method from an appropriate location in your program code. To play the operating system's default beep sound once, type

Beep

Or, you could wrap the Beep method inside a loop to play it more than once.

Playing Audio Files

If you want to do more than add a simple beep sound to your applications, REALbasic lets you do so using methods that belong to the Sound class. The Sound class provides access to the following methods:

- **Play**. Plays the selected sound file.

- **PlayLooping**. Repeatedly plays the selected sound file.

- **IsPlaying**. Returns a Boolean value of True if a sound file is playing.

- **Stop**. Stops sound-file playback.

- **Volume**. Provides control over the volume of sound playback. The supported range is 0 to 100, where 0 is mute and 100 is equal to the operating system's normal volume setting.

- **Pan**. Provides control over the volume played in the left and right speaker. The supported range is –100 to 100, where –100 plays sound only in the left speaker, 0 balances sound level equally in both speakers, and 100 plays sound only in the right speaker.

- **Clone**. Returns a copy of a sound. This allows an application to work independently with a copy of the same sound file without loading it a second time.

Importing a Sound File into Your Application

You can use the Sound class to play sounds in your applications in many different ways. For starters, you can add the sound to your REALbasic project by dragging-and-dropping it into the Project screen. You can then play the sound file by referring to it by name, and then calling on the Sound class's Play method, as the following shows.

```
Welcome.Play
```

Here, a sound file named Welcome was imported into the project making it available for play using the previous code statement. Similarly, you can play the sound file over and over again, as the following shows.

```
Welcome.PlayLooping
```

You can also stop playing the sound file at any time, as shown here.

```
Welcome.Stop
```

Playing an imported sound file is an effective option when you want to play custom sound files and distribute them as part of your application.

Pointing to External Sound Files

Another way to play sound files is to use the FolderItem class and the GetFolderItem function, as the following shows.

```
Dim TargetFile As FolderItem    'Declare a FolderItem object
Dim SoundFile As Sound    'Declare a Sound Object

TargetFile = GetFolderItem("Welcome.wav")  'Retrieve specified audio file

If TargetFile.Exists  = True Then  'User did not click on Cancel
  SoundFile = TargetFile.OpenAsSound   'Retrieve the audio file
  SoundFile.Play   'Play the audio file
Else
  MsgBox "Cannot find audio file."
End If
```

This example sets up the playing of a wave file stored in the same folder as the REALbasic application by instantiating a FolderItem object and specifying the path of the sound file. A check is then made to ensure the sound file exists before using the FolderItem class's OpenAsSound method to retrieve a reference to the sound file, which is then played.

Note The FolderItem class' OpenAsSound method provides you with the capability to open a sound file, which can then be programmatically played, paused, restarted, and stopped using methods and properties belonging to the Sound class. On Macintosh, you can play any Macintosh System 7 audio files. You can also play any sound file supported by QuickTime on Windows and Macintosh, including MP3 files. The Sound class can also play wave files on Windows using *DirectSound,* which is a component of Microsoft's *DirectX* (Microsoft's high-performance graphic and sound engine).

When you use this option for playing sound files, you must ensure in advance that the sound files exist in the specified location on the computer where the application will run. You can ensure this by installing copies of the sound files yourself in the appropriate folders or by using sound files that ship as part of the operating system (OS).

Playing User Selections

A third option for playing sound files is to let the user specify the location of their sound files, as the following example shows.

```
Dim AudioTypes As New FileType    'Declare a FileType object
Dim SoundFile As Sound    'Declare a variable representing a Sound object

AudioTypes.Name= "Audio Files"  'Specify string identifying supported files
AudioTypes.Extensions=".wav"    'Specify supported file types

'Declare variable representing a folder object
Dim TargetFile as FolderItem = GetOpenFolderItem(AudioTypes)

If TargetFile <> Nil Then  'Proceed if the user did not click on Cancel
   SoundFile = TargetFile.OpenAsSound   'Retrieve the selected audio file
   SoundFile.Play   'Play the audio file
End If
```

In this example, the GetOpenFolderItem function is used to display a generic Open window dialog, enabling the user to specify the name and location of the sound file to be played.

Giving Your Application a Voice

If you are developing your REALbasic applications exclusively for Macintosh or Windows, you might want to take advantage of REALbasic's Speak method. This method provides you with the capability to use the operating system's built-in speech synthesizer to pronounce text strings and has the following syntax.

```
Speak(TextPhrase, [Interrupt])
```

TextPhrase is a placeholder representing the text string to be pronounced. *Interrupt* is an optional parameter, which, when set equal to True, cancels any previous calls made to the Speak method.

The Speak method is easy to use. For example, start up a new REALbasic project and add an EditField control and three PushButton controls. Enable the EditField control's Multiline property and label the three PushButton controls as Instructions, Talk, and Clear, as Figure 11-1 shows.

Figure 11-1. *Creating a REALbasic application that pronounces text strings, as seen on Windows*

Add the following code statement to the PushButton labeled Instructions.

```
Speak "Type anything you wish into the entry field and click on the " _
  + "talk button to listen."
```

When clicked, this button pronounces the supplied text string. Next, add the following code statement to the button labeled Talk.

```
Speak EditField1.Text
```

When clicked, this control pronounces any text typed into the EditField1 control. Finally, add the following code statement to the PushButton control labeled Clear.

```
EditField1.Text = ""
```

When clicked, this button clears out any text entered into the EditField1 control, enabling the user to enter new text.

▪Note You can find a working example of this application on this book's companion CD-ROM.

Making Music

As you can see, REALbasic provides robust audio capabilities. In addition to playing Beeps, audio sounds, and supporting speech pronunciation on Macintosh and Windows, REALbasic also supports the playing of musical notes using the NotePlayer control (on Macintosh when QuickTime is installed and on Windows via MIDI functions).

To work with the NotePlayer control, you add a copy of it to your REALbasic application. This copy is visible in the REALbasic IDE, but it won't be visible to the end user when the application runs. To work with this control, you must specify the type of instrument to be used to play musical notes. You do this by setting the Instrument property to an Integer representing one of instruments listed in Table 11-1.

Table 11-1. *A Listing of Instruments with Which You Can Play Notes in a REALbasic Application*

Instrument	Integer	Instrument	Integer	Instrument	Integer
Acoustic Grand Piano	1	Harmonica	23	Tremolo Strings	45
Bright Acoustic Piano	2	Tango Accordion	24	Pizzicato Strings	46
Electric Grand Piano	3	Acoustic Nylon Guitar	25	Orchestral Harp	47
Honky-tonk Piano	4	Acoustic Steel Guitar	26	Timpani	48
Rhodes Piano	5	Electric Jazz Guitar	27	Acoustic String Ensemble 1	49
Chorused Piano	6	Electric Clean Guitar	28	Acoustic String Ensemble 2	50
Harpsichord	7	Electric Guitar Muted	29	Synth Strings 1	51
Clavinet	8	Overdriven Guitar	30	Synth Strings 2	52
Celesta	9	Distortion Guitar	31	Aah Choir	53
Glockenspiel	10	Guitar Harmonics	32	Ooh Choir	54
Music Box	11	Wood Bass	33	Synvox	55
Vibraphone	12	Electric Bass Fingered	34	Orchestra Hit	56
Marimba	13	Electric Bass Picked	35	Trumpet	57
Xylophone	14	Fretless Bass	36	Trombone	58
Tubular bells	15	Slap Bass 1	37	Tuba	59
Dulcimer	16	Slap Bass 2	38	Muted Trumpet	60
Draw Organ	17	Synth Bass 1	39	French Horn	61
Percussive Organ	18	Synth Bass 2	40	Brass Section	62
Rock Organ	19	Violin	41	Synth Brass 1	63
Church Organ	20	Viola	42	Synth Brass 2	64
Reed Organ	21	Cello	43	Soprano Sax	65

Instrument	Integer	Instrument	Integer	Instrument	Integer
Accordion	22	Contrabass	44	Alto Sax	66
Tenor Sax	67	Synth Lead 8	88	Kalimba	109
Baritone Sax	68	Synth Pad 1	89	Bagpipe	110
Oboe	69	Synth Pad 2	90	Fiddle	111
English Horn	70	Synth Pad 3	91	Shanai	112
Bassoon	71	Synth Pad 4	92	Tinkle Bell	113
Clarinet	72	Synth Pad 5	93	Agogo	114
Piccolo	73	Synth Pad 6	94	Steel Drums	115
10 Flute	74	Synth Pad 7	95	Woodblock	116
Recorder	75	Synth Pad 8	96	Taiko Drum	117
Pan Flute	76	Ice Rain	97	Melodic Tom	118
Bottle Blow	77	Soundtracks	98	Synth Tom	119
Shakuhachi	78	Crystal	99	Reverse Cymbal	120
Whistle	79	Atmosphere	100	Guitar Fret Noise	121
Ocarina	80	Bright	101	Breath Noise	122
Square Lead	81	Goblin	102	Seashore	123
Saw Lead	82	Echoes	103	Bird Tweet	124
Calliope	83	Space	104	Telephone Ring	125
Chiffer	84	Sitar	105	Helicopter	126
Synth Lead 5	85	Banjo	106	Applause	127
Synth Lead 6	86	Shamisen	107	Gunshot Table	128
Synth Lead 7	87	Koto	108	Drum Kit	16385

The NotePlayer class has only one method called PlayNote, which plays a note at a specified pitch level and velocity. *Pitch* and *velocity* are specified as integers, each of which has a range from 0 to 127. For pitch, each increment raises the pitch by a half step. Middle C begins at 60. For velocity, 127 specifies a hard key press and 0 represents a key no longer being pressed. For example, the following code statement demonstrates how to play a note on a Xylophone, using a medium pitch and velocity.

```
NotePlayer1.Instrument = 14
NotePlayer1.PlayNote(60,60)
```

Using the NotePlayer control, you can simulate the playing of many different musical instruments. This includes, for example, different types of pianos. Figure 11-2 shows a REAL-basic application that simulates the playing of six different minipianos.

Figure 11-2. *A small virtual piano implemented as a REALbasic application, running on Windows*

To create this example, open a new REALbasic application and add NotePlayer control, seven PushButton controls, and a StaticText control and align them as you see in Figure 11-2. Then, assign a title of RB Piano Player to the window's `Title` property and open the application's menu bar and remove the Edit menu. Next, add an Instruments menu and add the following menu items to it:

- Acoustic Grand Piano
- Bright Acoustic Piano
- Electric Grand Piano
- Honky-tonk Piano
- Rhodes Piano
- Chorused Piano

Next, add six event handlers, one for each of the specified instruments. Add the following code statements to the Instrument AcousticGrandPiano event handler.

```
NotePlayer1.Instrument = 1
txtPianoName.Text = "Acoustic Grand Piano"
```

As you can see, when executed, this menu handler sets the musical instrument to Acoustic Grand Piano and displays the name of the instrument in the StaticText control for the user to see. Next, add the following pairs of code statements to the appropriate menu handlers.

```
NotePlayer1.Instrument = 2
  txtPianoName.Text = "Bright Acoustic Piano"

NotePlayer1.Instrument = 6
txtPianoName.Text = "Chorused Piano"

NotePlayer1.Instrument = 3
txtPianoName.Text = "Electric Grand Piano"
```

```
NotePlayer1.Instrument = 4
txtPianoName.Text = "Honky-tonk Piano"
```

```
NotePlayer1.Instrument = 5
txtPianoName.Text = "Rhodes Piano"
```

Next, set the caption of the first PushButton control to *C* and double-click it to open its Action event handler in the Code Editor. Enter the following code statement.

```
NotePlayer1.PlayNote(60,127)
```

This statement plays a note with medium pitch at the maximum possible velocity. Assign the second PushButton control a caption of *D* and add the following code statement to its Action event handler.

```
NotePlayer1.PlayNote(62,127)
```

Assign the second PushButton control a caption of *E,* and then add the following code statement to its Action event handler.

```
NotePlayer1.PlayNote(64,127)
```

Assign the third PushButton control a caption of *F* and add the following code statement to its Action event handler.

```
NotePlayer1.PlayNote(65,127)
```

Assign the fourth PushButton control a caption of *G,* and then add the following code statement to its Action event handler.

```
NotePlayer1.PlayNote(67,127)
```

Assign the fifth PushButton control a caption of *A* and add the following code statement to its Action event handler.

```
NotePlayer1.PlayNote(69,127)
```

Assign the last PushButton control a caption of *B,* and then add the following code statement to its Action event handler.

```
NotePlayer1.PlayNote(71,127)
```

At this point, you have the programming logic defined for each of the PushButton controls and menu items. One last step remains, telling the application what instrument to set as the default instrument at startup. To do this, add the following code to the Piano window's Open event handler.

```
NotePlayer1.Instrument = 1
txtPianoName.Text = "Acoustic Grand Piano"
```

Now, save and run your application. You'll see you can switch between and play various types of pianos.

■**Note** You can find a working example of this application on this book's companion CD-ROM.

Working with Graphics

REALbasic provides strong support for working with graphics. For example, in previous chapters, you learned how to open and display graphic files using methods belonging to the FolderItem class and the ImageWell control. While the ImageWell control can be used to display graphic files, it does not provide any properties or methods that facilitate the creation of graphics. This chapter expands on your understanding of REALbasic's graphic support by teaching you how to create and draw graphics files by using the Canvas control, and properties and methods belonging to the Graphics class.

REALbasic's Coordinate System

To create custom graphics using REALbasic, you need to know a bit about REALbasic's coordinate system, which determines where graphics are drawn in a Canvas control or on the background of a window. This coordinate system is made up of a grid of pixels. The upper left-hand corner of Canvas controls or windows represents the origin of the grid and has coordinates of 0,0. That is, the first argument represents the distance from the left-hand side and the second argument represents the distance from the top of the Canvas control or window.

Most of the methods you use to draw graphics are based on two sets of information. The first set of information is the upper-left hand coordinate position of the graphic to be drawn. The second set of information required to draw most images is the height and width of the image to be drawn.

Displaying Graphic Files as a Window's Background Image

One way to liven the appearance of an application's window is to display a background color. You can do this by enabling the HasBackColor property, and then selecting a color by clicking the ellipsis icon located in the window's BackColor property to open and select a background color from the Color Picker window, as Figure 11-3, Figure 11-4, and Figure 11-5 show.

■**Note** To display a background color in a window, the HasBackColor property must be enabled.

Figure 11-3. *The Color Picker, as seen on Mac OS X*

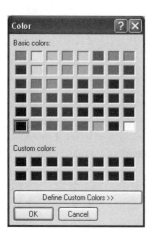

Figure 11-4. *The Color Picker, as seen on Windows*

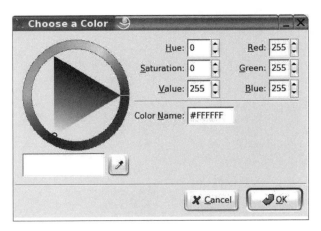

Figure 11-5. *The Color Picker, as seen on Linux*

Or, you can specify a window's background color via code, as the following shows.

```
Me.HasBackColor = True
Me.BackColor = RGB(255,0,0)
```

USING DIFFERENT COLOR MODELS

In REALbasic, you can specify a color value using any of three color models: RGB, HSV, or CMY. *RGB* is based on the selection of red, green, and blue values. *HSV* is based on the selection of hue, saturation, and value. *CMY* is based on the selection of cyan, magenta, and yellow. For each of these three models, you must specify a value in the range of 0–255. For example, you could specify a color of white using the RGB color model, as the following shows.

```
Dim CustomColor As Color
CustomColor = RGB(255, 255, 255)
```

Or, you could specify a color of black, as you see in the following.

```
Dim CustomColor As Color
CustomColor = RGB(0, 0, 0)
```

REALbasic also enables you to specify a color value by specifying a hexadecimal value of a color based on the RGB model, as you see in the following.

```
Dim CustomColor As Color
CustomColor - &cff0000
```

This example sets the window's background color to red (for example, RGB(255, 0, 0)).

You can also spruce up a window by displaying a picture as a background image. This can be done by importing a picture into your project and setting the BackDrop property in the window's Open event handler, as you see in the following.

```
Me.BackDrop = Mountains
Me.Width = BackDrop.Width
Me.Height = BackDrop.Height
```

In this example, a jpeg file named Mountains is displayed in the window's background. In addition, the height and width of the window were resized to match the height and width of the jpeg file.

Drawing Custom Graphics

You can programmatically draw graphics in windows and on canvas controls. Doing so requires you to use methods and properties belonging to the Graphics class. Using these properties and methods, you can draw individual pixels, lines, and numerous shapes, such as ovals and rectangles. You can also draw standard dialog icons, such as the Note, Caution, and Stop icons.

Both the window and Canvas control support a Paint event. The Canvas control and window's Paint event handler is the central location for any application that has program code used to draw. The *Paint event* executes any time a window or Canvas control needs to be drawn or redrawn. For example, the Paint event executes whenever a window or Canvas control is opened. The Paint event also executes whenever a Canvas control or window is resized or when a previously hidden portion of a Canvas control or window becomes exposed. The Paint event is set up as a Subroutine and is passed the Graphics object each time it is executed, as you see in the following.

```
Sub Paint(g As Graphics)
```

This provides your code statements with immediate access to all the properties and methods belonging to the Graphics class.

Drawing Pixels

Using the Pixel property belonging to the Graphics class, you can draw individual pixels to create extremely detailed graphics. As a quick demonstration, place the following code statements in the Paint event handler for a new project's window, and then run it.

```
Dim CustomColor As Color
CustomColor = RGB(255, 0, 0)
g.Pixel(50,100) = CustomColor
```

If you look closely at the window, you can see a pixel has been drawn in red (using the RGB function and a Color object named CustomColor) at a location that is 50 pixels from the left-hand side of the window and 100 pixels down from the top of the window.

Drawing Text

Using the Graphics class's properties and methods, you can also draw text on window and Canvas controls, as you can see in the following.

```
g.ForeColor = RGB(0,0,0)

g.Bold = True
g.TextFont = "Arial"
g.TextSize = 24

g.DrawString "Once upon a time ...", 25, 50
```

In this example, the Graphics class's ForeColor property is set equal to black. In addition, the Graphics class's Bold, TextFont, and TextSize properties are also specified. Finally, the DrawString method is executed. This method takes as parameters a text string and the upper left-hand coordinates at which the text string should be drawn. Figure 11-6 shows the output produced by this example.

Figure 11-6. *Drawing text, as seen on Linux*

Drawing Icons

The Graphics class also provides methods for drawing standard Caution, Note, and Stop icons. These methods are named as follows:

- DrawCautionIcon

- DrawNoteIcon

- DrawStopIcon

Each of these methods requires you to pass to it the coordinates at which the icon should be drawn, as you see in the following example.

```
g.ForeColor = RGB(0, 0, 255)

g.DrawStopIcon 90, 45
g.Bold = True

g.DrawString "Error: Something went wrong.", 90, 70
```

In this example, the DrawStopIcon method is used to draw a Stop icon at coordinates 90, 45. Next, the DrawString method is used to draw a descriptive text string just to the right of the icon, as Figure 11-7 shows.

Figure 11-7. *Drawing text and icon, as seen on Linux*

Drawing Lines

The Graphics class also provides you with the capability to draw lines on window and Canvas controls using its DrawLine method. This method requires four sets or arguments. The first two arguments represent the starting coordinates of the line to be drawn and the last two arguments represent the ending coordinates of the line. The following shows an example of how to use the DrawLine method.

```
g.ForeColor = RGB(255,0,0)

g.DrawLine 50, 50, 200, 200
```

Figure 11-8 shows the output generated by this example, which as you can see is a straight line. The beginning of the line is 50 pixels from the left-hand side of the window and 50 pixels from the top. The end of the line is 200 pixels from the left-hand side of the window and 200 pixels from the top.

Figure 11-8. *Drawing a line, as seen on Linux*

Drawing Shapes

The Graphics class also provides a number of different methods for drawing various types of shapes, including the following:

- Ovals

- Rectangles

- Polygons

- Round Rectangles

- Filled-in Ovals

- Filled-in Rectangles

- Filled-in Polygons

- Filled-in Round Rectangles

For example, the following code statements demonstrate how to draw a filled-in rectangle shape using the Graphics class's FillRect method. This method requires four sets of arguments. The first two arguments represent the left-hand coordinates of the rectangle to be drawn and the last two arguments represent the width and height of the shape. The following shows an example of how to use the FillRect method.

```
g.ForeColor = RGB(255,0,0)
```

```
g.FillRect 50, 50, 200, 200
```

Figure 11-9 shows an example of the output produced.

Figure 11-9. *Drawing a filled-in rectangle, as seen on Linux*

The Fun and Practical Side of Working with Graphics

As you've already seen, REALbasic provides you with all the tools you need to create custom graphics. By adding custom graphics to your windows, you can add personal touches to your applications. Using the Canvas control, you can create and display custom images, such as corporate logos. The possibilities are endless.

■Note Another way to use graphics in REALbasic is to create custom controls. For example, a Visual Basic programmer migrating an application over to REALbasic might run into a situation where a particular Visual Basic control, such as the ListView control, does not match up to a corresponding REALbasic control. One way of dealing with this situation is to build your own custom control that provides equivalent functionality. You can do this using the Canvas control, the Graphics class, and some custom code. The creation of custom controls is an advanced topic and beyond the scope of this book. To learn more, refer to REALbasic's *Reference Manual*.

Building an MP3 Player

This chapter wraps up by demonstrating how to create a custom-built MP3 player named the RB MP3 Player. While this chapter demonstrates the creation of this application using the Macintosh version of REALbasic, it can also run on Windows.

The RB MP3 Player, shown in Figure 11-10, provides users with the capability to select and play MP3 audio files. Users can also elect to repeatedly play a MP3 file. MP3 playback can be stopped at any time and the sound can be muted. The user also has the capability to control sound volume.

Figure 11-10. *A REALbasic MP3 player, as seen on Mac OS X*

Designing the User Interface

Begin the creation of the RB MP3 Player application by starting a new project. Resize Window1 as you see in Figure 11-10 and change its Title property to RB MP3 Player. Next, add three Push-Button controls, two StaticText controls, a Slider control, and a Checkbox control, and then align them, as Figure 11-10 shows.

Once you finish adding the required controls, modify the property values for the controls, as Table 11-2 specifies.

Table 11-2. *Property Modifications for the RB MP3 Player Application*

Object	Property	Value
PushButton1	Name	pbnPlay
	Caption	Play
	Enabled	False
PushButton2	Name	pbnStop
	Caption	Stop
	Enabled	False
PushButton1	Name	pbnMute
	Caption	Mute
	Enabled	False
StaticText1	Name	txtVolume
	Text	Volume:
StaticText2	Name	txtFileName
	Text	
Slider1	Name	sdrVolume
	Enabled	False
	Value	50

Object	Property	Value
CheckBox1	Name	chkLoop
	Enabled	False
	Caption	Loop

Setting Up the Menu System

The RB MP3 application has a simple menu system that consists of one menu and two menu items. To set it up, open the Project Screen and double-click Menubar1. Select the Edit menu that REALbasic automatically adds to the menu system and press Delete to remove it. Then, select the File menu and click the Add Menu Item button located on the editor's toolbar. Enter &Open MP3 File as the text for the menu item, and then press Enter. Next, drag-and-drop this menu item to the top of the File menu, so it is the first menu item displayed.

Setting Up Property Values

The RB MP3 Player application uses the Sound class to facilitate the playback of MP3 audio files, so you need to set up an instance of the Sound object that can be referenced by all parts of the application. Because the application consists of a single window, you can achieve this by using a custom window property to declare the Sound object. To set this up, open the Window Code editor, and then click the Add Property button located on the editor's toolbar. Enter SoundFile in the Declaration field and Sound in the As field.

```
SoundFile As Sound
```

Adding Program Code

Now, you're ready to start the coding process for this application. To begin, let's set up the menu handler for the FileOpenMP3File menu item. Do so by clicking the Add Menu Handler button located on the Code Editor's toolbar. Then, enter the following code statements.

```
Dim AudioTypes As New FileType    'Declare a FileType object

AudioTypes.Name = "Audio Files"    'Set a string identifying supported files
AudioTypes.Extensions = ".mp3"    'Specify supported file types

'Declare a folder object and retrieve the name and path of a MP3 file
Dim TargetFile as FolderItem = GetOpenFolderItem(AudioTypes)

'Perform the following as long as the user did not click on Cancel
If TargetFile <> Nil Then
  SoundFile = TargetFile.OpenAsSound    'Retrieve the audio file
```

```
'Enable interface controls
pbnPlay.Enabled = True
pbnStop.Enabled = True
pbnMute.Enabled = True
chkLoop.Enabled = True
sdrVolume.Enabled = True

'Display the name of the selected mp3 file
txtFileName.Text = TargetFile.Name
```

End If

When clicked, the FileOpenMP3File menu displays a standard Open window dialog, enabling the user to specify the name and location of a MP3 audio file. If the user specifies a MP3 file, it is opened and assigned to the SoundFile object. In addition, the interface controls on the window are enabled to let the user begin playing the MP3 audio file. The filename of the MP3 file is also displayed at the bottom of the window.

All that remains is to enter the code associated with each of the application's interface controls. Start by opening the Action event handler for the pbnPlay control and assigning it the following code statements.

```
'Determine whether to execute the play or playlooping method
If SoundFile.IsPlaying <> True Then   'If mp3 is already playing don't do anything
  If chkLoop.Value = False Then
     'Set sound level equal to slider control value
     SoundFile.Volume = sdrVolume.Value
   SoundFile.Play   'Play the mp3 file
  Else
    SoundFile.PlayLooping  'Repeatedly play the mp3 file
    chkLoop.Enabled = False  'Disable the CheckBox control
  End If
End If
```

When executed, the first statement checks to see if a MP3 file is already playing. If this is the case, the rest of the statements are skipped and the current MP3 file keeps playing. Otherwise, the next code statement checks to see if the user selected the CheckBox control (chkLoop), indicating the MP3 file should be played over and over again. Based on the result of this evaluation, the MP3 audio is played using either the Sound class's Play or PlayLooping method.

Next, open the Action event handler for the pbnStop control and add the following code statement.

```
SoundFile.Stop    'Stop mp3 file playback
```

When executed, the code in this event handler stops MP3 file playback. Next, open the Action event handler for the pbnMute control and add the following code statements.

```
'Toggle between mute and volume
If SoundFile.Volume <> 0 Then
  SoundFile.Volume = 0  'Mute the sound
Else
  SoundFile.Volume = sdrVolume.Value  'Resume sound
End If
```

These code statements toggle the value assigned to the Volume property between 0 and sdrVolume.Value, effectively muting and unmuting the sound playback. Finally, open the ValueChanged event handler for the sdrVolume control and add the following code statement.

```
SoundFile.Volume = Me.Value  'Adjust playback volume
```

This statement adjusts the volume level used to play the MP3 file, based on the value assigned to the Slider control (for example, Me.Value).

Testing the RB MP3 Player

That's it. The RB MP3 Player should be ready to run. Save and compile the application, and then make sure it works as advertised. If you encounter any errors when compiling the application, go back and look for typos.

Summary

In this chapter, you learned how to liven your REALbasic applications by adding different kinds of audio capabilities, including beeping, sound play, speech pronunciation, and musical notes. You also learned how to work with the Canvas control, and how to use methods and properties belonging to the Graphics class. On top of all this, you learned how to create a number of new REALbasic applications.

CHAPTER 12

■■■

Debugging REALbasic Applications

In Chapter 11, you learned how to integrate audio and graphics into your REALbasic applications. In this, the final chapter of this book, you learn what to do when your REALbasic applications won't compile. This includes learning how to use REALbasic's built-in debugger to track down and fix syntax errors, as well as learning how to trace program flow and track the status of variables, properties, and objects. You also learn how to set breakpoints to arbitrarily pause applications, after which you can manually control statement execution one line at a time. And, last, you learn how to programmatically handle errors to prevent them from crashing your applications or to present the user with friendlier and more useful errors messages.

Specifically, you learn how to

- Track down and fix syntax errors

- Use the REALbasic debugger to track logic flow and variable, property, and object values

- Set breakpoints to pause application execution

- Add code that handles run-time errors

Tracking Down and Fixing Errors

You have inevitably run into a problem or two as you worked with the various sample applications presented in this book. Specifically, you probably made a few typos here and there. Up to this point, you were advised to double-check your typing as the primary means to tracking down and fixing errors or *bugs*.

As you begin developing your own REALbasic applications from scratch and, as your applications grow larger and more complex, you are going to run into more errors. Even the most experienced and talented programmers have to deal with errors. This is an inevitable fact of programming.

REALbasic applications are subject to several different types of errors, which we explore in the following sections. These errors fall into three main categories as follows:

- Syntax

- Run-time

- Logical

■**Tip** As a programmer, you should always look for ways to write better, error-free code. One way of working toward this goal is adopting a number of good programming practices, including

- Using consistent naming standards for your variables, constants, objects, properties, subroutines, and functions

- Adding programming logic to your applications that validate all user input

- Adding programming logic to your applications to handle missing files or incorrect file paths

- Providing users with clear instruction on the proper use of your applications

- Anticipating places in your applications where errors are most likely to occur and developing exception-handling procedures to deal with these situations

- Testing your applications extensively, making sure every piece of functionality is verified

- When testing, try feeding your application erroneous input to ensure it handles the input correctly

---

Understanding Syntax Errors

Perhaps the most common form of programming error is the syntax error. *Syntax errors* occur when you fail to write programming statements that conform to REALbasic's rules. In many cases, syntax errors occur because of typos you make when keying in programming statements. Syntax errors also occur when you fail to provide required statement parameters or when you provide more parameters than are accepted by a method, function, and so on.

Eliminating Syntax Errors One at a Time

If a syntax error occurs when you are testing your application within the REALbasic integrated development environment (IDE), REALbasic stops executing the application and flags the error. REALbasic highlights the code statement where the syntax error occurred in the Code Editor and displays a small image of a bug to the left of the code statement, as Figure 12-1 shows.

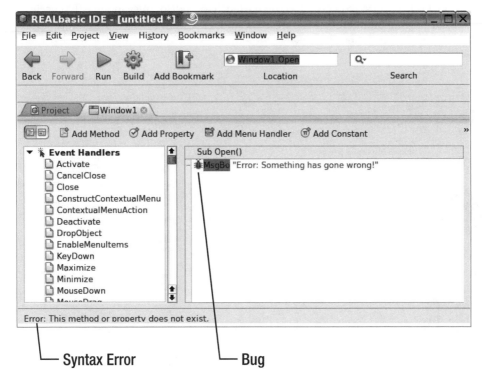

    └─ **Syntax Error**   └─ **Bug**

Figure 12-1. *REALbasic displays a message describing a syntax error at the bottom of the IDE as a Tip, as seen on Linux.*

REALbasic won't compile your application until every syntax error has been corrected. Each time you attempt to compile an application with one or more syntax errors, REALbasic stops compilation at the first syntax error it finds and highlights the error. By highlighting syntax errors in this manner and providing you with information about the error, REALbasic makes tracking syntax errors relatively painless.

Tackling Multiple Syntax Errors at a Time

If you are working on a relatively large and complex application, you are likely to come across multiple syntax errors at the same time. Rather than addressing them one at a time each time you try to compile your application, REALbasic enables you to configure it to display a list of all the syntax errors it discovers when it attempts to compile your applications. To set this up, click the Edit menu, and then select the Options menu item. This opens the Options window. Next, click the Build Process icon displayed on the left-hand side of the window. REALbasic responds by displaying Build Process settings, as Figure 12-2 shows. Select the Show multiple compile errors option, and then click OK.

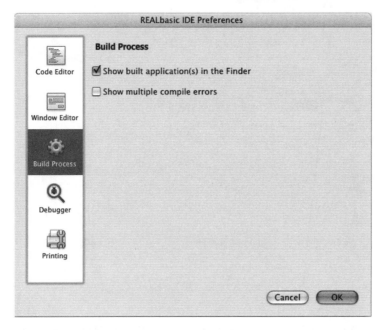

Figure 12-2. *Configuring REALbasic to display multiple compile errors, as seen on Mac OS X*

Once configured, REALbasic displays all the syntax errors it uncovers by adding an Errors screen to the REALbasic IDE, as Figure 12-3 shows. Each syntax error is reported as a separate entry. The data reported includes the type of error, its location within the application, and a descriptive error message. To fix the error, double-click its entry in the Errors screen, and then REALbasic switches over to the code editor and displays the statement where the error resides.

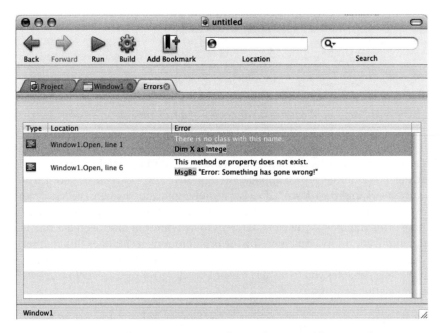

Figure 12-3. *Viewing all the syntax errors detected in a REALbasic application, as seen on Mac OS X*

Understanding Run-Time Errors

Another type of error you need to look for is run-time errors. *Run-time errors* occur when an application tries to do something illegal. For example, an OutOfMemoryException run-time error would occur if your application attempts to do something and insufficient memory is available to do so. Likewise, a TypeMismatchException run-time error would occur if a REAL-basic application attempts to assign the wrong data type to an object.

Unlike syntax errors, the REALbasic compiler is unable to detect every run-time error. It's up to you to find and fix them when testing your REALbasic applications. Be careful to test every part of your applications. Otherwise, a seldom-executed function or subroutine might produce a run-time error, which you might miss when testing. As a result, your users would be left to discover your error, which is the last thing a programmer wants to let happen.

If a run-time error occurs when you are testing your application within the REALbasic IDE, REALbasic stops executing the application and flags the error. REALbasic highlights the code statement where the error occurs in the Code Editor and displays a small image of a bug to the left of the code statement, just as it does with syntax errors.

If you fail to discover a run-time error during testing and a user discovers it in the final-release version of your application, REALbasic then displays a cryptic error (as Figure 12-4 shows) and immediately terminates the application.

Figure 12-4. *REALbasic terminates applications on discovery of a run-time error, as seen on Windows.*

Unfortunately, no matter how hard you may try, sometimes it's impossible to prevent errors from occurring. For example, if your application requires network access to perform a particular task, the network might go down. Likewise, if your application needs to access a particular disk drive on the computer, the disk drive might crash. Fortunately, as you learn in the section "Developing Error Handlers," you can take steps to help prevent unexpected errors from crashing your applications. By implementing the programming techniques this chapter shows you, you can often add programming logic to your applications that lets them recover from errors or, at the least, enables you to display a user-friendly error message before gracefully terminating application execution.

Understanding Logical Errors

A third category of error you might run into is logical errors. A *logical error* is caused by a mistake on your part. For example, you might attempt to add two numbers you meant to subtract, resulting in a logically correct, but completely useless, value. Another example of a logical error would be an endless loop.

REALbasic is unable to identify or detect logical errors. Instead, it's up to you to carefully analyze the output produced by your applications to ensure things are working as they should. The best way to deal with logical errors is to prevent them in the first place by taking the time to carefully plan out your applications.

Working with the REALbasic Debugger

REALbasic's built-in debugger does a lot more than simply highlight syntax and run-time errors. It provides you with the capability to set breakpoints at specific locations in your application to pause script execution. Once paused, you can track the values assigned to variables, properties, and objects to ensure they contain the values you expect. You can also track the order in which methods are executed to ensure the application's logical flow is proceeding in the order you expect. On top of all this, REALbasic lets you exercise line-by-line control over the execution of each statement in your application.

Setting Breakpoints

To set a *breakpoint,* all you have to do is click the dash located in the first column of the Code Editor, as you see in Figure 12-5. REALbasic identifies breakpoints by displaying a red circular marker. REALbasic automatically pauses application execution at any statement where a breakpoint is set.

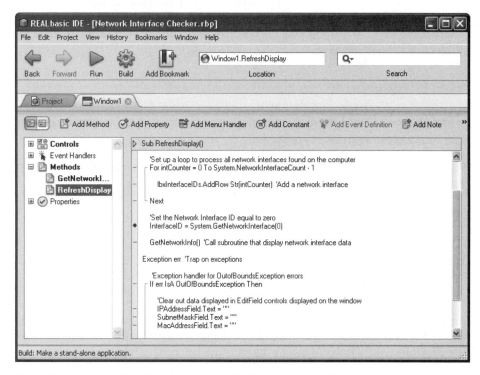

Figure 12-5. *Setting a breakpoint within a REALbasic application, as seen on Windows*

Note Any breakpoints you set are persistent, meaning they are saved with your REALbasic project and will not go away until you remove them. However, if you compile a stand-alone version of your applications, any embedded breakpoints are ignored.

When debugging your applications, you should add breakpoints in locations where you think errors are most likely to occur. REALbasic enables you to add as many breaks as you think necessary to your application. When you run your application within REALbasic's IDE and a breakpoint is reached, REALbasic pauses application execution, highlighting the statement containing the breakpoint. The highlighted statement represents the next statement to be executed. At this point, you can review the value of any variables, properties, and objects in your application, as well as take line-by-line control over the execution of your application.

Once you track down and resolve any errors existing within your application, you can remove any breakpoints you set by clicking the red circular marker that represents them or by clicking Projects ➤ Clear All Breakpoints.

■**Tip** As an alternative to setting breakpoints manually via the IDE, you can embed the Break keyword within your code statements. When the compiler reaches a Break keyword, it pauses application execution exactly as if a breakpoint had been manually established.

An advantage to using the Break keyword in place of a breakpoint is you can set up the conditional execution of the Break keyword, as the following shows.

```
If intCounter > 10 Then
   Break
End If
```

Tracking Values

When either a breakpoint or a Break keyword is reached, the REALbasic compiler pauses the application and displays the Run screen, as shown in Figure 12-6. Using this screen, you can investigate the values assigned to variables, properties, and objects, as well as monitor the logical flow of your application.

The Run screen is divided into two panes. The Code Editor pane, located in the left-hand pane, displays the currently executing method, highlighting the statement containing the breakpoint. Just above the Code Editor pane is the Stack drop-down list, which displays the name of the current method. In addition, you can examine the methods that were executed by the application. The methods are listed in the order they were executed. You can click any method in the drop-down list to display it. By examining the order in which methods are presented in this list, you can review the local flow of your application and make sure things are occurring in the order you expected.

The Variables pane, shown in Figure 12-7, located on the right-hand side of the screen, displays a list of all variables local to the selected method. This provides you with the capability to check the values currently assigned to variables as you debug your application. In addition, the Variables pane is dynamic, meaning the values displayed change as your applications execute.

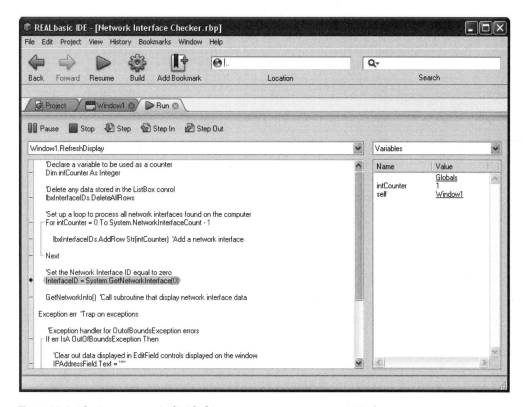

Figure 12-6. *The Run screen is divided into two panes, as seen on Windows.*

Figure 12-7. *The Variables pane displays a listing of all variables local to the currently selected method.*

Any objects displayed in the Variables pane are shown as links. You can click the link to open an object viewer and get more information about the state of the object. For example, Figure 12-8 shows the contents of the object viewer when the Window1 object is selected.

Figure 12-8. *You can open a link for an object in the Variables pane to view information about the state of the object.*

In addition to inspecting the values assigned to properties that belong to a selected object, you can click a link shown in an object viewer to drill down and view any objects associated with the object. As you can see, starting from the Variables pane, you can drill down and view values associated with any variables, properties, or objects.

■ **Note** The top entry on the Variables pane is always Globals. This link provides you with access to any global variables in your application.

Using Break Points to Control Statement Execution

Once the compiler pauses application execution at a break point, REALbasic provides you with a number of different options for stepping through the execution of your program statements. This way, you have total control over when statements execute, and you can pause to examine the values assigned to variables, properties, and objects, as necessary. To control statement execution, REALbasic provides you with access to a collection of five buttons located at the top of the Run screen, as Figure 12-9 shows.

Figure 12-9. *Using the debugger toolbar to control statement execution*

■**Note** You can also access the functionality provided by the Debugger toolbar from the Project menu.

The debugger toolbar on the Run screen consists of the following buttons:

- **Pause**. Pauses execution without stopping the application and returning to the IDE.

- **Stop**. Stops execution and exits the debugger.

- **Step**. Executes the currently selected statement and pauses before executing the next statement. However, if the selected statement is a call to a method, the entire method executes, after which the execution pauses on the next statement.

- **Step In**. Executes the currently selected statement and pauses before executing the next statement. If the next statement is a call to a method, the debugger displays the statements that make up the methods and lets you step through them line-by-line.

- **Step Out**. Executes the rest of the statements in a method without pausing for line-by-line execution. This lets you skip a step-by-step execution of code statements within methods you believe are bug free to speed the debug process.

As you use the Step, Step In, and Step Out buttons to control statement execution, the compiler continues to identify the next statement to be executed by highlighting it. In addition, you can resume normal application execution at any time by clicking the Resume button located on REALbasic's main toolbar.

Developing Error Handlers

As previously discussed, run-time errors (or exceptions) happen for many different reasons. If these errors are not handled, your REALbasic applications display cryptic errors and crash. This can leave your users confused and frustrated.

REALbasic provides you with different ways to trap errors and prevent them from wreaking havoc on your application. To develop exception handlers, you need to be able to anticipate the locations within your applications where run-time errors are most likely to occur. Likely candidate locations include anyplace within your applications where you accept freeform user input, as well as anywhere you access computer and network resources, which are subject to failure or temporary periods of unavailability.

You can take any number of different approaches when developing exception-handling routines for your REALbasic applications. For example, depending on the error, you might attempt to recover from an error by retrying a given task or by performing an alternate operation. For example, if your application needs to store a file on a network drive that is unavailable, the application might, instead, temporarily store the file locally, and then monitor the availability of the network drive, and save the file remotely when the drive comes back online. Other ways of handling run-time exceptions include

- Displaying user-friendly error messages

- Requesting users to report any errors that occur

- Providing users with additional instructions on how to properly work with the application

- Apologizing for errors that cannot be handled and cleanly terminating the application (after saving any unsaved work)

REALbasic provides you with access to two different techniques for setting up exception-handling routines—`Exception` and `Try` blocks—both of which are shown in the following sections.

Handling Run-Time Errors with Exception Blocks

`Exception` blocks are placed at the end of methods where you think run-time errors may occur. Every statement that occurs after the exception line is considered part of the `Exception` block. If REALbasic detects a run-time error in a method and that method has an `Exception` block, processing control immediately switches over to the `Exception` block.

Exception blocks trap (or catch) errors and provide access to information about the errors. `Exception` blocks begin with an `Exception` statement that has the following syntax.

```
Exception ErrorParameter As ErrorType
```

Both `ErrorParameter` and `ErrorType` are optional parameters. `ErrorParameter` is used to determine the type of error that was trapped. `ErrorType` can only be specified when `ErrorParameter` is used to trap a specific type of error.

The following series of examples demonstrates how to work with `Exception` blocks. For starters, create a new REALbasic project and add the following statements to the Window1 Open event handler.

```
Dim strCustomerArray(2) As String

strCustomerArray(0) = "Molly"
strCustomerArray(1) = "William"
strCustomerArray(2) = "Alexander"

MsgBox strCustomerArray(5)
```

In this example, an array named strCustomerArray has been set up to store three elements. However, the last statement generates a run-time error when it attempts to reference an array element that is out of bounds. If you try running this application within the REALbasic IDE, the compiler will identify the error as a bug and terminate the compilation process. However, if you go ahead and compile a stand-alone version of this application, and then run that version of the application, the error message shown in Figure 12-10 is displayed. After clicking OK, your application is closed.

Figure 12-10. *An example of a unhandled run-time error, as seen on Windows*

To prevent this error from terminating the application and from displaying the cryptic error message, you can add an Exception block to the bottom on the Open event handler as the following shows.

```
Dim strCustomerArray(2) As String

strCustomerArray(0) = "Molly"
strCustomerArray(1) = "William"
strCustomerArray(2) = "Alexander"

MsgBox strCustomerArray(5)

Exception err
  MsgBox "Something went wrong with the array"
```

In this example, an Exception block was added that traps any run-time errors occurring within the method. If you compile a new stand-alone version of this application and run it, the message shown in Figure 12-11 is displayed and the application is allowed to continue to execute.

Figure 12-11. *Allowing an application to continue running by adding an Exception block to the method where a run-time error occurred, as seen on Windows*

REALbasic also lets you create Exception blocks that trap specific run-time errors, as the following example shows.

```
Dim strCustomerArray(2) As String

strCustomerArray(0) = "Molly"
strCustomerArray(1) = "William"
strCustomerArray(2) = "Alexander"

MsgBox strCustomerArray(5)

Exception err
  If err IsA OutOfBoundsException Then
    MsgBox "Something went wrong with the array"
  Else
    MsgBox "Unknown Error!"
  End If
```

Note The previous example used the IsA operator to determine what type of run-time error occurred. The IsA operator returns a Boolean value of True when a match occurs.

In this example, the Exception block executes any time a run-time error occurs. Using the ErrorParameter, the Exception block executes an If…Then…Else block that processes the run-time error. One of two different error messages is then displayed based on whether an OutOfBoundsException error occurs.

Note Refer to the REALbasic Language Reference for a complete list of run-time errors.

If you prefer, you could rework the previous example as the following shows, listing multiple Exception blocks in place of an If…Then…Else block.

```
Dim strCustomerArray(2) As String

strCustomerArray(0) = "Molly"
strCustomerArray(1) = "William"
strCustomerArray(2) = "Alexander"

MsgBox strCustomerArray(5)

Exception err As OutOfBoundsException
  MsgBox "Something went wrong with with the array"
```

```
Exception err As NilObjectException
  MsgBox "Object does not exist"
```

    `Exception` blocks provide you with the capability to recover from many different run-time errors. For them to be effective, however, you must anticipate the locations within your REAL-basic application where they will be needed and take the appropriate actions.

Handling Run-Time Errors with Try Blocks

REALbasic also lets you trap and handle run-time errors using `Try` blocks, which have the following syntax.

```
Try
  Code statements where errors may occur
Catch[ErrorParameter] [As ErrorType]
  Code statements to execute
Finally
  Code statements run whenever a run-time error occurs
End [Try]
```

    To set up a `Try` block, you start by placing the `Try` keyword just before any code statements where run-time errors are likely to occur. Then, you add one or more `Catch` blocks following these code statements. You can add as many different `Catch` blocks as you want, each of which should trap a different type or error. If you choose, you can add an optional `Finally` block, which executes any time a run-time error is trapped by the `Try` block, regardless of whether a `Catch` block was executed.

    The following example demonstrates how to set up a `Try` block to trap and handle run-time errors.

```
Dim strCustomerArray(2) As String

strCustomerArray(0) = "Molly"
strCustomerArray(1) = "William"
strCustomerArray(2) = "Alexander"

Try
  MsgBox strCustomerArray(5)
Catch err As OutOfBoundsException
  MsgBox "Something went wrong with the array"
End Try
```

■**Tip** The order in which you define `Catch` blocks within your `Try` blocks is important. REALbasic only executes the first matching `Catch` block it finds. So, when defining multiple `Catch` blocks, be sure to define them so the more specific `Catch` blocks occur before the more general ones.

Building a Network Connection Checker Application

This chapter concludes by demonstrating how to create a small network connection utility that detects and displays information about every currently active network interface on a computer. To build this application, you need to learn how to work with properties and methods belonging to the System and NetworkInterface objects. In addition, you have the opportunity to put your newly acquired exception-handling experience to use.

■**Note**   The System object provides access to properties and methods that you can use to retrieve information about a computer. One System object property is the NetworkInterfaceCount property, which returns an Integer representing the number of network interface devices connected to a computer. The System object also provides access to the GetNetworkInterface method, which can be used to instantiate a NetworkInterface object, which can then be used to retrieve information about each network interface attached to the computer. Specifically, the NetworkInterface object provides access to the IPAddress, MacAddress, and SubnetMask properties, which return the IP address, Mac address, and Subnet Mask for a specified network interface.

The development of the Network Connection Checker is demonstrated here using the Windows version of REALbasic, although you can just as easily create this application using the Macintosh or Linux version of REALbasic. All the steps involved are the same. Figure 12-12 provides you with a look at the Network Connection Checker when it first starts.

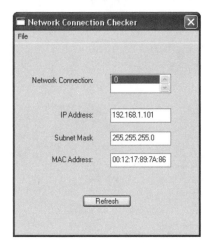

Figure 12-12. *The Network Connection Checker can be used to display information about every network interface currently set up on a computer, as seen on Windows.*

Setting Up the User Interface

The Network Connection Checker application is made up of a menu system and a single window that contains a ListBox, a PushButton, and three EditField controls, along with five StaticText controls used to label the other controls. To create this application, open a new REALbasic desktop application. Add the required controls to Window1 and align them as you saw in Figure 12-12. Next, modify the properties for the application's window and controls, as shown in Table 12-1.

Table 12-1. *Property Modifications for the Network Connection Checker Application*

Object	Property	Value
Window1	Title	Network Connection Checker
ListBox1	Name	lbxInterfaceIDs
EditField1	Name	IPAddressField
EditField2	Name	SubnetMaskField
EditField3	Name	MACAddressField
PushButton1	Name	pbnRefresh
	Caption	Refresh
StaticText1	Name	txtNetConnection
	Text	Network Connection:
StaticText2	Name	txtIPAddress
	Text	IP Address:
StaticText2	Name	txtSubnetMask
	Text	Subnet Mask:
StaticText4	Name	MacAddressField
	Text	MAC Address:

Now that Window1 and its controls are configured, let's set up the application's menu system. To do so, double-click the Menubar1 item located on the Projects screen. REALbasic responds by displaying the default menu system for the application in the MenuBar Editor. The application doesn't need the default Edit menu, so delete it by selecting it and clicking Delete. This leaves only the File menu, which is all this application requires.

Adding Custom Properties and Methods

The event handlers for the window of the Network Connection Checker application (Window1) are where most of this application's code will reside. Before you begin adding code to these event handlers, however, you need to add a property and two methods to the window. The property will be used to declare a variable representing an instance of the NetworkInterface object. Different event handlers use this property to retrieve network interface information.

The two methods you create will be responsible for displaying network interface data and for refreshing the display of all active network interfaces.

To add the property, open the Code Editor for Window1. Next, click the Add Property button located on the Code Editor's toolbar and then enter InterfaceID in the Declaration field and NetworkInterface in the As field.

To add the first custom method, click the Add Method button located on the Code Editor's toolbar. A method declaration area is displayed at the top of the Code Editor. Enter GetNetworkInfo in the Method Name field and add the following programming statements to the subroutine.

```
'Display the IP Address of the currently selected network interface
IPAddressField.Text = InterfaceID.IPAddress

'Display the Subnet Mask of the currently selected network interface
SubnetMaskField.Text = InterfaceID.SubnetMask

'Display the MAC Address of the currently selected network interface
MacAddressField.Text = InterfaceID.MACAddress
```

When called, this subroutine is responsible for updating the display of IP Address, Subnet Mask and MAC Address information for the currently selected network interface device (as specified by InterfaceID property).

To add the second custom method, click the Add Method button again, and then enter RefreshDisplay in the Method Name field. Next, add the following programming statements to the subroutine.

```
'Declare a variable to be used as a counter
Dim intCounter As Integer

'Delete any data stored in the ListBox control
lbxInterfaceIDs.DeleteAllRows

'Set up a loop to process all network interfaces found on the computer
For intCounter = 0 To System.NetworkInterfaceCount - 1

  lbxInterfaceIDs.AddRow Str(intCounter)  'Add a network interface

Next

'Set the Network Interface ID equal to zero
InterfaceID = System.GetNetworkInterface(0)

GetNetworkInfo()  'Call subroutine that displays network interface data

Exception err  'Trap exceptions
```

```
'Exception handler for OutofBoundsException errors
If err IsA OutOfBoundsException Then

  'Clear out data displayed in EditField controls displayed on the window
  IPAddressField.Text = ""
  SubnetMaskField.Text = ""
  MacAddressField.Text = ""

  'Display a user friendly error message
  MsgBox "There are no currently active network connections."

End If
```

As the embedded comments document, this subroutine sets ups a For…Next loop to generate a list of network interfaces installed on the computer, which is then displayed in the ListBox control. Based on the assumption that all computers where this application will run must have at least one active network interface, a default network interface is defined (for example, InterfaceID = System.GetNetworkInterface(0). The GetNetworkInfo() subroutine is then executed to display network interface data.

The subroutine ends by setting up an Exception handler designed to trap OutOfBoundsException errors. An OutOfBoundsException error can occur if a network interface displayed by the application is selected after becoming disabled. The event handler prevents this error from crashing the application and, instead, clears out the display area and displays a user-friendly error message.

Adding a Little Program Code

Once you finish configuring the application's user interface and its menu system, and you add its custom property and methods, it's time to start adding the program code associated with the application's controls. Begin by adding the following code statement to the new Open event handler for the lbxInterfaceIDs ListBox control.

```
RefreshDisplay
```

This code executes when the application starts or, more specifically, when the window (Window1) containing the ListBox control is loaded. It executes the RefreshDisplay method, which displays a list of all active network interfaces on the computer. Next, add the following code statements to the new Change event handler for the lbxInterfaceIDs ListBox control.

```
'Set the Network Interface ID equal to the interface selected by the user
InterfaceID = System.GetNetworkInterface(me.ListIndex)

GetNetworkInfo()  'Call subroutine that displays network interface data

Exception err  'Trap exceptions
```

```
'Exception handler for OutofBoundsException errors
If err IsA OutOfBoundsException Then

  'Clear out data displayed in EditField controls displayed on the window
  MacAddressField.Text = ""
  IPAddressField.Text = ""
  SubnetMaskField.Text = ""

  'Display a user friendly error message
  MsgBox "This connection is no longer active. Please contact the " _
  + "helpdesk for additional assistance."

End If
```

This code is responsible for calling the GetNetworkInfo() subroutine whenever the user selects a different network interface. Now, add the following code statements to the new Action event handler for the pbnRefresh PushButton control.

```
'Call subroutine that updates the display of network interface data
RefreshDisplay()
```

This code calls the RefreshDisplay() subroutine whenever the user clicks the PushButton control labeled Refresh.

Testing the Network Connection Checker

That's it. Go ahead and save the application, naming it Network Connection Checker. Then, put it through its paces to make sure it doesn't have any errors. Of course, to do so, you need to run it on a computer with at least one, but preferably two or more, network interfaces. If necessary, use the debugging instructions and tips presented in this chapter to track down and fix any errors you may come across. Also, when you do your testing, try disabling one or more network interfaces and see how the application handles it. For example, if you start the application, disable a network interface, and then select it within the application, the application should display the message you see in Figure 12-13. The application should continue running, instead of crashing with a run-time error.

Figure 12-13. *As seen on Windows, the Network Connection Checker application displays an informational message when the user selects a network interface that has become inactive.*

Here's another test you might want to try: disable all the computer's network interfaces before starting the Network Connection Checker application. In this situation, the application should respond by displaying the message you see in Figure 12-14 when it starts up.

Figure 12-14. *An informational message tells the user no active network interfaces were found, as seen on Windows.*

Assuming the user can enable any failed or disabled network interface devices, the application will correctly report on them when the Refresh button is clicked.

Summary

In this chapter, you learned how to debug your REALbasic applications. This included learning how to track down and fix one or more syntax errors at a time, as well as how to track program flow to ensure things are happening in the order you expect. You also learned how to track the status of variables, properties, and objects, in addition to learning how to set and remove breakpoints. On top of all this, this chapter taught you how to trap exceptions to be able to recover from run-time errors or to present users with friendly and meaningful error messages.

PART 4

■ ■ ■

Appendixes

Migrating Visual Basic Projects to REALbasic

If you are a Visual Basic programmer looking to make the jump to REALbasic, you probably have Visual Basic applications you want to migrate over as well. REALbasic and Visual Basic share a great many similarities. As such, there is no reason why you cannot convert most of your applications over to REALbasic. This way, not only can you run them on Windows, but you also can port them over to Macintosh and Linux.

Specifically, you learn

- How to prepare your Visual Basic code for migration

- How to import Visual Basic projects into REALbasic projects

- How to use the REALbasic Project Converter

Porting Visual Basic Projects to REALbasic

Depending on the size and complexity of your Visual Basic projects, the challenge of converting your applications may seem daunting. However, you can do a number of things to make the process go smoother and to save yourself considerable time and effort.

You should be able to reuse most of your Visual Basic code in your new REALbasic applications. However, many little differences exist between the two programming languages. This should not be surprising given Microsoft's Windows centric approach to programming language implementation. REALbasic, on the other hand, has been implemented using a cross-platform approach that stresses code portability.

A sampling of differences between Visual Basic and REALbasic include the following:

- **Differences in supported data types**. For example, Visual Basic supports the Long data type and REALbasic does not. Instead, you should use REALbasic Integer data type. Visual Basic also supports the Currency data type, for which REALbasic has no equivalent.

- **Differences in classes and data types**. For example, in REALbasic the Date is handled as a class, whereas in Visual Basic, the Date is made available as a built-in data type.

- **Differences in variable declaration**. REALbasic forces you to declare all variables using the Dim keyword. Visual Basic enables you to dynamically create variables, making Option Explicit an optional statement.

- **Differences in variable naming rules**. In REALbasic, variable names must begin with a letter and are made up of alphanumeric characters. However, Visual Basic variable names can also contain special characters (%, @, &, $, and so forth) leading to potential conflicts.

- **Differences in keywords**. A valid variable in one language may result in a keyword conflict in the other language.

- **Differences in operators**. For example, in Visual Basic, concatenation is performed using the ampersand (&) character, whereas REALbasic uses the plus (+) character.

- **Differences in the way some keywords are implemented**. For example, in Visual Basic, the Mid function can be used to return a substring or to perform a substring replacement. In REALbasic, the Mid function can only be used to return a substring.

- **Differences in the naming of the same functions**. For example, REALbasic has LowerCase and UpperCase functions, whereas Visual Basic has LCase and UCase functions.

- **Differences in the application of conditional logic**. Unlike Visual Basic, REALbasic does not support single line Case statements.

- **Differences in the formation of loops**. REALbasic does not support the setup of a loop index on the Next statement in a For...Next loop the way Visual Basic does. Visual Basic supports the creation of loops that iterate negatively, using the To and Step keywords. REALbasic replaces these keywords with the DownTo keyword.

- **Differences in how functions operate**. Visual Basic allows functions to return a result by setting a value equal to the name of the function. REALbasic requires you to use the Return statement.

- **Differences in how parameters are supported**. Instead of supporting optional parameters, REALbasic provides the capability to set up default values for parameters.

- **Differences in file system access**. Visual Basic using a Windows-specific approach to accessing the file system, whereas REALbasic uses an operating system independent-access approach.

As you can see from this brief sampling, the differences between Visual Basic and REAL-basic are far too numerous to outline in this appendix. Instead, this appendix is designed to provide you with an overview of your options for converting Visual Basic projects to REALbasic projects and to outline the basic steps involved.

Doing a Little Prep Work

You can take a number of simple steps prior to converting your program code that can significantly simplify the migration process. For starters, review your Visual Basic code and, if necessary, change it so all variables are formally declared. Also, ensure that all variable names conform to REALbasic's rules. You should spend a little time checking on the data types being used, as well, and change them if necessary. And, while you're at it, keep an eye on variable names, as well as subroutine and function names to make sure they are not in conflict with any REALbasic keywords.

Importing Visual Basic Projects

REALbasic provides you with the capability to import any Visual Basic 2 or later form, along with all associated code into REALbasic projects. In doing so, REALbasic automatically re-creates Visual Basic forms as REALbasic windows. In addition, REALbasic creates event handlers and methods to store any program code imported along with the Visual Basic forms.

The following procedure outlines the steps involved in importing a Visual Basic form into a REALbasic project:

1. Locate the Visual Basic form you want to import.

2. Create a new REALbasic project or open the REALbasic project into which you want to import a Visual Basic form.

3. Drag-and-drop the Visual Basic form into the REALbasic Project Editor screen.

Depending on the complexity of the program code imported along with a Visual Basic form, you may not need to do anything else to get your project to compile under REALbasic. In most cases, though, you'll have some code statements that REALbasic was unable to convert. To find out, try to compile your new REALbasic application and, if necessary, fix any reported errors.

REALbasic's Project Converter Utility

In addition to importing your Visual Basic forms directly into REALbasic projects, you can use the Visual Basic Project Conversion Utility to assist in the conversion of entire Visual Basic projects to REALbasic projects. This utility is available free: simply download it from the REALbasic website (`www.realbasic.com/downloads/`). According to its documentation, the Visual Basic Conversion Utility is designed to assist in converting Visual Basic 4.*x* to 6.*x* projects to REALbasic projects. This utility is *not* intended as a tool for converting Visual Basic .NET applications.

You install the Visual Basic Project Conversion Utility by downloading and decompressing it in the desired location on your computer. Once installed, you can use it to convert Visual Basic projects by dragging-and-dropping the Visual Basic projects on to the utility. The utility then analyzes all the Visual Basic project's files. The Visual Basic Project Converter Utility automatically converts Visual Basic projects, forms, classes, modules, and program code into equivalent REALbasic projects, windows, classes, modules, and program code.

Although, this utility can completely convert simple Visual Basic projects to REALbasic projects, it cannot convert most projects without a little help on your part. For example, you will probably have to rewrite certain portions of program code. In addition, any controls found in Visual Basic applications for which corresponding controls do not exist in REALbasic need to be converted to Canvas controls, leaving it up to you to create your own replacement controls or equivalent functionality. The Visual Basic Project Converter Utility's database support is limited. Any database connections found in a Visual Basic project will not be re-created within REALbasic projects. Neither will a database be added to your REALbasic project. Instead, you must go back and reestablish the database connection, and then reset the DataField and DataSource properties for all controls bound to the database.

■ ■ ■

What's on the CD-ROM?

When it comes to being a good REALbasic programmer, no substitute exists for hands-on experience in creating and testing REALbasic applications. It helps to have a collection of application source code from which you can learn and experiment. By studying and copying code examples from other REALbasic projects, you can also save time when creating new applications. This book's companion CD-ROM provides access to all the sample applications presented in this book.

This book's companion CD-ROM also provides you with convenient access to copies of REALbasic 2006 for Macintosh, Windows, and Linux.

REALbasic Program Source Code

This book was written with the intention that you create and experiment with each of the sample applications presented in the chapters as you make your way through the book. However, in the event that you may not have had the time to create and test every application presented, you can find copies of each sample application on this book's companion CD-ROM.

Table B-1 provides you with a quick review of each of the sample applications you will find.

Table B-1. *REALbasic Projects Available on This Book's Companion CD-ROM*

Chapter	Application/Project	Description
Chapter 1	Hello World.rbp	A Hello World! Application
Chapter 2	RBBookFinder.rbp	The RBBookFinder Browser
Chapter 3	RBClock.rbp	A Desktop Clock Application
Chapter 4	RBQuickNote.rbp	The RBQuickNote StickyPad Application
Chapter 5	RBCalculator.rbp	A Desktop Calculator
Chapter 6	RB NumberGuess.rbp	The RB Number Guess Game
Chapter 7	RB Movie Player.rbp	The RB Movie Player
Chapter 8	Picture Viewer.rbp	The RB Picture Viewer
	StatesListbox.rbo	A custom ListBox Control of State Names
Chapter 9	RB Word Processor.rbp	The RB Word Processor

Continued

Table B-1. *Continued*

Chapter	Application/Project	Description
Chapter 10	DBBuilder.rbp	The RB Book Database Setup Application
	DBAdd.rbp	The RB Book Database Add New Books Front End
Chapter 11	RB Painter.rbp	The RB Draw Application
	RB MP3 Player.rbp	The RB MP3 Player
	RB Speech.rbp	A Speech Synthesizer Application
	RB Piano Player.rbp	A Minivirtual Piano
Chapter 12	Network Interface Checker.rbp	The Network Connection Checker

APPENDIX C
■ ■ ■

What's Next?

Congratulations on completing *Beginning REALbasic*. Learning a new programming language is a significant achievement and represents a major effort. But, don't look at the completion of this book as the end of your REALbasic education. You have plenty more to learn! To help keep your momentum going, this appendix provides you with information about different resources you may want to consider pursuing to further develop your REALbasic programming skills.

Locating REALbasic Resources Online

Many websites are dedicated to REALbasic, and some are better than others. The following sections outline a number of good sites. Along with the name and web address of each site, you'll find a brief description of what you can expect to find.

REALbasic University

The REALbasic University website, located at `www.applelinks.com/rbu/`, provides access to a weekly online column dedicated to Macintosh software development using REALbasic. This website is a great source for learning new programming techniques and getting tips on how to do things differently.

RBDocs

The RBDocs website, located at `www.rbdocs.com`, is an online community where you can find a collaborative collection of REALbasic documentation. This website's goal is to provide more detailed documentation than is provided in the REALbasic Reference.

RBGarage

The RBGarage website, located at `www.rbgarage.com`, provides access to over 1,000 different links to REALbasic resources, including links to plug-ins, modules, sample code, and tutorials.

VBZone

The VB Zone RB website, located at `rb.thevbzone.com/`, provides access to sample REALbasic projects and tons of sample code. You'll also find a good collection of programming lessons and links to other REALbasic resources.

REALbasic Gazette

The REALbasic Gazette website, located at `rbgazette.com/`, is a web log where you can go to find REALbasic news. This website also provides a huge supply REALbasic programming tips and program code.

Really Basic REALbasic

The Really Basic REALbasic website, located at `www.ttpsoftware.com/ReallyBasicRB/`, is devoted to providing beginner REALbasic programmers with sample projects, code snippets, and tutorials, as well as other useful resources for those just getting started.

REALOPEN

The REALOPEN website, located at `realopen.org/`, is a public open-source repository for REALbasic code. The REALOPEN website's main function is to provide a collaborative environment in which REALbasic software developers can organize and share access to projects. But, this is also a great place to find plenty of REALbasic news.

Realgurus.com

The Realgurus.com website, located at `realgurus.com/board/`, provides access to forums where you can access thousands of online discussions about REALbasic programming.

REALbasic Developer Magazine

Another excellent source for cutting-edge information and REALbasic is the *REALbasic Developer* magazine, which you can subscribe to by visiting `www.rbdeveloper.com`, as shown in Figure C-1. *REALbasic Developer* magazine provides access to an assortment of articles of interest to both beginner and professional programmers, and it provides an essential resource for serious REALbasic programmers.

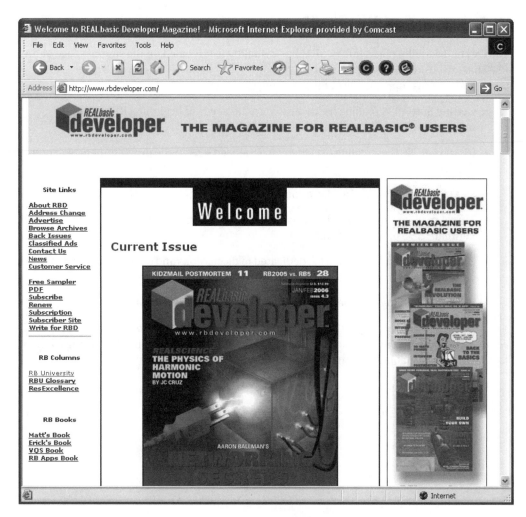

Figure C-1. REALbasic Developer *magazine provides access to REALbasic articles and advertisements sponsored by third-party developers.*

Joining REALbasic Mailing Lists

You can find a Mailing Lists link to REALbasic mailing lists located on the support page at the REALbasic website (www.realbasic.com/support/). Go to this URL and you'll be given the opportunity to sign up with any of the following mailing lists.

- **Getting Started**. A mailing list dedicated to the needs of beginning REALbasic programmers.

- **REALbasic NUG**. A mailing list where experienced REALbasic programmers post questions and share answers.

- **REAL News**. A mailing list where you can sign up to receive REALbasic announcements.

- **Tips**. A mailing list that provides access to useful information and tips provided by Geoff Perlman, CEO of REAL Software.

- **REALbasic Games**. A mailing list dedicated to discussions and questions related to game development using REALbasic.

- **Plugins**. A mailing list where you can get information about REALbasic plug-ins.

To sign up with one or more of these mailing lists, all you need to do is provide your e-mail address, and then specify whether you want to receive individual mailing-list postings or messages in digest format before you click the Submit Request button.

Index

Find it faster at http://superindex.apress.com

Find it faster at http://superindex.apress.com

You Need the Companion eBook

Your purchase of this book entitles you to its companion eBook for only $10.

We believe this Apress title will prove so indispensable that you'll want to carry it with you everywhere, which is why we are offering the companion eBook for $10 to customers who purchase this book now. Convenient and fully searchable, the eBook version of any content-rich, page-heavy Apress book makes a valuable addition to your programming library. You can easily find, copy, and apply code—and then perform examples by quickly toggling between instructions and the application. Even simultaneously tackling a donut, diet soda, and complex code becomes simplified with hands-free eBooks!

Once you purchase this book, getting the $10 companion eBook is simple:

❶ Visit **www.apress.com/promo/tendollars/**.

❷ Complete a basic registration form to receive a randomly generated question about this title.

❸ Answer the question correctly in 60 seconds and you will receive a promotional code to redeem for the $10 eBook.

2560 Ninth Street • Suite 219 • Berkeley, CA 94710

Apress®

Apress License Agreement (Single-User Products)

THIS IS A LEGAL AGREEMENT BETWEEN YOU, THE END USER, AND APRESS. BY OPENING THE SEALED CD PACKAGE, YOU ARE AGREEING TO BE BOUND BY THE TERMS OF THIS AGREEMENT. IF YOU DO NOT AGREE TO THE TERMS OF THIS AGREEMENT, PROMPTLY RETURN THE UNOPENED DISK PACKAGE AND THE ACCOMPANYING ITEMS (INCLUDING WRITTEN MATERIALS AND BINDERS AND OTHER CONTAINERS) TO THE PLACE YOU OBTAINED THEM FOR A FULL REFUND.

APRESS SOFTWARE LICENSE

1. GRANT OF LICENSE. Apress grants you the right to use one copy of the enclosed Apress software programs collectively (the "SOFTWARE") on a single terminal connected to a single computer (e.g., with a single CPU). You may not network the SOFTWARE or otherwise use it on more than one computer or computer terminal at the same time.

2. COPYRIGHT. The SOFTWARE copyright is owned by Jerry Lee Ford, Jr., with portions owned by REAL Software, Inc. and is protected by United States copyright laws and international treaty provisions. The SOFTWARE contains licensed software programs, the use of which are governed by English language end user license agreements inside the licensed software programs. Therefore, you must treat each of the SOFTWARE programs like any other copyrighted material (e.g., a book or musical recording) except that you may either (a) make one copy of the SOFTWARE solely for backup or archival purposes, or (b) transfer the SOFTWARE to a single hard disk, provided you keep the original solely for backup or archival purposes. You may not copy the written material accompanying the SOFTWARE.

3. OTHER RESTRICTIONS. You may not rent or lease the SOFTWARE, but you may transfer the SOFTWARE and accompanying written materials on a permanent basis provided you retain no copies and the recipient agrees to the terms of this Agreement. You may not reverse engineer, decompile, or disassemble the SOFTWARE. If SOFTWARE is an update, any transfer must include the update and all prior versions. Distributors, dealers, and other resellers are prohibited from altering or opening the licensed SOFTWARE package.

4. By breaking the seal on the disc package, you agree to the terms and conditions printed in the Apress License Agreement. If you do not agree with the terms, simply return this book with the still-sealed CD package to the place of purchase for a refund.

DISCLAIMER OF WARRANTY

NO WARRANTIES. Apress disclaims all warranties, either express or implied, including, but not limited to, implied warranties of merchantability and fitness for a particular purpose, with respect to the SOFTWARE and the accompanying written materials. The software and any related documentation is provided "as is." You may have other rights, which vary from state to state.

NO LIABILITIES FOR CONSEQUENTIAL DAMAGES. In no event shall Apress be liable for any damages whatsoever (including, without limitation, damages from loss of business profits, business interruption, loss of business information, or other pecuniary loss) arising out of the use or inability to use this product, even if Apress has been advised of the possibility of such damages. Because some states do not allow the exclusion or limitation of liability for consequential or incidental damages, the above limitation may not apply to you.

U.S. GOVERNMENT RESTRICTED RIGHTS

The SOFTWARE and documentation are provided with RESTRICTED RIGHTS. Use, duplication, or disclosure by the Government is subject to restriction as set forth in subparagraph (c) (1) (ii) of The Rights in Technical Data and Computer Software clause at 52.227-7013. Contractor/manufacturer is Apress, 2560 Ninth Street, Suite 219, Berkeley, California, 94710.

This Agreement is governed by the laws of the State of California.

Should you have any questions concerning this Agreement, or if you wish to contact Apress for any reason, please write to Apress, 2560 Ninth Street, Suite 219, Berkeley, California, 94710.